Economy and Economics of Ancient Greece

Whilst modern economists are primarily concerned with how people behave, classical writers such as Plato, Aristotle, and Xenophon were more interested in how people should behave, thus marking the ethical difference between economics now and economics in Ancient Greece. Partly a piece of economic history, partly a critique of utilitarianism, Takeshi Amemiya presents a complete model of the Athenian economy.

Exploring all areas of this economy including public finance, banking, manufacturing, and trade, Amemiya discusses the historical, cultural, political, and sociological condition of ancient Greece as well as the ethical background in which the economy developed. Such a broad and comprehensive survey is unprecedented in this field.

Takeshi Amemiya has taught an undergraduate course for the last five years at Stanford on Economy and Economics of ancient Greece and this text would be perfect for those and other students interested in this period. It would also be a useful reference point for graduates and of considerable interest to classicists at any level.

Takeshi Amemiya teaches econometrics and Greek economy and economics at Stanford University.

Routledge explorations in economic history

1 **Economic Ideas and Government Policy**
   Contributions to contemporary economic history
   Sir Alec Cairncross

2 **The Organization of Labour Markets**
   Modernity, culture and governance in Germany, Sweden, Britain and Japan
   Bo Stråth

3 **Currency Convertibility**
   The gold standard and beyond
   Edited by Jorge Braga de Macedo, Barry Eichengreen and Jaime Reis

4 **Britain's Place in the World**
   A historical enquiry into import controls 1945–1960
   Alan S. Milward and George Brennan

5 **France and the International Economy**
   From Vichy to the Treaty of Rome
   Frances M. B. Lynch

6 **Monetary Standards and Exchange Rates**
   M.C. Marcuzzo, L. Officer, A. Rosselli

7 **Production Efficiency in Domesday England, 1086**
   John McDonald

8 **Free Trade and its Reception 1815–1960**
   Freedom and trade: Volume I
   Edited by Andrew Marrison

9 **Conceiving Companies**
   Joint-stock politics in Victorian England
   Timothy L. Alborn

10 **The British Industrial Decline Reconsidered**
   Edited by Jean-Pierre Dormois and Michael Dintenfass

11 **The Conservatives and Industrial Efficiency, 1951–1964**
Thirteen wasted years?
Nick Tiratsoo and Jim Tomlinson

12 **Pacific Centuries**
Pacific and Pacific Rim economic history since the 16th century
Edited by Dennis O. Flynn, Lionel Frost and A. J. H. Latham

13 **The Premodern Chinese Economy**
Structural equilibrium and capitalist sterility
Gang Deng

14 **The Role of Banks in Monitoring Firms**
The case of the Crédit Mobilier
Elisabeth Paulet

15 **Management of the National Debt in the United Kingdom, 1900–1932**
Jeremy Wormell

16 **An Economic History of Sweden**
Lars Magnusson

17 **Freedom and Growth**
The rise of states and markets in Europe, 1300–1750
S. R. Epstein

18 **The Mediterranean Response to Globalization Before 1950**
Sevket Pamuk and Jeffrey G. Williamson

19 **Production and Consumption in English Households 1600–1750**
Mark Overton, Jane Whittle, Darron Dean and Andrew Hann

20 **Governance, The State, Regulation and Industrial Relations**
Ian Clark

21 **Early Modern Capitalism**
Economic and social change in Europe 1400–1800
Edited by Maarten Prak

22 **An Economic History of London, 1800–1914**
Michael Ball and David Sunderland

23 **The Origins of National Financial Systems**
Alexander Gerschenkron reconsidered
Edited by Douglas J. Forsyth and Daniel Verdier

24 **The Russian Revolutionary Economy, 1890–1940**
Ideas, debates and alternatives
Vincent Barnett

25 **Land Rights, Ethno-Nationality, and Sovereignty in History**
Edited by Stanley L. Engerman and Jacob Metzer

26 **An Economic History of Film**
   Edited by John Sedgwick and Mike Pokorny

27 **The Foreign Exchange Market of London**
   Development since 1900
   John Atkin

28 **Rethinking Economic Change in India**
   Labour and livelihood
   Tirthankar Roy

29 **The Mechanics of Modernity in Europe and East Asia**
   The institutional origins of social change and stagnation
   Erik Ringmar

30 **International Economic Integration in Historical Perspective**
   Dennis M. P. McCarthy

31 **Theories of International Trade**
   Adam Klug
   Edited by Warren Young and Michael Bordo

32 **Classical Trade Protectionism 1815–1914**
   Edited by Jean Pierre Dormois and Pedro Lains

33 **Economy and Economics of Ancient Greece**
   Takeshi Amemiya

Economy and Economics of Ancient Greece

Takeshi Amemiya

LONDON AND NEW YORK

First published 2007
by Routledge
2 Park Square, Milton Park, Abingdon, Oxon OX14 4RN

Simultaneously published in the USA and Canada
by Routledge
270 Madison Avenue, New York, NY 10016

Routledge is an imprint of the Taylor & Francis Group, an informa business

© 2007 Takeshi Amemiya

Typeset in Baskerville by Bookcraft Ltd, Stroud, Glos.
Printed and bound in Great Britain by MPG Books Ltd, Bodmin

All rights reserved. No part of this book may be reprinted or reproduced or utilised in any form or by any electronic, mechanical, or other means, now known or hereafter invented, including photocopying and recording, or in any information storage or retrieval system, without permission in writing from the publishers.

British Library Cataloguing in Publication Data
A catalogue record for this book is available from the British Library

Library of Congress Cataloging in Publication Data

Amemiya, Takeshi.
Economy and economics of ancient Greece / Takeshi Amemiya.
  p. cm
 Includes bibliographical references.
 1. Greece–Economic conditions–To 146 B.C. I. Title.
 HC37.A44 2007
 330.938–dc22   2006026697

ISBN10: 0–415–70154–6 (hbk)
ISBN10: 0–203–79931–3 (ebk)

ISBN13: 978–0–415–70154–9 (hbk)
ISBN13: 978–0–203–79931–4 (ebk)

Contents

List of illustrations	ix
Preface	x
Acknowledgments	xv
Map of Ancient Greece	xvi
Map of Attica	xvii
Chronology up to 600 BC	xviii
Chronology of sixth- and fifth-century Athens	xx
Chronology of fourth-century Athens	xxii
Weights, measures, and units	xxiv

PART I
History, society, culture   1

1   History   3

2   Society and culture   13

3   Athenian democracy   37

4   Was Athenian democracy a success?   45

PART II
Economy   55

5   Modernist–primitivist and formalist–substantivist controversy   57

6   The Athenian economy of the fifth and fourth century   62

PART III
Economics   115

7 Xenophon's economics   117
8 Plato's ethics   120
9 Aristotle's ethics   131
10 Plato's economics   138
11 Aristotle's economics   150
12 Utilitarianism   158

Glossary of Greek names and terms   169
References   174
Index   179

Illustrations

Figures

11.1 Edgeworth diagram   153

Tables

2.1 Size of workshops   35
2.2 Population estimates   36
3.1 Characteristics of Athenian institutions   43
6.1 Estimates of grain production   74
6.2 Slave import under varying assumptions   90
6.3 Slave import under the Isager-Hansen assumptions   91

Appendices

6.1 Calorie percentage in grain, grain–other food ratio, food–expenditure ratio   113
6.2 Annual consumption of grain   114
6.3 Transfer payment by the government (only adult male)   114

Preface

This book will start with a brief introduction to the history of Greek civilization from the Mycenaean period to the fourth century BC, then present a detailed account of the Athenian economy and society in the fifth and fourth centuries, and conclude with the economic thoughts of Xenophon, Plato, and Aristotle.

A study of the Athenian economy is not only interesting for its own sake but also useful as it will shed light on the primitivist–modernist controversy and the formalist–substantivist controversy. These two pairs of opposing concepts are closely related to each other, though conceptually different. A formalist believes that the Athenian economy can be analyzed by the basic behavioral assumptions of modern economics, namely, utility maximization and profit maximization, whereas a substantivist believes that a different set of behavioral assumptions, such as status maximization, must be substituted. A formalist is more likely to be a modernist, and a substantivist a primitivist, although not necessarily so. For example, one who believes that even the modern American economy should not be explained by utility maximization and profit maximization may be said to be both, a modernist and a substantivist, with regard to the modern American economy. Consideration of these problems will, therefore, be relevant not only for the Athenian economy but also for the modern economy and will force us to think deeply about the role of economic theory in general.

Finley, following Weber and Polanyi, suggested that there was no "separate" economy in ancient Greece; it was "embedded" in society. He called this idea "substantivism," thus shifting the emphasis of the debate from primitivist–modernist to substantivist–formalist. In order to understand the Athenian economy, we need to study various aspects of its society such as its religion, laws, customs, institutions, and political organizations. These are important to understand any economy, modern or ancient, but more so for ancient economies because the degree of "embeddedness" is more pronounced for them.

A study of the Athenian economy and society will provide a background for understanding the economic thoughts of Plato and Aristotle. Both Plato and Aristotle extolled a small self-sufficient economy and disapproved of greedy profit-taking in reaction to the burgeoning market economy in fourth-century Athens. They were more concerned with justice than market equilibrium. They found value in what is good in itself rather than what is conducive to pleasure. A study of the economic thoughts of Plato and Aristotle, and their ethical theories of which their economic thoughts constitute a part, will help us to rethink our accustomed values. In particular, it will help clarify the arguments for and against utilitarianism, which forms the ethical foundation of modern economic theory.

The book is organized into chapters as follows.

1. History
This chapter will present the history of Greek civilization beginning with the Indo-European invasion of 1600 BC to the end of the Athenian democracy in 322 BC, with a discussion of important events and personalities. A brief chronology of the Hellenistic age is given at the end, although this book primarily deals with the Classical Age.

2. Society and culture
This section will set forth characteristics of Greek society and culture extending over religion, literature, and popular morality through original authors such as Homer, Herodotos, Thucydides, Xenophon, Lysias, Demosthenes, and tragedy and comedy poets, as well as commentators such as Finley, Easterling, Muir, and Dover. The attitude of society toward women, slaves, and money is especially important and will be discussed in detail.

3. Athenian democracy
4. Was Athenian democracy a success?
These chapters describe how Athenian democracy started and how the State endured the Peloponnesian War and the war with Macedonia until it ended in 322 BC. What were the institutions and the characteristics? What were the instances of success and failure? The balance of power between the elite and the mass is discussed here.

5. Modernist–primitivist and formalist–substantivist controversy
6. The Athenian economy of the fifth and fourth century
On the basis of both literary and epigraphic evidence we demonstrate that fifth- and fourth-century Athens had an extensive monetary and market system. Manufacturing was also well developed. Chapter 6 is subdivided into sections discussing market, agriculture, trade, public finance, and money and banking. The results of these sections are combined and organized into a comprehensive whole in the section where a model of the Athenian economy of the fourth century BC is presented. The model starts with estimates of population and grain production in Attica. These lead to an estimate of grain import and what Athens had to export to pay for the imported grain. Although estimates of grain production vary, scholars agree that Athens had to import a considerable proportion of its grain need. There is disagreement, however, as to how Athens paid for the grain import. Finley thought that most of it was paid by silver. The current consensus, however, is that the

export of manufactured goods occupied a central part. This latter view will be substantiated in my model of the Athenian economy.

The basic building blocks of the model are the revenues and expenditures of the five sectors of the economy – the poor farmers, the rich farmers, the manufacturing and service sector, the government, and foreign trade. Many separate studies of various aspects of the economy – agriculture, trade, public finance, etc. – exist, but a study presenting an overall picture is rare, and that is what I plan to attempt here. Scholars have shied away from this attempt because they were not able to come up with an appropriate behavioral model that explains the Athenian economy. I will show in this book that a set of simple accounting identities alone, with minimal behavioral and institutional assumptions, can go a long way toward understanding an overall picture of the Athenian economy.

7. Xenophon's economics

Xenophon's *Oikonomikos* consists of two parts: a conversation between Socrates and Critobulos and another between Socrates and Ischomachos. The first part contains a very original price theory. For example, a flute does not have use value for those who cannot play it but has market value which is lost, however, if the money earned by selling the flute is spent immorally. The second part contains a treatise on how to train a young wife in the art of household management and another one on agronomy. Xenophon also has a work called *Ways and Means*, in which he proposes ways to rebuild the Athenian economy in the middle of the fourth century. One of the proposed plans was to develop the port of Peiraieus by providing benefits to foreign residents and traders. Another was to increase investment in Laureion silver mines. It is obvious that Xenophon was well aware of the principle of diminishing productivity and the principle that supply follows profit.

8. Plato's ethics

The central features of Plato's ethics are (1) that it is person-centered rather than action-centered and (2) that good and pleasure are different. In both respects it differs significantly from utilitarianism. The implication of (1) is that Plato believes that once good character is developed through education, good action naturally follows. The second theme appears in many works but most forcefully in *Gorgias*. Another important characteristic of Plato's ethical theory is that it is firmly grounded in his metaphysics of forms.

9. Aristotle's ethics

Aristotle's ethical theory is fundamentally the same as Plato's, even though one might say that he is slightly more sympathetic to pleasure. The theory of *eudaimonia* he developed in the *Nicomachean Ethics* should not be mistaken for utilitarianism because the Greek word *eudaimonia* is much closer to good than to pleasure. Aristotle believed that everything has its own proper function and the state in which this function is fully developed is called *aretē*. For example, the *aretē* of an eye is to see well, and the *aretē* of a horse is to run fast. But, interestingly, the *aretē* of a man is not just to be fully like a man, but rather, to try to reach beyond man. Thus, Aristotle believed the highest *eudaimonia* is *theōria* – looking toward God.

10. Plato's economics

In Book II of the *Republic*, Plato explains how the division of labor arises in human society. His theory of the division of labor has both similarities and differences with that of Adam Smith. They agree that the division of labor brings about efficiency of production but differ in that, whereas Plato says the division of labor is a result of rational decision, Smith says it is a result of human instinct.

In *Laws* Plato goes to great lengths to emphasize the harm of greed for money. He also sets many regulations in his ideal state to constrain economic activities, such as upper and lower limits to individual wealth, price regulations, prohibition of interest-taking and credit sale, etc.

11. Aristotle's economics

Aristotle presents his controversial theory of price determination in Book V of the *Nicomachean Ethics*, which was variously interpreted as utility theory, labor theory, and others. Here he seems to be more interested in the concept of just price than the price determined in the impersonal market. After all the main topic of Book V is justice.

Aristotle's rebuke of a greed for money is just as strong as Plato's. In Book I of *Politics*, Aristotle discusses the art of household management (*oikonomikē*) and states that its aim is to procure necessary goods for the household and strongly admonishes against any attempt to obtain goods beyond what is necessary, calling it the art of retail trade (*kapēlikē*). Aristotle abhors the limitless nature of acquisition according to the art of retail trade, whereas the art of household management sets a natural limit by necessity. According to Aristotle, the worst form of the art of retail trade is lending money with interest. As is well known, this idea persisted throughout the Middle Ages.

12. Utilitarianism

Utilitarianism, as originally proposed by Bentham, is the ethical theory in which the value of an action is measured solely by the utility, happiness, and pleasure (including psychological pleasure) it produces as its consequence. Bentham's goal was to maximize the social sum of individual utilities. In this sense it should not be identified with selfishness. In fact, several authors such as Rawls criticized it on the grounds that it sacrifices too much individual happiness for the sake of social welfare. As stated earlier, it differs essentially from Platonic or Aristotelian ethics in that it only considers the consequence of an action regardless of the motive or other mental conditions of the person who performs the action, and does not recognize values aside from utility.

Utilitarianism has been the cornerstone of modern economics. Individuals are assumed to behave so as to maximize utility. In reality, however, it is not clear whether they actually do, let alone whether they should. Some economists, notably Amartya Sen, have criticized it saying that in certain situations people act on the basis of belief or commitment rather than maximizing utility.

This book is primarily intended to be an introductory textbook for undergraduate students but may also be used as a reference for graduate students. It is based on the lecture notes I have used in the last five years at Stanford in the course titled "Economy and Economics of Ancient Greece." I know of no other book quite like this. There are a few books on the economy alone: for example, Finley, *The Athenian Economy*, 2nd edn (UC Berkeley 1985); Austin and Vidal-Naquet, *Economic & Social History of Ancient Greece* (UC Berkeley 1977); and Cartledge, Cohen, and Foxhall, eds, *Money, Labour and Land* (Routledge 2002). The first two are written from the primitivist perspective and are somewhat out of date. The third book is a collection of essays, many of which reflect recent scholarship. There are many books on certain aspects of the economy, among which important ones are: Andreades, *History of Greek Public Finance* (Harvard 1933); Buchanan, *Theorika* (J. J. Augustin Publisher 1962); Cohen, *Athenian Economy and Society: A Banking Perspective* (Princeton 1992); Davies, *Wealth and the Power of Wealth in Classical Athens* (Arno Press 1981); Gabrielsen, *Financing the Athenian Fleet* (Johns Hopkins 1994); Garlan, *Slavery in Ancient Greece* (Cornell 1988); Garnsey, *Cities, Peasants and Food in Classical Antiquity* (Cambridge 1998); and Isager and Hansen, *Aspects of Athenian Society in the Fourth Century B.C.* (Odense University Press 1975). In addition there are many journal articles and chapters of edited books. The results in these books have been combined and a total picture of the Athenian economy presented in this book.

Concerning Greek economics, there are two excellent treatises by Langholm: *Price and Value in the Aristotelian Tradition* (Universitetsforlaget 1979) and *The Legacy of Scholasticism in Economic Thought* (Cambridge 1998). They are, however, concerned only with the scholastic interpretation of Aristotelian economics and its effects on scholastics. Lowry's *The Archaeology of Economic Ideas* (Duke 1987) is written from a utilitarian perspective and presents an interpretation of the ethical theories of Plato and Aristotle quite different from mine. There are, of course, many excellent books and articles on the ethics of Plato and Aristotle from which I learnt a great deal. In particular I should mention the works of Julia Annas, which I quote liberally in this book.

This preface is followed by maps of Greece and Attica, chronological tables, and the Greek units of measurement. The main text is followed by a glossary of names and terms and the references used.

Acknowledgments

During the course of writing this book, Julius Moravcsik, Michael Jameson, Ian Morris, Sadao Ito, and Mariko Sakurai have given me much encouragement and useful advice, for which I am very grateful. I would also like to thank Shigenari Kawashima, who fostered my interest in ancient Greece as I participated in his Greek tours many times. I am also grateful to Annatassios Karayiannis, who read the whole manuscript, and Julia Annas, who read a part. Both of them gave me valuable comments. I am afraid, however, that due to the lack of my abilities I have not been able to make full use of the advice of all these people. My daughter Naoko Amemiya has read the whole manuscript and made my English much more idiomatic.

Map of Ancient Greece

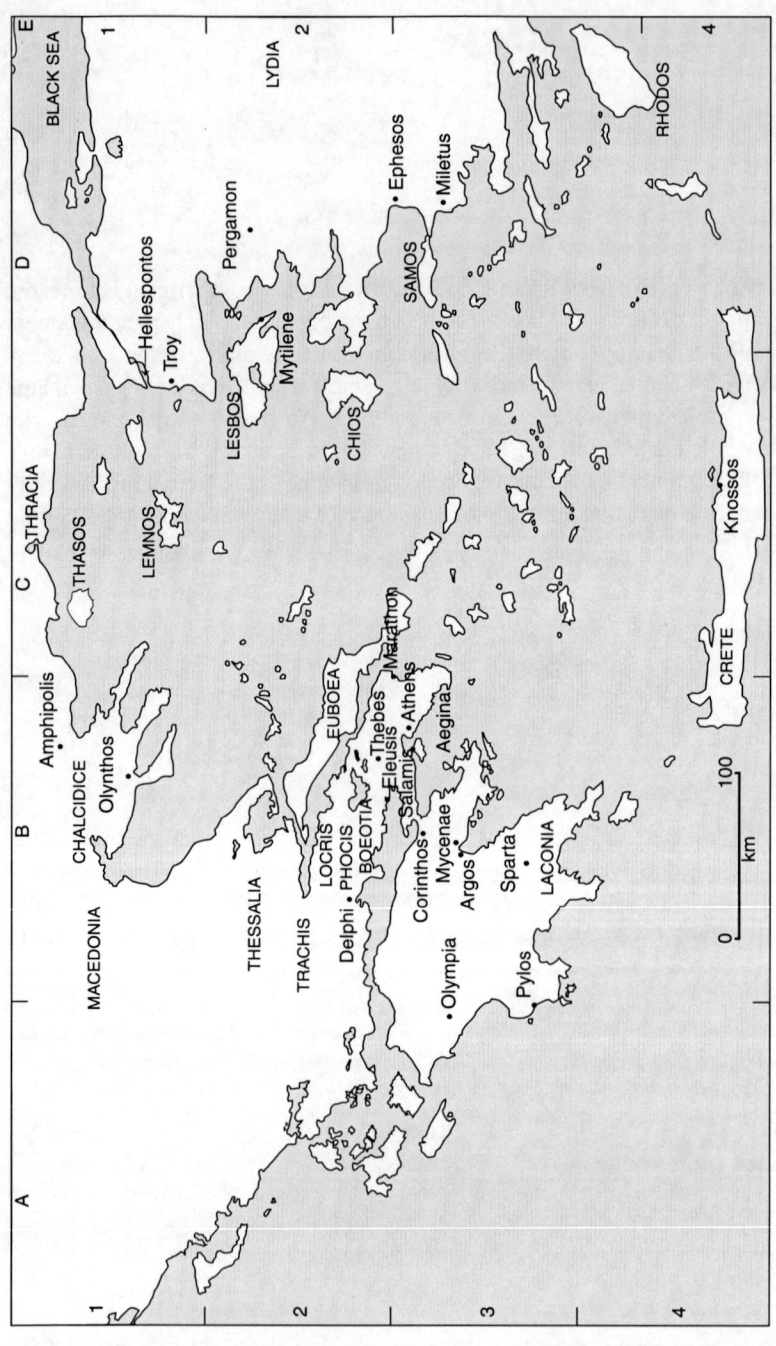

Map of Attica

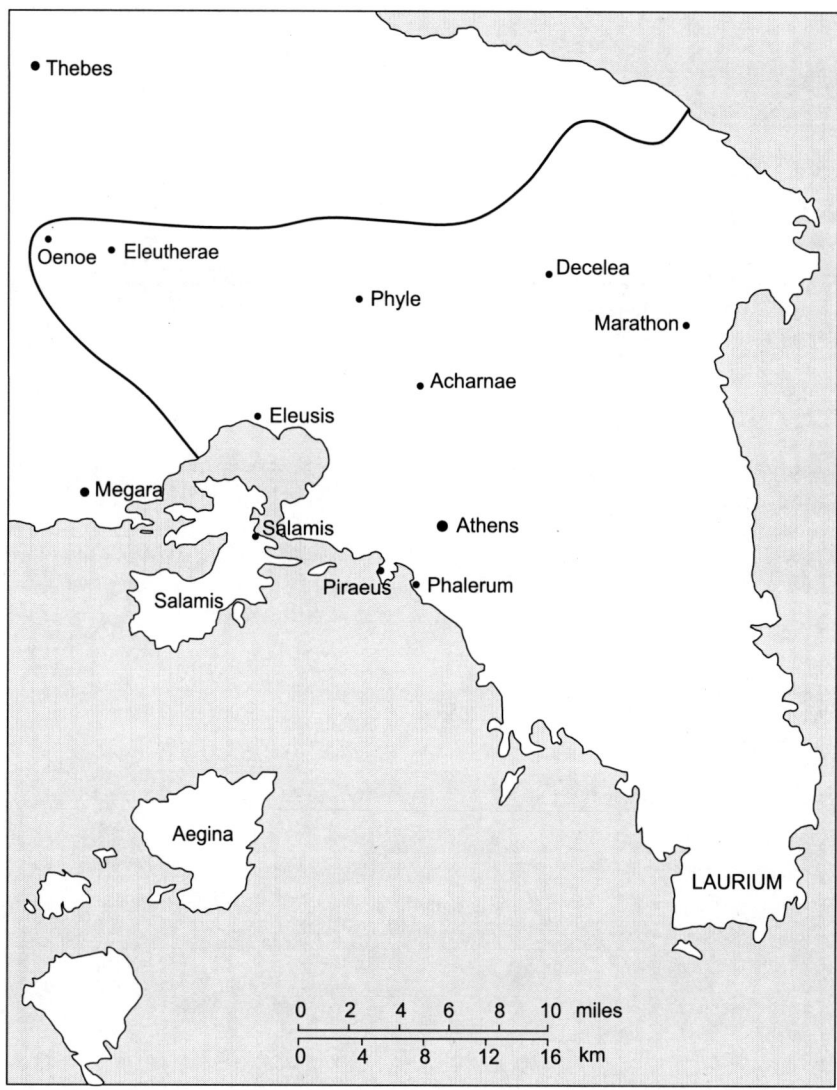

Chronology up to 600 BC

	MESOPOTAMIA	EGYPT	GREECE
3,300	Writing in Sumer		
3,200			
3,100		Hieroglyphic writing	
3,000		Old Kingdom	Early Bronze Age begins
2,950			
2,900			
2,850			
2,800	Akkadian conquest		
2,750			
2,700			
2,650			
2,600			
2,550			
2,500			
2,450			
2,400			
2,350	Sargon I		
2,300			
2,250	Fall of Sargon dynasty		
2,200			
2,150			
2,100		Middle Kingdom	Middle Bronze Age begins
2,050			
2,000			Old Palace of Knossos
1,950			
1,900			
1,850			
1,800			
1,750	Hammurabi of Babylon		
1,700		▲	New Palace of Knossos
1,650	▲	⋮ Hyksos Reign	1,630 Earthquake in Thera
1,600	⋮ Fall of Hammurabi	▼	▲ Late Bronze Age begins
1,550	⋮	New Kingdom	⋮
1,500	⋮		⋮
1,450	⋮		Conquest of Crete

1,400	Kassite Reign of Babylon			Mycenaean Greece
1,350				
1,300				Destruction of Palace of Knossos
1,250		Ramses II (1279–12)		
			1,220	Troy destroyed
1,200	Collapse of Hittite Kingdom			
1,150		Ramses III (1186–55)		Dorian Invasion
1,100				
1,050				
1,000				Ionian migration to Asia Minor
950			950	Iron Age begins
900				
850				
800			800	Colonization begins
			776	First Olympiad
750	Assyrian Empire		750	Homer
700			700	Hesiod
650				
600			620	Law Code of Dracon

Chronology of sixth- and fifth-century Athens

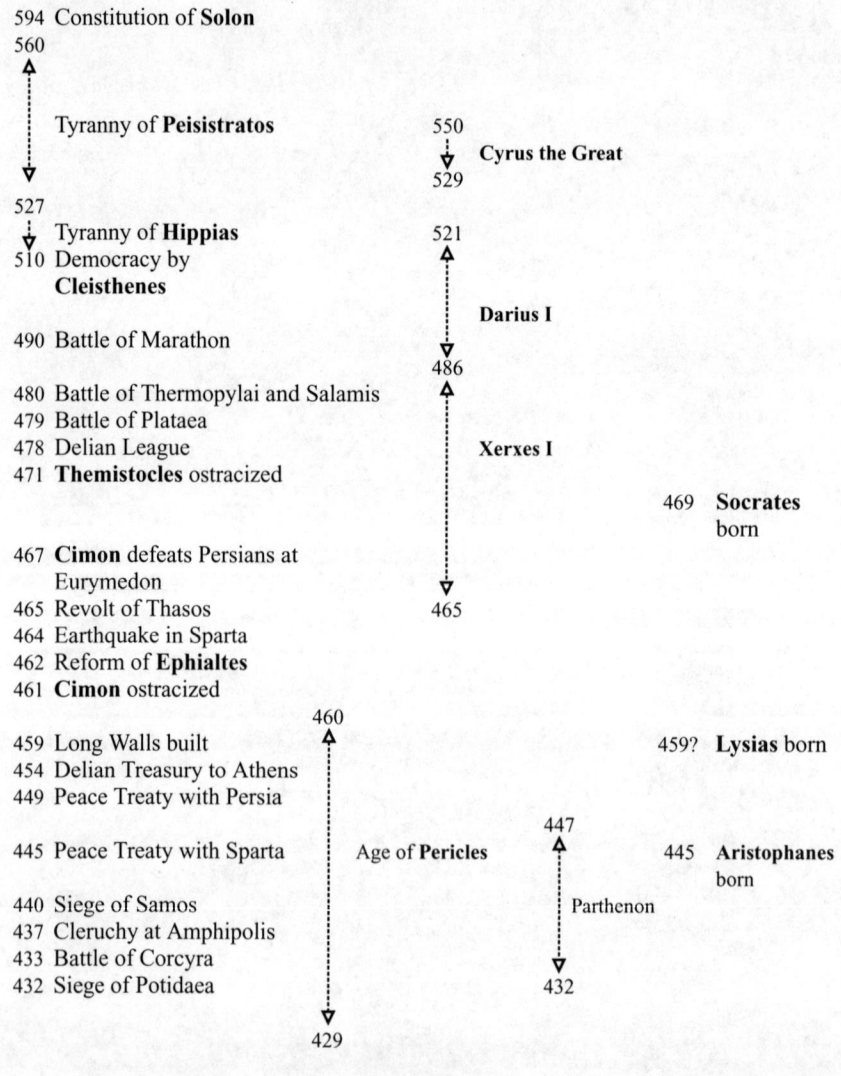

594 Constitution of **Solon**
560

    Tyranny of **Peisistratos**   550
                                          Cyrus the Great
                               529

527
    Tyranny of **Hippias**   521
510 Democracy by
    Cleisthenes
                                    Darius I

490 Battle of Marathon
                                 486
480 Battle of Thermopylai and Salamis
479 Battle of Plataea
478 Delian League   **Xerxes I**
471 **Themistocles** ostracized

                                                                 469 **Socrates**
467 **Cimon** defeats Persians at   born
    Eurymedon
465 Revolt of Thasos   465
464 Earthquake in Sparta
462 Reform of **Ephialtes**
461 **Cimon** ostracized
                     460

459 Long Walls built   459? **Lysias** born
454 Delian Treasury to Athens
449 Peace Treaty with Persia
                                          447
445 Peace Treaty with Sparta   Age of **Pericles**   445 **Aristophanes**
                                                                     born
440 Siege of Samos
437 Cleruchy at Amphipolis   Parthenon
433 Battle of Corcyra
432 Siege of Potidaea   432

                     429

Chronology of sixth- and fifth-century Athens

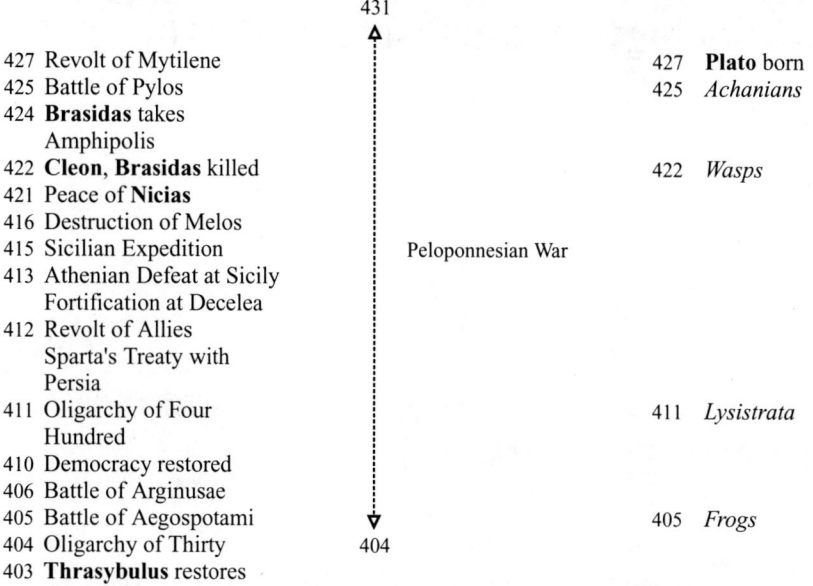

427 Revolt of Mytilene		427 **Plato** born
425 Battle of Pylos		425 *Achanians*
424 **Brasidas** takes Amphipolis		
422 **Cleon, Brasidas** killed		422 *Wasps*
421 Peace of **Nicias**		
416 Destruction of Melos		
415 Sicilian Expedition	Peloponnesian War	
413 Athenian Defeat at Sicily Fortification at Decelea		
412 Revolt of Allies Sparta's Treaty with Persia		
411 Oligarchy of Four Hundred		411 *Lysistrata*
410 Democracy restored		
406 Battle of Arginusae		
405 Battle of Aegospotami		405 *Frogs*
404 Oligarchy of Thirty		
403 **Thrasybulus** restores democracy		

Chronology of fourth-century Athens

			399	**Socrates** dies
		395 ▲		
394	Athens & Persia defeat Sparta			
392	Long Walls rebuilt		Corinthian War (Everyone against Sparta)	
			392	*Ecclesiazusae*
		▼	388	*Plutus*
387	King's Peace	387		
	(Persia gets Asia Minor and the		384	**Aristotle** and **Demosthenes** born
	Greeks get the autonomy.)			
382	Sparta seizes Theban acropolis			
			380	**Lysias** dies
379	Liberation of Thebes from Sparta			
377	Second Athenian League			
375	Spartan navy crushed			
371	Thebes defeats Sparta in Leuktra			
	Peace of Athens (Thebes replaced			
	Sparta as the principal adversary)			
369	Independence of Messenia			
			364	*Against Aphobus I*
			362	*Oeconomicus*
		359 ▲		
357	Phocian War (Thebes expelled			
	from Euboea)			
357–5	Social War (Revolt of Byzantium,		355	*Ways and Means*
	Chios, Kos, Rhodes)		354	*On the Navy-Boards*
349–8	**Demosthenes** *Olynthiaces*			
348	**Philip** conquers Olynthos	Philip	348	**Plato** dies
347	**Philip** replaces Phocians in the			
	Amphictiony			
346	Peace of **Philocrates**			
340	**Philip** attacks Perinthos; Peace			
	treaty repealed			
		▼		
338	Battle of Chaeronea	336		

333	**Alexander** defeats Persia	
		325? *Athenian Politeia*
323	**Alexander** dies	323? *Against Dionysodorus*
323–2	Lamian War	
322	**Antipater** conquers Athens	**Aristotle** and **Demosthenes** die

Weights, measures, and units

Length: 1 stadion (στάδιον) = 203 yards
            1 plethron (πλέθρον) = 100 feet

Area: 1 plethron (πλέθρον) = 0.235 acres
         1 hectare = 10,000 m^2 = 2.471 acres

Volume: 1 *medimnos* (μέδιμνος) = 48 *choinixes* (singular χοῖνιξ, plural χοίνικες) = 51.8 liters = 1.47 bushels
             1 *metretes* (μετρητής) = 10 gallons (liquid) = 12 *choes* (χόες)
             1 *chous* (χοῦς) = 12 *kotylai* (κοτύλαι)
             1 *kotyle* (κοτύλη) = 2.23 ounces

Coins: 1 talent (τάλατον) = 60 minas (μναῖ)
          1 mina (μνᾶ) = 100 drachmas (δραχμαί)
          1 drachma (δραχμή) = 6 obols (ὀβολοί)
          1 obol (ὀβολός) = 3 copper coins (χαλκοί)
          1 Persian gold coin (Δαρεικός στατήρ) = 20 drachmas
          1 Cyzicos gold coin (Κύζικος στατήρ) = 28 drachmas

Part I
History, society, culture

1 History

Introduction

I will present a brief outline of ancient Greek history, covering a period roughly from 1600 BC (the time of the first Indo-European invasion of Greece) to 322 BC, the year Athens was conquered by Macedonia. This period is further divided into the following four sub-periods: 1600–1200 Mycenaean Age, 1200–800 Dark Age, 800–510 Archaic Age, and 510–322 Classical Age. In this book I will be concerned mostly with the Classical Age and the history of Athens, the time and place for which, by far, the greatest amount of information is available. The reader should consult the chronology table given at the beginning of the book. Some of the references that cover this whole period are Green (1973), Fine (1983), Starr (1991), and Pomeroy *et al.* (2004).

Mycenaean Age 1600–1200

Greek history can be said to have started around 1600 BC, when the Indo-Europeans invaded the Greek mainland. The so-called Indo-Europeans were the group of people sharing the same language but not necessarily of the same ethnic race, who lived in the region between the Black Sea and the Caspian Sea. They started migrating beginning around 4000 BC. Some migrated toward Europe and some toward Iran and India. A branch of the migrants moved into Greece around 1600 BC. People had lived in Greece for a long time before that event and an advanced Minoan culture had flourished in the Aegean islands, centering in Crete. These indigenous people are believed to have been of a different race from the Indo-Europeans, both culturally and linguistically. The palace of Knossos in the northern part of Crete, excavated by Arthur Evans in 1899, was the center of the Minoan civilization. Clay tablets bearing a linear script called Linear A were found there. It has not been deciphered but is believed to be a non-Indo-European language. Unlike Roman alphabets, each symbol of Linear A represents either a vowel, or a combination of a consonant and a vowel. In this sense it is like Japanese *hiragana*.

The Indo-Europeans who invaded Greece established many towns in places such as Mycenae, Tiryns, Pylos, Thebes, and Athens, each ruled by a king living in a well-fortified palace ruling a hierarchical bureaucracy. We can see the extent of the power and wealth enjoyed by the kings in the remains of the walled palace of Mycenae and the treasures excavated there by Heinrich Schliemann in 1874. Since Mycenae was the most powerful among these kingdoms, the civilization founded by these Indo-Europeans is called Mycenaean. Within 150 years after their invasion into the Greek mainland, the Mycenaeans invaded Crete and destroyed the palace of Knossos thereby putting an end to the Minoan civilization. This age is characterized by the extensive use of bronze artifacts. For more detailed study of the Mycenaean civilization, the reader should consult Drews (1988), Chadwick (1976), and Dickinson (1994). This last reference covers the Minoan civilization as well.

Clay tablets bearing the Mycenaean script have been excavated from the remains of the above-mentioned cities, notably Pylos and Knossos. It is called Linear B and it uses essentially the same script as Linear A, yet the language it represents is different from Linear A and was deciphered by Michael Ventris in 1952 and found to contain characteristics of the Greek language. The writings found in most of the clay tablets excavated so far describe the various roles of personnel and workers, and the inventories of produce and goods collected and distributed by the central administration. Aside from the names of a few gods and goddesses, not much cultural and social information can be obtained from the writings. See the aforementioned Chadwick (1976) for the nature of Linear B script and what we can learn about Mycenaean society from it.

The major differences between Minoan and Mycenaean civilizations besides the difference in language are as follows: (1) The palaces of Mycenaean cities were strongly fortified whereas the palace of Knossos was not. Many weapons have been excavated from the remains of Mycenaean cities whereas hardly any were found from Minoan sites. From this we might surmise that the Minoan world was more peaceful. (2) In the Minoan society, the status of women seemed to be higher than in the Mycenaean society. Some argue that the Minoan society was matriarchal but there is no hard evidence for it. The Mycenaean society, on the other hand, was patriarchal. (3) The most powerful god of the Mycenaeans was the male god Zeus whereas goddesses seem to have played a much more important role in the Minoan civilization, judging from the large amount of female figurines excavated from Minoan sites. The Mycenaean conquest of the Minoans is symbolized by mythological epics such as the marriage of Zeus and Hera, the defeat of the Amazons by Achilles, and the killing of Gorgon Medusa by Perseus. (4) The Minoans were more artistic than the Mycenaeans. We can still see the beautiful wall paintings excavated from the palace of Knossos, now exhibited in the Heraklion Museum. The paintings of Mycenaean origin are inferior.

The conquest of the *Jōmon* tribes by the *Yayoi* tribes that took place in Japan approximately two thousand years ago has a certain parallel to the Mycenaean conquest of the Minoans. For example, *Jōmon* was a matriarchal society whereas *Yayoi* was patriarchal, and the *Jōmon* tribe was more peaceful than *Yayoi*.

The Mycenaean civilization came to an abrupt collapse around 1200. Several causes for the collapse have been proposed such as natural disasters, famines, and foreign invasions. It is not known, however, whether one of these causes or their combination was the true culprit. Whatever the cause, all the major cities of the Mycenaean age suffered great physical damage and their population began to decline suddenly around this time. The catastrophe was not limited to the Greek mainland and extended to Anatolia and Egypt. Scholars used to believe this was caused by the invasion of the Dorians, a group of Greeks from northern Greece, different from those who sustained the Mycenaean civilization. They spoke the Doric dialect. It is true that there was a southward movement of the Doric race sometime between 1200 and 900, but it is doubtful that it occurred with such great force as to destroy the whole of Greece in such a short time. The Dorians eventually made Sparta their stronghold but archaeological evidence suggests that the establishment of Sparta did not occur long before 900. See Drews (1993) for an excellent discussion of the causes of the catastrophe.

Many of the inhabitants of the destroyed Mycenaean cities migrated to other regions such as Achaea, Arcadia, and the western coast of Anatolia, called Asia Minor. A majority of those who migrated into Asia Minor lived in its central area called Ionia and the dialect of the region is called the Ionic dialect. This migration is attested by the fact that the Ionic dialect is similar to the dialect of Attica.

Dark Age 1200–800

The next 400 years following the collapse of the Mycenaean civilization is called the Dark Age because archaeological finds from this era are scant compared to the preceding era. Houses are smaller, pottery is of an inferior quality, and graves are smaller with fewer buried treasures. Linear B seems to have disappeared and there is no sign of any written language. However, it would be far from the truth to conclude that nothing happened in this period. During those 400 years, there was gradual recovery from the initial devastation and there were signs of development which culminated in the later flourishing of the Greek civilization. The development of this period may be characterized by the following occurrences: (1) The emergence of city-states (*polis*). Compared to Mycenaean palace-centered kingdoms, city-states were characterized by a sense of citizenship and community under common law and common religion. (2) Closely related to the above, there was a transition from monarchy to aristocracy. (3) Toward the latter period of the Dark Age continuing on to the next age, an oriental influence on Greek culture started to make an impact. (4) A new type of pottery with geometric patterns emerged.

Archaic Age 800–510

The trends mentioned in the last paragraph continued in this period and came to their fruition. Among the city-states that started emerging in the preceding period, Athens developed into the most populous and prosperous *polis*. It was the only community that survived the devastation of the Dark Age. Hence Athenians prided themselves as *autochthonos* (springing from the earth), meaning they had always been there. According to Athenian tradition, Dracon introduced laws about homicide and other offences in 620. Not much about Dracon is known, however. In the beginning of the sixth century, Solon contributed a great deal to the development of the Athenian *polis*. He compiled a new code of laws, superseding most of the more severe laws of Dracon, established the foundation of the Athenian constitution (which will be discussed in detail in Chapter 3, "Athenian democracy"), abolished debts incurred by *thētes* (the lowest income class), made the enslavement of citizens illegal, and stimulated the economy and trade by bringing foreign residents (metics) to Athens and letting them engage in manufacturing and trade. This tradition of metics and slaves primarily engaging in manufacturing and trade persisted throughout the Classical Age. Solon's constitution was more aristocratic than democratic. Nevertheless, it seems correct to say that he planted the seeds of democracy that culminated in the establishment of democracy by Cleisthenes in 510 after 50 years of tyranny by Peisistratos and Hippias in the intervening years.

This was the period in which population grew in city-states throughout Greece and trade with outside regions expanded. As the result of overpopulation, many Greek city-states established colonies in regions such as Sicily and the Black Sea area.

The cultural influence from the Levant and Mesopotamia continued to increase. (See Burkert (1992) for the extent of this oriental influence.) One of the most significant events of this age was the introduction of the Phoenician alphabet into Greece in the ninth century. There is no evidence of scripts before this after Linear B disappeared. Homeric poems were the first writings to be written in the Greek alphabet created by adapting the Phoenician alphabet. (It is believed that Homer did not write them himself, however.) The alphabet turned out to be much more suited to express the Greek language than scripts like Linear A and B.

It is believed that Homer was active in Asia Minor in the middle of the eighth century. His *Iliad* depicts the heroic deeds of warlords from various Greek kingdoms in the war against Troy. The oral tradition about the Trojan War had existed long before Homer fabricated it into a majestic epic poem. The Trojan War of this oral tradition is supposed to have taken place shortly before the collapse of the Mycenaean civilization in 1200. Whether or not such a war actually took place is uncertain. Schliemann believed it did and excavated Troy several times in the early 1870s. He thought he found the remains of the ancient city of Troy sacked by the Greeks. Unfortunately he dug too deep into the layers of the successive cities and mistook the ancient city that existed in 2200 as Homer's Troy. (For a further discussion of the Trojan War and a search for Troy, see Wood (1985).) Homer's recitation of the *Iliad* must have been extremely popular among the Greeks living in Ionia because it reminded them of the glorious days when the Ionians lived on the Greek mainland. Since Homeric poems are based on oral tradition, the world they describe must to some extent reflect the reality of the Mycenaean age, but there is no way of knowing the precise extent. Some aspects of the poems must undoubtedly correspond more closely to the period closer to when Homer lived. For example, the *Odyssey* contains stories that may symbolize Greek colonization and the expansion of foreign trade of the eighth century.

The replacement of pottery with geometric designs by Attic black-figure vases by 600 also occurred in this age.

Classical Age 510–322

I consider the Classical Age to have begun in 510, the year Cleisthenes put an end to the tyranny of Hippias and established democracy in Athens, and to have ended in 322, the year the Athenian democracy ceased to exist as a result of her capitulation to Macedonia. I will list and give brief comments on the major events of the Classical Age in chronological order:

510   **Cleisthenes' Constitution.** I discuss this in detail in Chapter 3, "Athenian democracy'.
494   Miletos was subjugated by Persia.
490   **Battle of Marathon.** Athenian hoplites, led by Athenian general Miltiades, defeated the Persian army. According to Herodotos, 6,400 Persian and 192 Athenian soldiers were killed in the battle.
483   Productive silver mines were found in Laureion. Following Themistocles' suggestion, Athenians built a hundred warships using the money from the mines. They also built the port of Peiraieus.
480   Thirty-one united Greek states led by the Spartan king Leonidas fought against Xerxes' invading army. Leonidas was killed in the battle of Thermopylai but the Athenian navy destroyed the Persian navy in the battle near Salamis.
479   The united army of Sparta and Athens led by the Spartan king Pausanias defeated the Persian army led by Mardonios, nephew and son-in-law of Xerxes.
478   **Delian League.** Athens organized it in defense against the Persians, with its headquarters first at Delos and later at Athens. Chios, Samos, and Lesbos provided ships, and the other states money. In its heyday, around 467, 200 states joined the league. The reasons why Athens, rather than Sparta, organized such a league are that the former played a more important role in the war against Persians and that it was anxious to secure the region around Hellespontos for the safety of grain importation from the Black Sea region. The league gradually developed into an Athenian hegemony with Athens controlling the political and judicial affairs of the other members. In the 440s it became an economically unified entity with a unified system of currency and weights and measures.
462   **Reform of Ephialtes.** Democracy started by Cleisthenes was made complete.
461   **Cimon ostracized.** See "Glossary of Greek names and terms" at the end of the book for Cimon and ostracism. His ostracism ushered in the age of Pericles, his major political rival.
460   **Age of Pericles** began. It lasted till his death in 429. The Parthenon was built during the period 447–32. This is also called the golden age of Greece.
431   **Peloponnesian War** started. What prompted it initially was a dispute between Athens and Corinth but it soon developed into a war between the

Athenian League and the Peloponnesian Alliance headed by Sparta. The major members of the Athenian League were Lesbos, Chios, Samos, cities in Asia Minor, the Hellespont, the Thracian cities, most of the islands except Melos and Thera, and Corcyra. The major members of the Spartan Alliance were Corinth, all the cities in Peloponnesos except Argos and Achaea which were neutral, Megara, Boeotia, Locris, Phocis, and Leucas. It lasted until 404 with a brief interlude after the Peace of Nicias in 421. Soon after the beginning of the war, Pericles ordered Athenian citizens to abandon their farms and move from the countryside of Attica into the center of the city within the walls. During the winter they were able to go back to their farms because the Spartan army too went back home. The overcrowding of the city caused a high death rate when plague broke out in 430, eventually killing one-third of the population, including Pericles himself.

416 **Destruction of Melos.** See the section "Examples of failure" in Chapter 4, "Was Athenian democracy a success?".

415 **Sicilian Expedition.** Alcibiades, driven by personal greed and ambition, was the major advocate of the expedition and persuaded the Assembly in spite of Nicias' well-advised opposition. Alcibiades and Nicias were chosen to be the generals that led the expedition consisting of 40,000 (according to Thucydides) people. Right before the ships left for Sicily, a certain act of sacrilege was discovered. Several of Hermes' statues were destroyed and a secret of the Eleusinian mystery was revealed. Alcibiades was indicted and sentenced to death for this act, with his property confiscated and auctioned off. It is not known, however, whether he was actually guilty of the act. Hearing this news, Alcibiades went ashore and defected to Sparta revealing all the military secrets to the Spartans. After a while, however, he fell into disfavor with the Spartans and defected to Persia.

413 **Athenian Defeat at Sicily.**

411 **Oligarchy of Four Hundred.** See Theramenes and Thrasybulos in "Glossary". It was brought about by Alcibiades' cunning plot. When democracy was restored in the next year, Alcibiades, in a characteristic flip-flop, joined the democrats and was rehabilitated as an Athenian citizen a few years later.

406 **Battle of Arginusai.** Arginusai are small islands between Lesbos and Asia Minor. Athenians won a decisive sea battle there against Spartans, but six of the eight Athenian generals who fought there were later recalled home and executed for not rescuing Athenian sailors who were drowning and for not collecting the dead. Actually the sea was so rough that it was not possible to save them. On the day this motion was approved, Socrates was the chairman of the Assembly and opposed the motion against popular sentiment. For a detailed account of the battle of Arginusai and the ensuing debate in the Assembly regarding the motion to execute the generals, see *Hellenica* (I. vi and vii) of Xenophon.

405 **Battle of Aigos Potamoi.** Aigos potamoi is on the eastern shore of Chersonesos. As a result of a military blunder, 171 Athenian ships were

captured by Spartans led by General Lysander. It effectively ended the war in Sparta's favor.

404 **Oligarchy of Thirty.** Athens accepted all of Sparta's conditions. The Long Walls were dismantled and Athens was allowed to have only 12 vessels. An oligarchy was set up by Lysander and headed by Socrates' former pupil Critias. See Theramenes in "Glossary".

403 Democracy was restored. See Thrasybulos in "Glossary".

399 **Trial and Execution of Socrates.** The ostensible reason for the indictment stated that Socrates did not believe in traditional Greek gods and corrupted the youth. Both accounts were contrary to the truth and the accusers knew it themselves. Some, like Stone (1988), argue that Socrates was executed for inciting a plot against democracy. As evidence they point out that Critias, a leader of the Oligarchy of Thirty, was once Socrates' pupil. Xenophon (*Memorabilia*, I. ii. 12–16) correctly argues that Socrates should not be accused if some of his pupils, like Alcibiades and Critias, turned out to be bad in spite of his education. Stone's thesis is contrary to Socrates' statement in Plato's *Crito* to the effect that he values the laws of Athens and therefore should obey them. Stone's book views Socrates as a third-rate politician, rather than a first-rate philosopher. Socrates was executed because he was ahead of his time by so many years. For example, he was against war for the sake of gain and against slavery. (Note that even Plato took slavery for granted.) Xenophon (*Memorabilia*, I. ii. 1) writes:

> No less wonderful is it to me that some believed the charge brought against Socrates of corrupting the youth. In the first place, apart from what I have said, in control of his own passions and appetites he was the strictest of men; further, in endurance of cold and heat and every kind of toil he was most resolute; and besides, his needs were so schooled to moderation that having very little he was yet very content. Such was his own character: how then can he have led others into impiety, crime, gluttony, lust, or sloth?
>
> (Trans. E. C. Marchant, Loeb Classical Library)

Xenophon (*Memorabilia*, IV. viii. 11) concludes as follows:

> All who knew what manner of man Socrates was and who seek after virtue continue to this day to miss him beyond all others, as the chief of helpers in the quest of virtue. For myself, I have described him as he was: so religious that he did nothing without counsel from the gods; so just that he did no injury, however small, to any man, but conferred the greatest benefits on all who dealt with him; so self-controlled that he never chose the pleasanter rather than the better course; so wise that he was unerring in his judgment of the better and the worse, and needed no counsellor, but relied on himself for his knowledge of them; masterly in expounding and defining such things; no less masterly in putting others to the test, and convincing them of

error and exhorting them to follow virtue and gentleness. To me then he seemed to be all that a truly good and happy man must be.

Even though Socrates was condemned to death by the Athenian court, he could have gone free by paying a fee or could have fled to a foreign country, but Socrates calmly accepted death as he believed it to be a just thing to do. His last hours are movingly portrayed in Plato's *Phaedo*. After sending home his wife and children, Socrates engages in philosophical discussions with several of his disciples. All his disciples are emotionally upset and in tears; only Socrates remains calm and behaves as if it were any other day.

395–87 Corinthian War. After the end of the war the balance of power among Greek states quickly changed. Sparta suddenly became unpopular as the domineering new leader of Greece, forcing an oligarchic form of government on the other states. In the Corinthian War, the allied forces of Athens, Thebes, Corinth, Argos, as well as Persia fought against Sparta. At the conclusion of the war, King's Peace was arranged by Artaxerxes II of Persia, and cities in Asia and Cyprus came under Persian control in exchange for the autonomy of the Greeks.

392 Long Walls were rebuilt with the help of Persian money.

377 Second Athenian League. At the beginning, Athens was less domineering over the members of the league. For example, the monies paid by the members, which were previously called "tributes," were called "contributions" instead. But it soon started to acquire its former characteristics and aroused the animosity of its members.

371 Thebes defeated Sparta in Leuktra. From this time on, Thebes replaced Sparta as the main adversary of Athens.

359 Philip became the king of Macedonia. In 357 he besieged Amphipolis and in 352 defeated Thessalian tyrants and Phocians. At this stage, however, Philip had not yet posed a major threat to Athens. In two of Demosthenes' speeches, *Against Aristocrates* (XXIII), written in 352, and *For the Liberty of the Rhodians* (XV), written in 351, Philip is mentioned only as an insignificant menace (Sealey 1993, pp. 125–6).

357–5 Social War (Revolt of Byzantium, Chios, Kos, and Rhodes). It was caused more by ambitions of the revolting cities than by Athenian imperialism (Sealey 1993, p. 110).

355 The End of the Second Athenian League. Isocrates' *On the Peace* and Xenophon's *Ways and Means* proposed ways to manage Athenian finance without the league, and *Eubulos* (see "Glossary") put their proposals into practice.

348 Philip captured and destroyed Olynthos. Earlier, in 349–8, Demosthenes in his *First, Second, and Third Olynthiac* (I, II, and III) argued for resisting Philip in defense of Olynthos.

347 Philip replaced Phocia in the Delphic Amphictiony (a league of Greek states formed for the purpose of protecting Delphic sanctuary). He took control of

Thermopylai, a strategic pass on the major path from the north into central and southern Greece.
- 346 Peace of Philocrates between Philip and Athens. Demosthenes initially supported it but later criticized it claiming that he had been deceived by Philocrates and Aischines (XIX, *On the Embassy*, written in 343).
- 340 Philip attacked Perinthos and seized the grain fleets. Consequently, Athens repealed the Peace of Philocrates.
- 338 **Battle of Chaironea.** Philip and Alexander defeated the combined force of Athens and Thebes.
- 333 **Battle of Issus.** Alexander defeated the Persian army led by Darius III.
- 323 Alexander died.
- 322 **Lamian War.** Macedonia defeated the Greek forces. Antipater, successor to Alexander, conquered Athens.

Hellenistic Age 322–30

The period from 322 to 30, the year Cleopatra took her own life after Octavius (later Augustus) conquered Alexandria, is called the Hellenistic Age. Even after the end of the Athenian democracy in 322, Athens remained an influential political and cultural center of the Hellenistic empire along with Alexandria in Egypt and Pergamon in Asia Minor. Even though the Hellenistic Age is signified by an important new cultural development, in this chronology I concentrate on its political aspects concerning Athens. During most of this period, the Hellenistic empire covering a vast area including Greece, Macedonia, Egypt, Asia Minor, the Levant, Mesopotamia, and India was ruled by Macedonian kings or generals. Therefore, Athenian democracy in the classical sense of ruling Athens as an independent nation did not exist. Nevertheless, there were many revivals of democracy in this period as a form of local government. After 30, Greece became a subject state of Rome. Even under Roman control, however, Athens remained an important cultural center.

- 322 Antipater established oligarchy in Athens. He imposed the 2,000 drachma property qualification for the oligarchy.
- 319 The death of Antipater was followed briefly by democracy until Cassander, Antipater's son, again imposed oligarchy and Demetrius of Phaleron ruled Athens as virtual regent on Cassander's behalf. Demetrius of Phaleron reduced the property qualification to 1,000 drachmas. He instituted the office of *nomophylakes* (the guardians of the laws), which practically replaced the institution of *graphē paranomōn* (see "Glossary"). He also established the office of *gynaikonomoi* (the superintendents of women), who supervised not only the conduct of women but also all the household activities. Economically Athens prospered under the rule of Demetrius of Phaleron.
- 307 Local democracy was restored as Demetrius of Phaleron was ousted with the help of another Hellenistic ruler called Antigonus the One-Eyed and his

son Demetrius Poliorcetes (Polis Sieger). Athens passed a decree honoring Lycurgos, the Athenian hero of the final years of the classical period who had fought vigorously against Macedonia. Within a matter of a few years, however, Demetrius Poliorcetes started exerting authoritarian power.

295 Demetrius Poliorcetes regained control of the city.

287 The Athenians defeated Demetrius' forces with the help of the other Hellenistic rulers including Ptolemy I of Egypt. Democracy was restored.

260 Demetrius' son Antigonus Gonatas recaptured the city. After that, a succession of Macedonian kings controlled Athens.

201 Rome defeated Hannibal of Carthage in the Second Punic War. After that, Rome turned their guns on Greece.

146 Rome conquered Macedonia. Athens also came under Roman control and an oligarchic tendency was strengthened.

31 Octavius conquered Alexandria, the last stronghold of the Hellenistic empire.

2 Society and culture

I will present various aspects of Greek society and culture primarily in the Classical Age but sometimes from the earlier periods as well.

Religion

A good introduction to Greek religion without a rationalistic bias is by Easterling and Muir (1985). There is a striking resemblance between ancient Greek religion and the Japanese traditional religion called Shinto. In the list that follows, a comparison is made between the two religions.

1   Polytheism. Many gods, especially Olympian, had specific roles associated with them. Zeus was the most powerful god of thunder; Haides, of the underworld; Poseidon, of the sea; Apollo, of music, medicine, archery, and prophecy; Artemis, of wild life and virginity; Aphrodite, of love; Hermes, of travel; Hephaistos, of crafts and smiths; Dionysos, of wine and theater; and Demeter, of fertility. Villages, households, and trades worshiped specific gods closely associated with them. Gods were not necessarily models of virtue. They possessed certain human characteristics such as playfulness, envy, fraud, and lust. Nor were they creators of the world and people, unlike the all-powerful god of Judaism and Christianity. Shinto too is a polytheistic religion sharing the above characteristics with the Greek religion. It had gods representing heavenly bodies, gods representing natural phenomena, gods of animals, gods in charge of various human activities, gods signifying abstract concepts, men turned into gods because of their heroic deeds, and so on. There are, however, some differences between Greek and Japanese gods: (1) Greek gods have more colorful personalities. (2) Gods and goddesses representing abstract concepts are more abundant in Greece. (3) Gods representing artificial objects exist only in Japan.
2   In addition to temples, each household had a shrine at the *hestia* (hearth) where specific gods were worshiped. It was the duty of the head of the household to offer food and drink to the gods before each meal. The hearth was sacred; Euphiletos in Lysias, *On the Murder of Eratosthenes*, implies that he would not have killed Eratosthenes if he had taken refuge at the hearth (see

below). In many Japanese houses too, one finds altars where gods are enshrined and offered libation and food.

3   Both the ancient Greeks and the Japanese love festivals. According to one source, every other day was a festival in Athens, of which 54 days were state holidays when the Assembly was closed. According to the latest Tokyo guidebook, one can find a festival somewhere in Tokyo almost every week. Nowadays some of these festivals are totally secular, such as a cherry-blossom festival, but in old Japan and classical Athens, all the festivals were religious in origin, many of which originated as agricultural rites. They were not solely religious in nature, however. In the festival of Panathenaia, Athenians enjoyed games, horse races, musical contests, and poetical recitation, and in Dionysia they attended performances of tragedies and comedies. Everybody attended festivals, not just citizens but also women, children, metics (resident aliens), and slaves. There was a festival, Thesmophoria, managed and attended only by women. Anybody who has watched a Japanese festival, even the one connected with a shrine or a temple, will notice how gay and rowdy the celebration is. Watching men, women, and children zigzagging through narrow streets carrying a little shrine on their shoulders while exchanging joyous shouts reminds one of the gay procession of the initiates in the Eleusinian festival described in Aristophanes' *Frogs*. This coexistence of sacred and secular is a characteristic of both, the ancient Greek and the Japanese Shinto religion. Unlike Judaism and Christianity, there were no sacred books, no central ecclesiastical organization, and no common worship at temples in both these religions. Religion was a part of everyday life. The Greeks, but not the Japanese, performed sacrificial rituals. In sacrificial rituals cattle, sheep, goats, and pigs were sacrificed. Afterward, roasted meat was distributed among citizens. Most of the meat consumption occurred at such rituals.

4   As one can see from the preceding section to some extent, Greek and Japanese religions originally affirmed the importance of the present life and did not say much about life after death. Through prayers and sacrifices, people expected favors from gods. Dover (1994, p. 265) states that there is only one known epitaph in the classical period which mentions that a dead person's soul is on Olympos with the gods, but many such were found in the later periods. The Eleusinian Mysteries and the Orphic cult, which started gaining popularity in the Classical Age and culminated in the Hellenistic and Roman period, emphasized the reward after death and a proper preparation in the present life through secret initiation and good deeds. In Japan the introduction of Buddhism in the sixth century made the notion of heaven and hell more conspicuous. Ancient Greek and Japanese religions did talk about heaven and hell though. *Kojiki* (the oldest book of Japanese history compiled in the beginning of the eighth century) mentions *yomi*, the underworld, where *Izanami* (the primary goddess of Japan) went after death, and *Tokoyo no Kuni* (a place of abundance where people neither grew old nor died), but the description is quite vague, and I do not think they occupied an important place in the minds

of people. The same was true of Hades and Elysian Fields mentioned by Homer.

5 Oracles, especially those of Delphi, and soothsaying played important roles in the daily decisions of individuals as well as states. What happened in Delphi was as follows: The priestess of Apollo called Pythia lived in the sanctuary of Delphi in permanent chastity. When presented a question, she would utter words of prophecy, which were written down by an attending male priest and given to the questioner. Blue Guide, in a typical rationalistic bias, states that Pythia was intoxicated by munching on a laurel leaf and inhaling vapor from a chasm below where she sat. This explanation has been convincingly refuted (Easterling and Muir 1985, p. 129). It is a part of the long tradition of shamanism popular all over Asia and Siberia throughout the ages. The custom of women in trance giving prophecies is still practiced in Japan.

6 Greeks were keenly aware of the insurmountable boundary between immortals and mortals. Two contradictory aspects coexisted in gods. In one aspect gods were familiar beings who granted favors if people prayed to them and practiced acts of piety through rituals and sacrifices. In the other aspect they were strange alien beings to be warded off so they would not afflict people with curses. There was a festival called Anthesteria held in in honor of Dionysos in February for three days. On the first two days of the festival, people drank wine and on the last day, the doorposts of all houses were smeared with pitch as an apotropaic sign and people uttered words: "Outside! It is no longer Anthesteria" (Easterling and Muir 1985, pp. 19–20). A similar custom is practiced in Japan on February 4, the day of *Setsubun*. On this day the Japanese pierce a sardine's head with a small branch and put it on the front porch to ward off imaginary daemons and throw roasted beans at them while shouting "daemon out!" Closely tied with the notion of the otherworldliness of gods is the notion that gods love purity and abhor pollution. In both ancient Greece and Japan, purification with water was an important ritual. The Japanese call it *misogi* and originally it meant washing away sins and impurities by the spiritual power of water, especially seawater. In Eleusinian mystery-rites held every September in Athens, the initiates were required to bathe in the sea to purify themselves before they could participate in the rituals.

7 Consistent with the affirmation of the present life, what was more important to the Greeks and the Japanese was not where the dead went but how they affected the living. A proper burial was considered a sacred duty of the living kin as one can see in Sophocles' *Antigone*. One of the most important duties of a son was to bury his father and carry on the family cult. The dead were believed to protect the living kin if they were properly buried and worshiped and, otherwise, to bring a curse upon them. Thus, ancestor worship was important in both cultures.

Honor and shame

Benedict (1948) stated that the basis of Japanese ethics is a sense of shame, whereas that of the Americans, a sense of guilt. She meant that a Japanese is more concerned about how others might think of him than how to follow his own moral code or a god's will. Dodds (1951, p. 17) quotes Benedict and asserts that ancient Greece in the world of Homer was also a shame culture. He writes

> Homeric man's highest good is not the enjoyment of a quiet conscience, but the enjoyment of *tīmē,* public esteem. ... And the strongest moral force which Homeric man knows is not the fear of god, but respect for public opinion, *aidōs*.

This last Greek word *aidōs* (αἰδώς) may be translated either as shame or respect for others. It was *aidōs* which compelled Hector to face Achilles. Dodds goes on to argue that it gradually changed to guilt culture through the Dark Age and the classical period, but his argument is not convincing. Modern Greeks themselves say that shame culture has persisted to the present day.

As evidence of the importance of shame during the classical period, see the following quotation from Demosthenes IV, *First Philippic*, 10: "For my own part I think that for a free people there can be no greater compulsion than shame for their position" (trans. J. H. Vince, Loeb Classical Library). Here the Greek word translated as shame is *aischynē* (αἰσχύνη), synonymous with *aidōs*.

One's failures and sins shamed not only himself but his family and descendants, and similarly the achievements of one's ancestors were a source of pride. Thus, a Greek felt strong ties to family and ancestors. Note Glaukos' proud account of his family lineage in *Iliad,* Book 6. When a member of a family became a house guest of another family, it created a strong bond, called *xenia*, between the two families over many generations. Thus, when Diomedes found out that an ancestor of Glaukos was once a guest in the house of his ancestor, the two warriors threw away arms and embraced each other.

Oikos and *polis*

It was important for the Greeks to maintain the family estate without squandering what they had inherited from their ancestors. See Pericles' speech in 430, reported by Thucydides (*The Peloponnesian War*, II. 62)

> Your fathers receiving these possessions not from others, but from themselves, did not let slip what their labor had acquired, but delivered them safe to you; and in this respect at least you must prove yourselves their equals, remembering that to lose what one has got is more disgraceful than to be baulked in getting.
>
> (Trans. Richard Crawley)

Dover (1994, pp. 301–6) states that although, in general, a Greek was supposed to put public interests before his private interests, there were occasions where one's obligation to the state conflicted with the obligation to his parents, guests, or supplicants, or with any other unwritten moral and social law. The resolution of this dilemma was not easy. Antigone put her religious duty to bury her brother above a state decree that prohibited it, but she paid for it by her death. Dover cites many oratorical speeches which allude to this dilemma. As Dover points out, duty to one's parents could potentially come into conflict with duty to the city, but not the protection of one's wife and children. The latter had to be sacrificed for the sake of the city.

Helping friends and harming enemies

Greeks lived in a world in which there was a clear-cut separation between those within a circle to which one belonged and those outside. A Christian ideal of loving one's enemy was unthinkable. Socrates was way ahead of his time when he said you should not harm even your enemies (*Republic*, Book I, 335E). Dover (1994, pp. 273–5) writes that an Athenian felt that his first private duty was to his parents, his second to his kinsmen, and his third to his friends and benefactors, that maltreatment of one's parents was regarded as the worst offence, and that respect for parents merged into respect for the older generation as a whole.

Competition

Greeks loved competition and contests in many facets of life – in athletic games, drama competitions, and law courts. Athenian litigiousness is well known. Ischomachos tells Socrates that he practices defending himself against accusations of sycophants (villains who sue rich people in the hope of a gain, see "Glossary") every day at home (*Oikonomikos*, xi. 23). Plato laments the existence of too many doctors and lawyers in Athens, an indication of a sick city (*Republic*, 405A). At the same time there were institutions that prevented competition from going to extremes. The institution of selecting officers by lottery was one. Ostracism (see "Glossary") was another. Litigiousness was checked by the institution of *epōbelia* (see "Glossary"). The driving force of competition was *tīmē* (honor) or *philotimia* (love of honor, ambition). Ambivalent attitudes toward *philotimia* indicate the Greeks' awareness of both the advantages and the disadvantages of a competitive spirit. In the positive sense, *philotimia* was synonymous with unselfish service to the public (Dover 1994, p. 231). In the negative sense, it was a manifestation of greed almost as bad as a desire for gain (Dover 1994, p. 232).

The worst manifestation of a competitive spirit was characterized by the term *hybris*. Liddell and Scott translate it variously as wantonness, wanton violence, insolence, and grievous assault. Dover (1994, p. 54) writes, "Hybris, behaviour in which a citizen treats a fellow-citizen as if he were dealing with a slave or a foreigner, was an indictable offence under Attic law." In order to check the tendency for competitiveness, the Greeks emphasized the importance of *sōphrosynē* (soundness of mind, moderation). Dover (1994, p. 46) states that the adjective *sōphrōn* may be variously translated as "careful," "intelligent," "law-abiding," "sober," "chaste," "sensible," "prudent," or "wise." The words posted at the gate of the Temple of Apollo in Delphi, "μηδὲν ἄγαν" (nothing in excess) and "γνῶθι σεαυτόν" (know thyself), were meant to remind human beings of their mortality and insurmountable separation from gods. Those who exceeded this limit committed the sin of *hybris*.

Wealth and poverty

Compared to the present-day mentality, the Greeks did not glorify wealth or downgrade poverty. In fact, they regarded both wealth and poverty as bad. Thucydides in *The Peloponnesian War* (III.45.4) states that poverty can lead to evil because of necessity, and wealth because of *hybris*. "There was a strong tendency to regard both wealth and poverty as matters of luck" (Dover 1994, p. 174). Of course anyone would prefer to be rich than poor. But there was a general suspicion that the rich got rich by being dishonest.

> People who acquired wealth do not seem to have been admired by the Greeks for commercial acumen, inventiveness, flair for the exploitation of opportunities, or the single-minded pursuit of profit which causes the self-made millionaire to be an object of admiration in some modern societies.
> (Dover 1994, pp. 172–3)

Thus, the rich were always eager to placate the poor by pointing out in law courts that they were contributing a great deal of money to various public expenditures for the benefit of the poor. Acquiring wealth was not praised, but preserving inheritance or increasing the value of farms by hard work was regarded as virtuous (see, for example, Xenophon, *Oikonomikos*, xx). Gaining profit by trade and finance was good to the extent that the *polis* benefited from it (Dover 1994, p. 173).

Unlike Christian ethics, labor itself was not regarded as a virtue in classical Greece. There were two reasons for this. First, it was believed that citizens should have as much free time as possible so that they could devote their time to participation in government. (Note that a Greek word for labor is *ascholia*, a negation of *scholē*, leisure.) Second, it was believed that it was not good for a free man to work for others. Thus, ideally, most work was supposed to be done by metics and slaves. In reality, however, many poor citizens had to work, and that, though undesirable, was not a sin. If there was a need for work, diligence was certainly better than sloth. Demosthenes (LVII, *Against Eubulides*, 35) says, "Pray, men of Athens, do not scorn the needy (their poverty is misfortune enough), and scorn still less those who choose to engage in trade and get their living by honest means" (trans. A. T. Murray, Loeb Classical Library). The same speech (Demosthenes, LVII, *Against Eubulides*, 30) refers to a decree that stipulated that anyone who reproaches those who do business in the market is liable to the penalties for evil speaking. Pericles praises those who attend to their private businesses while serving in civic duties (Thucydides, *The Peloponnesian War*, II.40.2).

Xenophon (*Memorabilia*, II. vii) tells of the advice Socrates gave Aristarchos. During the difficult years of the Peloponnesian War, many female relatives of Aristarchos came to live with him, but he could not support them, nor was he willing to make them work because he believed free persons should not work. Socrates convinced Aristarchos that it was no disgrace for women to earn money by using respectable talents, such as weaving and cooking. Aristarchos followed Socrates' advice, and, as a result, both Aristarchos and his female relatives were happier.

I will discuss this topic further under the section entitled "Elite and mass" in Chapter 4, "Was Athenian democracy a success?".

Theater and art

Tragedies

Tragedies were performed in festivals, the biggest of which was City Dionysia. They were staged in the Theater of Dionysos which could hold 14,000 spectators. In the Dionysian tragic festival, three tragedies and a satyr play (a grotesque and obscene play with a chorus of satyrs, spirits of the woods and hills and attendants of Dionysos) were performed. The expenses of staging plays were borne by rich citizens as a part of their *leitourgia* (see "Glossary"). Ten judges, selected from the ten *phylai* (tribes) of Attica, determined the first, second, and third prizes. There were many playwrights but only the plays of Aeschylus, Sophocles, and Euripides remain to this day. These three playwrights wrote 80 (6), 123 (7), and 92 (19) tragedies respectively, with the number of surviving complete plays given in the parentheses. All the surviving plays were performed during the fifth century. The themes of the tragedies were taken from mythology, except *The Persians* by Aeschylus, whose theme came from the Persian defeat at the battle of Salamis. Masked actors played the roles of men, women, and gods, with one actor often playing many roles in a single play. The origin of the Greek word for tragedy, τραγῳδία, is either that a goat (τράγος) was given as a prize or that a goat was sacrificed in the festival of Dionysos.

The presentation of tragedies in City Dionysia dates back to 538 BC during the reign of Peisistratos. It was revived and reorganized by the democratic Athenian *polis* in 502 after the reform of Cleisthenes. The practice of a wealthy Athenian citizen, called *chorēgos* (chorus leader), paying for the expense of staging tragedies started at this time. The fact that *chorēgos* was also called *didaskalos* (teacher) indicates the idea that tragedies played a role in educating Athenian citizens and instilling a sense of unity and pride. The chorus usually represented the voice of the Athenian citizens. *The Persians* by Aeschylus, staged a few years after the defeat of the Persians, must have directly appealed to Athenian nationalism. Aeschylus' play, however, is in no way based on a vulgar nationalistic theme. It recounts the tragic plight of man and his alienation from gods; as such, it appeals to people of every age and place. The plays of Sophocles and Euripides have the same universal theme. Plato questioned the usefulness of tragedies for the education of citizens (*The Republic*, 606D). Aristotle, however, recognized their beneficial effect saying they acted as catharsis, a cure for the emotions of pity and fear (*Poetics*, 1449B24–28).

Comedies

In the Dionysian comedy festival, five comedies were performed. Only Aristophanes' works have survived. Of the 33 plays that he wrote, 11 have survived in their entirety. His comedies are vulgar and obscene but beneath their façade one can detect his humanism (sympathy with average citizens and passion for peace) and incredible genius. Comedies, like tragedies, sometimes played a role in educating citizens. An example is Aristophanes' *Frogs* (686–7), where the chorus declares that its duty is to educate citizens and goes on to make political suggestions such as giving amnesty to those who participated in the Oligarchy of Four Hundred and criticizing copper coins minted in 406. Another example is a long speech by Dikaiopolis (meaning Just City and representing Aristophanes himself) in *Acharnians* (497–501), where an argument for ending the Peloponnesian War is presented.

Toward the end of the fourth century there was an important comedy poet named Menander. His genre of writing is called New Comedy. He wrote about one hundred plays, but only a handful of fragments have survived. His political overtone is more implicit than Aristophanes, reflecting his time. The Greek word for comedy, κωμῳδία, is derived from κώμη (village) and ᾠδή (song).

Pottery

The earliest pottery from Greece goes back to about 6000 BC. Both Minoan and Mycenaean cultures produced beautiful pottery. Toward the end of the Dark Age, geometric designs started to appear. In the seventh century, Corinth was noted for its pottery which had a distinct style. Athenian pottery, with which we are most familiar because a sizable quantity has survived to this day, started in the sixth century. Initially, black figures were painted on a red background, but around 530 a new style of red figures on a black background started to appear and soon replaced the old one. The names of some painters or potters are known from their signatures on vases. A majority of Athenian pottery makers and painters were metics or slaves and they worked in a district called Kerameikos (from the Greek word κέραμος meaning clay). A great amount of Athenian pottery was exported abroad.

Sculpture

The best and most famous Athenian sculptor was Pheidias, who created the Parthenon Frieze. It is said that he supervised the entire construction of the Parthenon. He is also famous for gigantic statues of Athena in the Parthenon and Zeus in Olympia. Both statues were made of gold and ivory over a wooden core, with embellishments in jewels, silver, copper, enamel, glass, and paint. Neither has survived but one can read a description of them in *Guide to Greece* (Penguin Classics) written by Pausanias, who traveled to Greece in the second century AD.

Education

In the section titled *Heredity and Environment*, Dover (1994, pp. 83–95) asks which of the two the Greeks regarded as more important. The answer is not straightforward, but the Greeks, in general, thought environment more important: hence, the importance of education.

Normally, boys from rich families went to private schools when they reached the age of seven, although fathers were free to choose whatever form of education for their sons they saw fit. A male slave called *paidagōgos* would often accompany a boy to the school. A *paidagōgos* sometimes played the role of a private tutor. There was no public school in Athens. Generally, girls did not go to school and were educated at home. However, Pomeroy (1997, p. 133) states that in the fourth century some women began to receive an education similar to that of men and pursued careers in the liberal arts and the professions. Reading and writing, gymnastics, and music constituted the major parts of education. These subjects were taught in the private houses of teachers. Higher education was started by sophists in the fifth century. The sophists were often foreigners traveling widely through the Greek world, charging fees for their teaching. The subjects they taught included science, philosophy, mathematics, history, geography, and anthropology. Protagoras (born 485) and Gorgias (c.485–375) were among the most famous sophists of the day. Socrates (Plato) criticized their practice of taking fees, Protagoras' relativistic philosophy, and Gorgias' teaching of rhetoric which was more an art of persuasion than of finding truth.

At some time in the 390s, Isocrates (see "Glossary") set up the first "university" at Athens, essentially a school of advanced rhetoric, and his example was soon followed by Plato and his more philosophically based Academy.

Philosophy and science

Much of my brief survey in this section is taken from Guthrie (1975). For a deeper analysis, the reader is referred to Heidegger (1984), which is short but highly inspirational.

There was no clear demarcation between philosophy and natural science in ancient Greece. Both emerged in the sixth century in Ionia and a little later in Sicily. The early philosophers sought nonmythological explanations for celestial and other natural objects and their movements. The fact that in Greek religion there was no myth about creation and that there were no important gods associated with celestial bodies, must have contributed to the appearance of the first study of philosophy and science in Greece rather than somewhere else. Another reason may be that the ports on the Ionian coast such as Miletos were the centers of Mediterranean trade and the observation of stars was important for the sea traders. However, this does not mean that their philosophy was materialistic. The early Greek philosophers did not clearly distinguish matter and spirit. Even Democritos, the founder of atomic physics, talked about an atom of spirit. Socrates, Plato, and Aristotle will be discussed separately in Part III.

Thales

Thales was active in Miletos in the early sixth century. He left no written work but was credited with the prediction of a solar eclipse in 585. He made a lot of money by predicting a big harvest of olive oil and buying up oil presses.

Anaximander

Anaximander was active in Miletos at about the same time as Thales. He "saw this world as a warring concourse of opposite qualities, of which four were primary – hot and cold, wet and dry" (Guthrie 1975, p. 26). By this principle he tried to explain the genesis of the universe and the evolution of man from fish.

Anaximenes

Anaximenes was active in Miletos in the second half of the sixth century. He said that air trapped in the body is the soul, very much like the Chinese doctrine of *Qi*. He also believed that air released from the body becomes one with the air in the universe. This is reminiscent of Eastern philosophy.

Heraclitus

Born in Ephesos, Heraclitus was active around 500. Only fragments of his work remain. His writings are cryptic and enigmatic; nevertheless, they are highly interesting. He is famous for having said or being believed to have said, "πάντα ῥεί" (everything flows). Another famous remark "ἕν πάντα πάντα ἕν" (one is all, all is one) also reminds one of Eastern philosophy.

Pythagoras

Pythagoras was born in Samos in the mid-sixth century, migrated to Croton in southern Italy in *c*.530, and founded a popular religious sect there. Later he was expelled for political reasons and, as a result, Pythagorean communities spread all over Greece. He believed in the reincarnation of souls, emphasized the idea of *kosmos* (order, fitness, beauty), and regarded numbers to be the central existence in the universe. He influenced Plato in all these beliefs. In the case of Pythagoras, the center of attention of the philosopher shifted from matter to form and structure.

Parmenides

Parmenides was born in Elea (southern Italy) and was active in the first half of the fifth century. He argued that movement is an illusion and that only the mind, not senses, can reach the truth.

Anaxagoras

Anaxagoras was born in Ionia in 500 but lived in Athens. He is known to have said that the sun was not a deity but a white-hot stone. He was prosecuted for impiety and forced to leave the city.

Democritos

Democritos was born around 460. He said that all objects consist of atoms, which were so small that man could not see them and they were indestructible, and the differences of perceptible objects resulted from the sizes and shapes of the atoms and their relative positions and motions. He influenced both Plato and Aristotle in his emphasis on virtue and admonition against greed. He preceded Plato in his idea on the division of labor originating from the different inclinations and skills of men. He is also regarded as the father of psychological hedonism (see Karayiannis (1988) for a more detailed discussion).

Status of women

The status of women in ancient Greece was certainly much lower than in modern Western countries. There are disagreements, however, about how low it was. I will present both arguments below. I will first present arguments for and against the proposition that women stayed home most of the time. In writing this section I am greatly indebted to Sakurai (1992). Standard English references about the status of Greek women are Pomeroy (1975) and Blundell (1995). But before that, a brief synopsis of Lysias' speech *On the Murder of Eratosthenes* will be given, as it contains useful information about the status of women as well as about family life in classical Athens.

Lysias, On the Murder of Eratosthenes

At first Euphiletos watched his wife as much as possible, but after a child was born, he came to trust her and put her in charge of household affairs. He regarded her as an efficient housekeeper and "the best wife." Euphiletos' house had two floors of the same size. At first he slept downstairs and his wife upstairs, but after the child was born, he and his wife switched floors as it was more convenient to nurse the baby downstairs.

Eratosthenes saw Euphiletos' wife for the first time when she went out to attend the funeral of Euphiletos' mother. After that, Eratosthenes tried to seduce her by having her housemaid carry messages to her. One day another woman having an affair with Eratosthenes sent an old woman to tell Euphiletos that Eratosthenes was having an affair with his wife. This other woman was angry with Eratosthenes because he came to see her less frequently than he used to. Upon hearing this, Euphiletos spoke to his servant girl and forced her to confess about the affair his wife was having with Eratosthenes.

After learning about the affair, Euphiletos recalled certain incidents which took on new meanings although at the time of their happening he did not suspect any wrongdoing. One day when Euphiletos came back from the country earlier than expected (like many wealthy gentlemen of the day Euphiletos must have owned a farm in the country to which he often attended), the servant girl made the baby cry to warn the wife. Another time he heard the door open in the middle of night and asked his wife about it. She explained that as the lamp went out, she had to go to the next-door neighbor to get a light.

One day Euphiletos invited his friend Sostratos for dinner. That night after Sostratos had gone home and Euphiletos had gone to sleep, the servant girl signaled to Euphiletos that Eratosthenes had entered the house. Euphiletos then went out to summon his friends, caught the seducer in the act of adultery, and killed him on the spot.

In this speech Lysias has written the defense for Euphiletos, who was accused of murder. (Even though Euphiletos asked Lysias to compose the defense, it is he himself who is speaking in the court in the first person.) Euphiletos defends himself by saying that he did not kill Eratosthenes either for profit or out of rancor. He argues that he was acting according to the age-old law that permitted the killing of the adulterer. In Athenian law a seducer faced a more severe penalty than a rapist. He also argues that it was not a premeditated murder saying that if he had known Eratosthenes was coming to the house that night, he would not have let Sostratos go home because rounding up friends in the middle of the night was not easy.

Proposition: Women stayed home most of the time

1. Xenophon's *Oikonomikos* is a story of a 30-year-old man educating his young wife of less than 15 to manage his household. "She was not yet fifteen years old when she came to me, and up to that time she had lived in leading-strings, seeing, hearing and saying as little as possible" (vii. 5, trans. E. C. Marchant, Loeb Classical Library). "Thus, to the woman it is more honourable to stay indoors than to abide in the fields, but to the man it is unseemly rather to stay indoors than to attend to the work outside" (vii. 30).
2. The wife of Euphiletos in Lysias' *On the Murder of Eratosthenes* seldom left the house. Shopping was done by the servant girl (8). When, on a rare occasion, she went out to attend the funeral of Euphiletos' mother, she was seen by her seducer Eratosthenes (8).
3. Pericles' citizenship decree of 451 made daughters of citizens very valuable and hence protected inside the house.
4. When *symposion* was held in a house, *hetaira* (female companions) entertained men and wives were not invited.
5. Even now, when one travels to rural Greece, one seldom sees Greek women in cafes.
6. In Aristophanes' *Lysistrata*, 15–19, Kalonike says, "It is hard, you know, for women to get out. One has to mind her husband: one, to rouse her servant:

one, to put the child to sleep: one, has to wash him: one, to give him pap" (trans. A. B. Rogers, Loeb Classical Library).

Proposition: Women went out often

1 Many Athenian women from poor families had to work outside. Demosthenes (LVII, *Against Eubulides*, 35) writes, "for you will find today many Athenian women who are serving as nurses ... If we were rich we should not be selling ribbons nor be in want in any way." Again in paragraph 45 he writes, "many women have become nurses and labourers at the loom or in the vineyards owing to the misfortunes of the city in those days" (trans. A. T. Murray, Loeb Classical Library).
2 Aristophanes (*Lysistrata*, 640–5) recounts the participation of a well-to-do girl in various festival activities: "Bore, at seven, the mystic casket; Was, at ten, our Lady's miller; then the yellow Brauron bear; Next (a maiden tall and stately with a string of figs to wear) Bore in pomp the holy Basket" (trans. B. B. Rogers, Loeb Classical Library).
3 There was a festival planned and attended only by women. It was a three-day festival in honor of Demeter called Thesmophoria. Aristophanes' *Thesmophoriazusae* describes this festival. The wife of Euphiletos in Lysias, *On the Murder of Eratosthenes*, 20, also went to Thesmophoria.
4 From Demosthenes LV, *Against Kallikles*, 23, we learn that women in neighboring houses in the country often visited one another.

Proposition: Women's status was relatively low

1 Women could not vote or appear in public courts as either a plaintiff or a defendant.
2 Family property was to be bequeathed to a male descendant; therefore, boys were valued more than girls, and sometimes girls were abandoned in the mountains within ten days after birth. Such an act was not punishable by law. If there was only a female child, she became an heiress and had to marry a relative of her father. The husband then merely managed the family property until a male child was born and reached adulthood.
3 The Greek word *andreia* (courage) is derived from the word *andres* (men). The Greeks used another word *tharsos* to denote the courage of barbarians and women. In Xenophon's *Oikonomikos* (IX. 19), Socrates, upon hearing Ischomachos' praise of his wife, says "your wife has a mind as good as a man's!"
4 In the funeral speech of 431, Pericles advises women that it is best for them not to be talked about for good or bad (Thucydides, *The Peloponnesian War*, II. 35).
5 There are many passages in Thucydides which are derogatory of women, while Herodotos is more open-minded. Aristotle says women have imperfect

reasoning power (*Politics*, 1260A10). Plato would include some women among the guardians of his ideal republic, but he has several derogatory remarks about women in *Laws*.

Proposition: Women's status was relatively high

1 Dowry (*proix*) was the possession of the wife. After a certain legal procedure, a wife could divorce a husband (MacDowell 1978, p. 88) and, when she did so, she could take her dowry with her. Until the divorced husband returned the dowry, he had to pay an 18 percent annual interest. The amount of dowry could be considerable. Demosthenes' father, who bequeathed an estate of 14 talents at the time of his death, set aside two talents as the dowry of his five-year-old daughter (Demosthenes, *Against Aphobos I*, 4–5).
2 In Xenophon's *Oikonomikos* and Lysias' *On the Murder of Eratosthenes*, wives are entrusted with household management. In Aristophanes' *Ecclesiazusae* (205–40), Praxagora boasts of the managing ability of women. In *Lysistrata* (486), Lysistrata says, "Don't we manage household money?"
3 In *Lysistrata,* women go on a sexual strike in order to force men to conclude a peace treaty. In *Ecclesiazusae* women take over the Assembly. Of course, these are unrealistic fictions. However, in order for the Athenian audience to find such comedies funny, there must have been deep-seated fear of women and, at least in some households, there must have been henpecked husbands.
4 Aspasia, Pericles' mistress, was a metic and a woman of such intellect and literary talent that Socrates is said to have studied rhetoric from her.
5 In Lysias' speech *Against Diogeiton*, Diogeiton married his daughter to his brother Diodotos. Two sons and a daughter were born, but Diodotos was killed in a battle. Then Diogeiton usurped most of the family property and did not give a proper share to the children of Diodotos even after they became adults. Thus, Diodotos' daughter's husband sued Diogeiton. Before the case went to court, Diogeiton's daughter (she herself could not sue because of an Athenian law which prohibited suing by women) summoned her family and relatives including Diogeiton and admonished her own father in a stately manner.
6 Priestesses of Athena and Demeter occupied positions of great authority.
7 Pseudo-Aristotle's *Oikonomikos*, believed to be written by a disciple of Aristotle, contains both derogatory and meritorious remarks about women; therefore, the author is more positive about women than the real Aristotle. For example, he writes that a husband should honor his wife next to his own parents (Book I, Chapter VIII), and a husband and a wife are equal (Book I, Chapter IX).
8 In the fourth century some women began to receive an education similar to men and pursued careers in liberal arts and the professions (Pomeroy 1997, p. 133).

Citizenship, marriage, and inheritance

In 451, Pericles passed a decree that certified a child as an Athenian citizen if and only if both parents were citizens. In order for the decree to make sense, it seems that a female citizen was defined to be a child of a citizen father. In reality, of course, an adult male citizen enjoyed all the political and legal rights that a female citizen, as defined above, did not. A male citizen was called *politēs* and a female citizen *politis* or *astē*. Before Pericles' decree, citizenship required only the father to be a citizen. After the middle of the fifth century, it was illegal for an Athenian citizen, male or female, to marry a noncitizen. A noncitizen found guilty of this act was sold as a slave, and an Athenian man married to a noncitizen was fined 1,000 drachmas (Demosthenes LIX, *Against Neaira*, 16). Living with a noncitizen woman as a mistress, as Pericles did with Aspasia, was permitted. Thus, Demosthenes says, half facetiously, "Courtesans (ἑταίρας) we keep for the sake of pleasure, mistresses (παλλακάς) for the daily care of our persons, but wives (γυναῖκες) to bear us legitimate children and to be faithful guardians of our households" (ibid. 122, trans. A. T. Murray, Loeb Classical Library; Greek words are my insertions). Mistresses were of two kinds: those kept to produce citizen children and those not. The former must have been necessarily citizens themselves in view of Pericles' decree, except in the case of Aspasia, whose children were granted citizenship by a special decree. The latter were usually slaves and their children also became slaves (MacDowell 1978, p. 89). According to Diogenes Laertios (*Lives of Eminent Philosophers*, II. 26), a law of 406 allowed a married man to have legitimate children with a woman other than his wife. Because of a decline in the citizen population during the Peloponnesian War, the Periclean citizenship decree was practically ignored until it started being enforced again at the end of the war and remained in effect until the end of the Athenian democracy.

Marriages were usually arranged by fathers. Sons sometimes had some say in their marriage, but daughters never did. A woman could not be legally married to a direct ascendant or descendant, nor to her brother or half-brother by the same mother. She could be married to her half-brother by the same father, or to her uncle or cousin (MacDowell 1978, p. 86).

There was no written record or registration of marriage. A proof for legitimate marriage quoted in a court was a promise of marriage called *engyē* between a man and a bride's father. To register a child in the registry of *phratria* (clan), the father had to swear that the child was born from a citizen wife through *engyē* (ἐξ ἄρτες καὶ ἐγγυήτες).

When the head of a household died, his estate was equally divided among his surviving sons. If he had no sons but had a daughter (called *epiklēros*), she was married to the nearest male relative of the deceased father. The husband would then manage the estate until a son was born. The son would eventually inherit the estate. If a man had neither son nor daughter, he would normally adopt a son (MacDowell 1978, pp. 95–100). Widows were expected to live with their sons. Sixty-five percent of widows remained unmarried (Gallant 1991, p. 27).

Slavery

Slave population

Slaves played a significant role in classical Athens. Although an exact number is unknown and hard to estimate, Hansen (1991) guesses that there may have been over 150,000 slaves in Attica in the fourth century, compared to 100,000 citizens (including women and children) and 40,000 metics. This makes the slave population more than a half of the entire population of Attica. In contrast, the ratio was about one-third in the American South and one-tenth in ancient Rome. Hansen's estimate may be on the high side, but there is no doubt that slaves were ubiquitous in Athenian society (see ranges of population estimates in Table 2.2). Most of the Athenian slaves were barbarians (non-Greeks), although not all. For example, women and children were brought home as slaves after the destruction of Melos in 416. Most of the slaves came from regions such as Thracia, Scythia, Caria, Syria, Libya, Phrygia, Lydia, Sicily, the Black Sea region, and Egypt. Athens was the center of the slave trade and new slaves were constantly being imported into Athens (see the section "Athenian slave import" in Chapter 6, "The Athenian economy of the fifth and fourth century"). Homebred slaves were few. In Xenophon, *Oikonomikos* (ix. 5), Ischomachos tells Socrates that in his estate the female servants' quarters are divided from the men's quarters by a bolted door in order to stop the servants breeding without his permission. The manumission record at Delphi shows 217 out of 841 (roughly one-quarter) slaves were homebred, but this seems upward-biased because the slaves born at home were more likely to be manumitted (Pritchett and Pippin 1956, p. 281). In the list of slaves in the confiscated estate in 414, only 3 out of 40 (0.075) were homebred (Pritchett and Pippin 1956, p. 281). Pomeroy (1994, p. 299) observes, however, that female slaves probably outnumbered male in classical Athens, and the existence of slave wet nurses (Demosthenes ILVII, 56) indicates that some slaves gave birth. She conjectures that the proportion of the homebred slaves may have been somewhat less than 12 percent (p. 30).

Manumission in classical Greece seems to have been infrequent, at least in comparison with the Roman practice (Cartledge 1985, p. 38), although there were certainly instances of it. Toward the end of the Peloponnesian War, however, many slaves who served as rowers of triremes were manumitted. A manumitted slave was called *apeleutheros* (freed man) and had the status of a metic. Only after going through this stage, could he acquire the full status of a citizen, which was rare.

Manumission List of 320s (reported by Davies 1981, p. 48, based on Lewis 1959):

- 72 domestic (50 wool-spinners or spinsters)
- 36 retailing
- 28 craftsmen (shoemakers, goldsmiths, tanners, etc.)

13   agriculture
6   service (barbers, seamstress, etc.)
4   transport
12   miscellaneous
171   total

Manumission List of 403 (Reported by Jameson (1977/1978, p. 134), based on IG 2^2 10 and 2403. This is an inscription rewarding supporters of the democracy after the overthrow of the Oligarchy of Thirty, and the status before and after the recognition is uncertain.):

18   agriculture (farmers, gardeners, nurserymen)
41   craftsmen
23   retailing
8   transport
5   skilled services (cooks, seers, scriveners)
5   miscellaneous
100   total

Occupations

There were different kinds of slaves depending on the kind of work they performed. In descending order of the agreeableness of their conditions, there were

1   Slaves with independent workshops, who paid a fee (*apophora*) to the owners. They rarely appear in written documents. Slaves who were skilled shoemakers paid a fee of two obols (see "Weights, measures, and units") a day to their master, and the superintendent of a shop paid three obols (Aeschines, *Against Timarchos*, 97). A slave of this kind lived in his own house with his wife and children and even had slaves of his own. An example of such a slave was Pasion (see "Glossary"), who was eventually granted citizenship. He was one of the richest men in Athens bequeathing an estate worth 80 talents. The slave he owned, Phormion, was also eventually granted citizenship. Menekles was a slave who had property worth 7,000 drachmas (Isaios II, 29 and 35). Another slave, Stratokles, bequeathed a property worth five talents and 3,000 drachmas (Isaios XI, 42). Pseudo-Xenophon (*Athenian Constitution*) says that one cannot tell whether a person is a slave or a citizen only from his dress.
2   House slaves and agricultural slaves. There are stories of house slaves being treated almost like family members. In addition to doing housework, many of them must have also worked as farmhands (Jameson 1977/1978, p. 137). According to the Attic Stelai record of the sale of 53 slaves in the year 414, 40 were given no occupation and were therefore presumably domestic (Davies 1981, p. 47). This constitutes roughly three-quarters of the total. In the manumission list of 320s given above, 72 (42 percent) were domestic, of whom 50

were wool-spinners or spinsters. Both Jameson (1977/1978, pp. 124–5) and Garlan (1988, p. 64) believe that a significant number of agricultural slaves existed in Athens and cite various literary works for evidence. In the manumission list of 320s, only 13 are listed as working in agriculture, but Jameson (1977/1978, pp. 133–4) believes there is a downward bias because slaves working in agriculture were less likely to earn enough money to purchase their freedom, compared to those who worked in the manufacturing or service sector.

3 Slaves who worked in manufacturing shops, trade, and the service industry. In some cases, shops occupied rooms of the private house of a master. See the manumission list of 320s and 403 above. Lysias and his brother employed 120 slaves in their shield factory (Lysias XII, *Against Eratosthenes*, 19). Pasion employed 60 slaves in his shield factory (Demosthenes XXXVI, *For Phormion*, 11). Demosthenes Senior employed 32 slaves in his sword factory and 22 slaves in his bed factory (Demosthenes XXVII, *Against Aphobos I*). Timarchos employed 12 slaves in his leather works, and Kerdon 13 in his cobbler shop (Aeschines, *Against Timarchos*, 97) (see Table 2.1).

4 Public slaves. Their duties included testing coins at the market, assisting magistrates and officers, serving as under-rowers of triremes (τριήρης), road cleaners, mint workers, and the 300 Scythian archers who kept order in the Assembly and the courts.

5 Slaves in Laureion silver mines. These were by far the greatest in number. When the Spartan occupation of Decelea (413–4) crippled mining operations, more than 20,000 slaves were said to flee to the Spartans (Thucydides, VII. 27. 5). Although an exact number cannot be trusted, it is an indication of the existence of a great number of slaves who worked in the mines. Isager and Hansen (1975, p. 43) estimate the number of slaves working in the silver mines at the end of the fifth century to be 30,000. The basis of this estimate is as follows: when mining operations reached their peak in about 340, the state leased approximately 140 mines annually for a period of three or seven years, which means that at least 400 mines were being worked at a time. It has been estimated that the working of a mine required about 50 slaves, and the running of the related workshop, about 30. Thus, they calculate $80 \times 400 \cong 30{,}000$ (p. 44). It should be noted, however, that some wealthy people used many more slaves – Nicias 1,000; Hipponikos 6,000; and Philemoniedes 300 (Davies 1981, pp. 42 and 79). J.A.C.T. (1984, p. 185) estimates the number of slaves in Laureion at as many as 40,000 at the peak. On the other hand, Osborne (1991, p. 134) gives a low figure of 10,000. The working conditions in the mines were abysmal.

Slave ownership

Some say that slaves made Athenian democracy possible because citizens did not have to work so much and could spend their free time participating in government and civil service. To shed light on the plausibility of this statement, we must see what proportion of citizens owned slaves. Cartledge (1985, p. 32) writes, "The 5000 or so citizens who at the close of the fifth century owned no land no doubt mostly owned no slaves either ... (but) the ownership of slaves here by families above the pauper line was very widespread indeed." Since the number of male citizens at that time was roughly 50,000, it means that 90 percent of the citizens owned slaves.

Some rich citizens owned a large number of slaves. Nicias had 1,000 slaves working in Laureion mines (Xenophon, *Ways and Means*, IV.14), as mentioned earlier. In addition to 34 slaves working in the factories, Demosthenes Senior had ten or so slaves at home (Garlan 1988, p. 62). In the late fifth century, a man rich enough to defray the cost of a public chorus owned ten slaves at his home (ibid.). In 375, a man worth two talents owned two female servants and a young slave girl (ibid.). Plato had five slaves, Aristotle thirteen, and Theophrastos nine (ibid.). Garlan (p. 61) has listed nine instances where Aristophanes mentions the number of slaves owned by various people. According to his list, a rich man owned 5–8 slaves, and an average citizen 2–4 slaves.

Some poor citizens who wanted to work for wages could not, partly because of the low esteem with which working for others was held and partly because employers preferred to hire slaves at a much lower wage rate. It was to help these poor citizens that Pericles started a big building project and instituted pay for serving in the public court. Later, pay for attending the Assembly and the Council meetings was also instituted. It has been argued that slavery prevented technical progress because the availability of cheap slave labor minimized the incentive for technological inventions.

Demosthenes, Against Aphobos I

I will give a brief description of this speech as it is relevant to the following discussion on the price and productivity of slaves. I will also refer to this speech later in the section entitled "Money, lending, and borrowing" in Chapter 6, "The Athenian economy of the fifth and fourth century".

When Demosthenes was seven and his sister five, his father bequeathed him 13 talents and 46 minas; however, his guardians Aphobos, Demophon, and Therippides spent a great part of it and gave Demosthenes only 70 minas (14 slaves, house worth 30 minas, and 30 minas in silver) when he reached the age of eighteen. To demonstrate the magnitude of his father's estate, Demosthenes shows that the guardians paid the 20 percent tax levied on *symmoriai* (the 1,200 richest men of Athens) on behalf of Demosthenes, which amounted to three talents.

Aphobos received a dowry of 80 minas on the condition that he were to marry the widow. He took the 80 minas but married someone else. In such a case he should have paid 18 percent interest for the ten years between the death of Demosthenes Senior and the time Demosthenes came of age, but Demosthenes says he was willing to reduce the rate to 12 percent (paragraph 17). Later, in paragraph 35, Demosthenes says that the amount of money his three guardians had confessed to receiving were 108 minas for Aphobos, two talents for Therippides, and 87 minas for Demophon. (I presume that the 108 minas Aphobos received included the dowry of 80 minas.) Together, it adds up to five talents and 15 minas, from which Demosthenes subtracts 77 minas' worth for maintenance (paragraph 35), leaving approximately four talents. This is followed by the following sentence: "Now, if you add to this last sum the interest for ten years, reckoned at a drachma only, you will find that the whole, principal and interest, amounts to eight talents and four thousand drachmae" (trans. A. T. Murray, Loeb Classical Library). Murray puts a footnote here and states that "reckoned at a drachma only" means 12 percent interest. In the same footnote Murray points out that "eight talents and four thousand drachmae" was calculated as an approximation of $0.12 \times 240 \times 10 + 240 = 528$ minas = 8 talents and 48 minas. It is interesting to note that Demosthenes does not use compound interest here. If he had, he would calculate $240 \times 1.12^{10} \cong 745$ talents = 12 talents and 25 minas, which is a far greater number. I suppose Demosthenes wanted to simplify the calculation for the sake of the jurors. There is reason to believe he himself knew about compound interest because, in paragraph 59, he says his father's estate would have trebled in ten years, which follows from calculating $1.12^{10} \cong 3.1$.

Demosthenes sued Aphobos after studying rhetoric with Isaios for two years. The court awarded Demosthenes 10 talents, but apparently he eventually got only a portion of it back. The other two settled out of court. The case took place in the year 364.

The items of Demosthenes' father's estate of 13 talents and 46 minas are as follows. This is a minor revision of what is given in the introduction of the Loeb volume translated by A. T. Murray.

32 or 33 slaves in the sword factory	190 minas
22 slaves in the bed factory	80*
Ivory, iron, wood, gall, and copper used in the factory	150
House	30
Furniture, utensils and cups, jewelry, apparel, ornaments	100
Cash (silver)	80
Money loaned at 12%	60
Maritime loan	70
Loan without interest	60
Deposit in Pasion's bank	24
Deposit in Pylades' bank	6
Deposit in Demomeles' bank	16
Total	866

* Murray puts this value as 40 because he uses the value of the loan whereas I use the value of the security.

Prices of slaves

415   The average price of 25 slaves from confiscated properties was 174 drachmas (Pritchett and Pippin 1956, p. 276). There was little difference in the prices of male and female slaves.

E 4c   A house slave (*oiketēs*), 2 minas (Demosthenes XLI, 8).

E 4c   Domestic slaves cost from 50 to 1,000 drachmas. Nicias bought an overseer of his silver mine for one talent (Xenophon, *Memorabilia*, II. 5. 2).

380   The value of the 32 or 33 slaves in the sword factory of Demosthenes' father was on average 5–6 minas each, the least being 3 minas. The value of 22 slaves in the bedmaking factory can be deduced to be approximately 3.6 minas each (Demosthenes XXVII, *Against Aphobos I*, 9).

4c   A slave working in a silver mine cost 125 drachmas (Demosthenes LIII, *Against Nikostratos*, 1).

4c   A farm slave, 125–150 drachmas. A mining slave, less than 185 drachmas.

4c   Cost of a slave (maintenance and amortization), 300 drachmas a year (Andreades 1933, p. 257).

330   Epicrates bought a slave boy, his father and brother for 40 minas from the perfume maker Athenogenes (Hyperides, *Against Athenogenes*).

Productivity of slaves

In the above-mentioned sword factory of Demosthenes Senior (380 BC), the total value of the slaves was 19,000 drachmas and the yield per year was 3,000 drachmas, implying an annual rate of 16 percent. In the bed factory, the total value is estimated to be 8,000 because the value of a property was normally twice the value of security with a yield of 1,200, implying an annual rate of 15 percent. In comparison, the return from the money loaned by Demosthenes Senior was 13 percent. The yield was about eight percent in agriculture (Casson 1976, p. 37). It was 33 percent in silver mines, and 20–25 percent for slaves owned by Timarchos in his leather workshops (Garlan 1988, p. 73).

The productivity estimates given above have been calculated as follows. For each item the numbers given in the text of *Against Aphobos I* are given in regular print; my calculations are given in bold print. The basis of my calculations is given in the numbered explanatory notes.

Sword factory

32–33 slaves	averaged 5 or 6 minas each none less than 3 minas
Value of slaves[1]	**190 minas**
Net income	30 minas a year
Rate of return	**30 ÷ 190 ≅ 0.16**

Bed factory

22 slaves	Given as a security for a debt of 40 minas
Value of slaves[2]	**80 minas**
Net income	12 minas a year
Rate of return	$12 \div 80 \cong 0.15$

Productive capital (this is listed as money loaned at 12 percent)

Value	60 minas
Net income[3]	more than 7 minas a year **8**
Rate of return	$8 \div 60 \cong 0.13$

Total

Value	290 minas
Net income	50 minas

Explanatory notes

1. This is calculated as "Total value (290) – Debt value in bed factory (40) – Value of productive capital (60)." Since $190 \div 33 \cong 5.76$, it is consistent with the statement that the value of each slave was 5 or 6 minas.
2. The value of security is estimated to be twice the value of the loan on the basis of Demosthenes XXXIV, *Against Phormion*, 6 and XXXV, *Against Lakritos*, 18.
3. This is calculated as "Total net income (50) – Net income of sword factory (30) – Net income of bed factory (12)." It is consistent with the statement that the net income was more than 7 minas a year.

Size of workshops

Table 2.1 is translated from Ito (1981, p. 7) with the kind permission of the author.

Harris (2002, p.81) reports the amounts of loans secured by the property and inscribed on eight *horoi* (stone tablets) placed next to workshops. The two highest amounts were 60 minas, the next highest 17, and the rest were 5–8 minas. In order to calculate the values of the workshops, one should double these numbers, since the value of the security is roughly twice the size of the loan.

Homosexuality

The ancient Greek mode of relationship between an adult male and a boy was different from the kind of homosexuality between two adult males known today. Homosexuality between adult males was less common and less accepted in classical Athens than it is now in much of the Western world. Those who adopted the submissive role in the adult homosexual relationship were especially condemned

Table 2.1 Size of workshops

Source	Owner	Slaves	Product	Yearly earnings	Independent workshop	Supervisor
Aeschines I, 97	Timarchos' father	9–10	Shoes	Approx. 12 minas	No	Yes
Demosth. XXVII, 9	Demosth.'s father	20	Beds	12 minas	No	Yes (?)
Demosth. XXVII, 9	Demosth.'s father	32–33	Knives	30 minas	No	Yes
Demosth. XXXVI, 11	Pasion	60–100	Shields	60 minas	Yes	Yes
Lysias XII, 8, 19	Lysias, Polemarchos	100–120	Shields	?	Yes	?

as *kinaidoi*. The Greeks were more tolerant, however, toward the relationship between an adult male and a boy, unless the boy was coerced to be sexually submissive or he offered sexual service in return for gain. Within these limits, it was considered normal for an adult male to be attracted by a beautiful boy. If these limits were exceeded, both parties were not only regarded with disgrace but also given penalties, the most severe of which was not being able to speak in the Assembly (see Aeschines, *The Speech Against Timarchos*, 13–20). There were various laws protecting young boys against indecent adults (ibid., 12). In classical Athens young unmarried women were not easily accessible. In 451, Pericles passed a decree that defined a person to be an Athenian citizen if and only if both his parents were citizens. This made daughters of citizens extremely valuable and all the citizen families carefully guarded their daughters until they were married off to citizens. Thus, some men sought their sexual gratification from prostitutes and boys.

A love affair between an adult male and a boy was sometimes considered a relationship in which the education of the youth was exchanged for a certain amorous gratification. Plato tells the following story in his *Symposium*: Young Alcibiades once invited Socrates to his home. Socrates wanted to leave before dinner but Alcibiades insisted he should stay for dinner. When Socrates was about to leave after dinner, Alcibiades again implored him to stay overnight, to which Socrates acquiesced. Then, Alcibiades invited Socrates into his own bed, but Socrates insisted on sleeping by himself on a sofa. In the middle of the night, however, Alcibiades slipped into the sofa. Alcibiades says next morning he woke up as if he had slept with his own father or brother. Socrates was happy to educate Alcibiades even if he did not receive anything in return.

Both Plato and Aristotle regarded love between a man and a woman as natural and that between a man and a man as unnatural (see *Laws* 836–841 and *Rhetoric* 1384A). In *Nicomachean Ethics* (1162A16–17), Aristotle states that the love (*philia*) between husband and wife is natural because man is by nature more of a pairing animal than a social animal (ἄνθρωπος γὰρ τῇ φύσει συνδυαστικὸν μᾶλλον ἢ πολιτικόν). One finds in Xenophon's *Symposium* (VIII. 3) a reference to a passionate love (*erōs*) between Nikeratos and his wife. Isocrates (III. 40) considered it a moral vice (*kakia*) for a man to seek sexual pleasure outside the home leaving a faithful wife at home.

Dover (1994, p. 206) thinks that Greeks in the classical period were more sexually inhibited than one would imagine from Aristophanes and vase paintings.

Population

Population estimates of Athens in the fifth and fourth centuries are extremely inaccurate. Table 2.2 presents the ranges of estimates (in thousands) by various authors (Andreades 1933, Garnsey 1988, Hansen 1986, 1991, 1992, J.A.C.T. 1984, Oliver 1995, and Whitby 1998).

Table 2.2 Population estimates (thousands)

	431	*Mid 4th cent.*	*322*
Adult male citzens	30–60	21–35	21–30
With families (×4)	120–240	84–140	84–120
Metics	24–25	20–30	10–25
With families (×2)	48–50	40–60	20–50
Slaves	30–100	50–150	50–150
Total	198–390	174–350	154–320

3   Athenian democracy

A good succinct reference on this topic can be found in Stockton (1990).

Solon's constitution

According to Aristotle's *The Constitution of Athens,* VII, Solon divided the citizens into the following four classes according to an annual yield of produce combining grain, olive oil, and wine:

- *Pentakosiomedimnoi.* More than 500 *medimnoi* (see "Weights, measures, and units").
- *Hippeis.* 300–500 *medimnoi.* Could furnish a horse for cavalry service.
- *Zeugitai.* 200–300 *medimnoi.* Constituted the main part of the hoplites army. (Hoplites are heavy-armed soldiers from the word *hoplon* meaning large shield.)
- *Thētes* (serfs). Remainder.

The *thētes* were allowed to sit only in the *ekklēsia* (assembly) and the *dikastēria* (public courts). It is not clear what the function of the assembly was in Solon's day; it certainly was not as important as after the reforms of Cleisthenes and Ephialtes. People may have just voted on the proposals put to it without debate. The most important officers were nine archons, which included archon *epōnymos,* somewhat like a modern prime minister (Solon himself occupied this position), archon *basileus* who performed religious duties, archon *polemarchos* who commanded the army, and the remaining six archons called *thesmothetai* (statute-setters). Only those belonging to the first two property classes could hold these positions. The next important office was Areopagus ("Αρειος πάγος), consisting of retired archons, who were guardians of the laws and had the power to purge and punish those who conspired to overthrow the constitution. The name Areopagus is derived from the Greek *Areios pagos,* which means the hill of Ares, northwest of the Acropolis. Finally, Solon instituted a *boulē* (council) of 400 members, 100 from each of the four *phylai* (tribes). Aristotle's description does not make clear the function of the council. Some guess its main function was the same as in the later period: namely, setting the agenda to be voted on in the assembly.

Cleisthenes' constitution

Administrative division

As I mentioned above, in Solon's days there were four *phylai* (singular, *phylē*), which were kinship groups. Cleisthenes instituted new *phylai*, ten in number, according to geographical divisions. A *phylē* consists of three *trittyes* (singular, *trittys*), each selected from one of the three zones of Attica – the city zone, the coast zone, and the inland zone. Further, a *trittys* consists of *dēmoi* (singular, *dēmos*). Each *trittys* consisted of one or more *dēmoi*, usually a block of neighboring *dēmoi*. The most important function of *dēmos* was the acceptance of new citizens. When a boy reached the age of 18, the *dēmos* assembly voted on the citizenship qualification and, if he was ascertained to have citizen parents, his name was registered on the *dēmos* registry. Henceforth, he was identified by three names – his own given name, his father's given name, and the name of his *dēmos*, as in "Demosthenes, son of Demosthenes, of *dēmos* Paiania." The other functions of a *dēmos* were mainly concerned with rituals and festivals. There were 139 *dēmoi* and their population sizes differed greatly, Acharnai (a big region in the north of Athens) being the most populated. A *dēmos* sent representatives to the Council (see below) roughly according to its population size.

There were also groups whose functions were more religious and social than political. Most important among them were *phratriai* (singular, *phratria*, brotherhood) and *genē* (singular, *genos*). *Genē* were probably subdivisions of *phratriai*. Support of members of these groups, as well as *dēmoi*, was important for success in national politics.

Assembly (*Ekklēsia*)

This became the most important political institution under Cleisthenes. All adult male citizens over the age of 18 could attend the Assembly and cast votes. Since a two-year military training for *ephēboi* (singular, *ephēbos*, see "Glossary") was instituted in 403, however, the *de facto* age of participation in the Assembly became 20 years old. The Assembly met 40 times a year, ten of which were called main sessions in which they took up *euthunai* (audit of state officials), impeachment, matters of food supply and national security. In one of these ten main sessions, ostracism (see "Glossary") was deliberated. Ostracism was devised as a way to reduce political strife but was abolished by the end of the fifth century because of its abuse and was replaced by the institution of *graphē paranomōn* (see "Glossary"). In the normal sessions they deliberated and voted on private matters, religious matters, and foreign policy. *Probouleumata* (agenda) of the Assembly were determined by the Council, but sometimes the Assembly gave instructions to the Council about the agenda to be taken up in the next session. The agenda was posted in the Agora four days before each session. There were two kinds of agenda: specific and open. The former concerned laws or decrees completely specified by the Council and sent to the Assembly to be voted upon. The latter concerned those whose specifics were to be drafted by the Assembly itself.

I should distinguish between a law (*nomos*), which laid down a permanent rule, and a decree (*psēphisma*), which pertained to a particular occasion. From around 410, efforts were made to remove obscurities or inconsistencies from existing laws and to inscribe the revised laws on stone; henceforth, no uninscribed law was to be enforced, and no decree could override a law. From around 403, new decrees were still made by the Assembly, but the making of new laws was handed over to groups of citizens known as *nomothetai* (lawgivers) chosen by lot from 6,000 jurors. I will discuss this point again later in Chapter 4, "Was Athenian democracy a success?".

Until about 360, the Assembly also functioned as a court judging grave offenses, but subsequently judicial matters were relegated to individual courts. Another function of the Assembly was the election of ten generals (*stratēgoi*) every year, one from each *phylē*. This position was one of the few which were selected by election rather than by lot. At first, a general had both political and military roles, but later he became solely a military leader of the army and the navy. Pericles was elected *stratēgos* almost every year from 443 until his death in 429. As I will mention later, however, Pericles' political influence was not solely, nor primarily, derived from occupying this position.

Although any male citizen over 18 had the right to attend the Assembly and participate in debates and voting, there were hindrances for some citizens. First, a majority of the citizens lived in the country on their farms and attending the Assembly sessions, which were normally held in the morning, required an overnight trip. Isager and Hansen (1975, p. 51) say, however, that peasants came to the city market for trade while attending the Assembly. According to Osborne (1985, pp. 68–72), some 39 percent of Athenians lived further than 15 miles from the city. Second, for those poor citizens who could not afford slaves and had to work at farms or shops, attending the Assembly sessions meant a loss of income. Partially to alleviate this problem, a payment of one obol for the attendance of Assembly sessions was instituted in 403 soon after the restoration of democracy. By 392 it was raised to three obols, and around 330 to one drachma (= six obols) for normal sessions and a drachma and three obols for main sessions. Note the following words sung by the chorus in Aristophanes' *Ecclesiazusae* (written in 392):

> We'll thrust aside this bothering throng which from the city crowds along, these men, who aforetime when only an obol they got for their pay would sit in the wreath-market, chatting away. Ah well, in the days of our noble Myronides now would have stooped money to take for attending the meetings, but hither they trooped, each with his own little goatskin of wine, each with three olives, two onions, one loaf, in his wallet, to dine. But now they are set the three-obol to get, and whene'er the State business engages, they clamour, like hodmen, for wages.
>
> (301–10, trans. B. B. Rogers, Loeb Classical Library)

As I will mention more fully under the section Council below, the Council consisted of 500 members, 50 from each of the ten *phylai*. A group of 50 from a *phylē* took turns to chair the Assembly sessions. They were called *prytaneis* (presidents) and they sat on the platform and were in charge of the proceedings of a session. They called Scythian archers whenever it was necessary to control disturbances. For a scene of an Assembly session, read the first scene of Aristophanes' *Acharnians*.

> Never, however, since I began to bathe, has the dust hurt my eyes as it does today. Still it is the day of Assembly; all should be here at daybreak, and yet the Pnyx is still deserted. They are gossiping in the marketplace, slipping hither and thither to avoid the vermilioned rope. The Prytanes even do not come; they will be late, but when they come they will push and fight each other for a seat in the front row. They will never trouble themselves with the question of peace. Oh! Athens! Athens! As for myself, I do not fail to come here before all the rest, and now, finding myself alone, I groan, yawn, stretch, break wind, and know not what to do; I make sketches in the dust, pull out my loose hairs, muse, think of my fields, long for peace, curse town life and regret my dear country home, which never told me to "buy fuel, vinegar or oil"; there the word "buy," which cuts me in two, was unknown; I harvested everything at will. Therefore I have come to the Assembly fully prepared to bawl, interrupt and abuse the speakers, if they talk of anything but peace. But here come the Prytanes, and high time too, for it is midday! As I foretold, hah! is it not so? They are pushing and fighting for the front seats.
>
> (www.perseus.tufts.edu/)

The Sessions of the Assembly were normally held in an outdoor semicircular space (called *Pnyx*) near the Acropolis, which could accommodate 6,000 people in the fifth century, but nearly double that number by 340. It is not difficult to imagine the amount of courage, charisma, strong voice, and oratorical skill, not to mention wisdom and knowledge, that one needed to convince a rowdy audience of 6,000 to vote one's way, especially as the attendees did not hesitate to heckle the speaker down if they so chose. Yet Pericles managed this at almost every session of the Assembly during his "reign" between 460 and 429. How was it possible? Besides the aforementioned personal traits, there were two ways of influencing the votes. One was through the support of the people of his own *dēmos*, *phylē*, and *phratria*. There were also upper-class clubs called *hetaireiai*, to which some prominent politicians belonged. (In Athens there were no political parties we are familiar with.) It is said, however, that Pericles shunned the upper-class clubs and tried to influence the populace directly. The other was through the monetary favors a politician offered people. Socrates tells Critobulos, "Secondly, it is your duty to entertain many strangers, on a generous scale too. Thirdly, you have to give dinners and play benefactor to the citizens, or you lose your following" (Xenophon, *Oikonomikos*, II. 5, trans. E. C. Marchant, Loeb Classical Library).

Before Cimon was ostracized, he and Pericles were major political rivals. Cimon was extremely wealthy and lavishly entertained his fellow Athenians. It is said that in order to counteract this, Pericles, who was from an aristocratic family but not as rich as Cimon, instituted a payment of two obols a day for jury duty in the public court (Aristotle, *The Constitution of Athens*, XXVII. 3). Pericles also started the construction of the Parthenon, employing many workers. The project was a good source of income for these workers. These acts made Pericles a popular figure among common people.

An increase in the power of democracy in the Periclean Age was partly caused by the increased importance of naval warfare. In Marathon 9,000 hoplites fought, whereas in Salamis 36,000 sailors manned 180 triremes (τριήρεις; singular, τριήρης; three-ranked galleys). Read the following encomium of democracy in Pericles' funeral speech of 431:

> Our constitution does not copy the laws of neighboring states; we are rather a pattern to others than imitators ourselves. Its administration favors the many instead of the few; this is why it is called a democracy. If we look to the laws, they afford equal justice to all in their private differences; if to social standing, advancement in public life falls to reputation for capacity, class considerations not being allowed to interfere with merit; nor again does poverty bar the way, if a man is able to serve the state, he is not hindered by the obscurity of his condition.
> (Thucydides, *The Peloponnesian War*, II. 37, trans. Richard Crawley)

In the Periclean Age, the emergence of democracy went hand in hand with patriotism and imperialism. In the following quotation from the speech given in 430, Pericles makes an unabashed admission of Athenian imperialism:

> Again, your country has a right to your services in sustaining the glories of her position. These are a common source of pride to you all, and you cannot decline the burdens of empire and still expect to share its honors. You should remember also that what you are fighting against is not merely slavery as an exchange for independence, but also loss of empire and danger from the animosities incurred in the exercise. Besides, to recede is no longer possible, if indeed any of you in the alarm of the moment has become enamored of the honesty of such an unambitious part. For what you hold is, to speak somewhat plainly, a tyranny; to take it perhaps was wrong, but to let it go is unsafe.
> (Thucydides, *The Peloponnesian War*, II. 63, trans. Richard Crawley)

Council (*Boulē*)

Cleisthenes established the Council of five hundred (*boulē*) comprising 50 members from each of the ten *phylai*. The Council members (*bouleutai*; singular, *bouleutēs*) were chosen by lot from male citizens of 30 years or older belonging to the first three classes of Solon. By the latter part of the fourth century, however, the property qualification was *de facto* nonexistent. Members were chosen from *dēmoi* roughly in proportion to their population size. Acharnai, the biggest *dēmos*, sent 20 members to the Council, whereas there were many small *dēmoi* with only one senator each. Citizens could not serve in the Council more than twice and not two years in a row. The Council members lived in Athens for a year and held meetings at the *Bouleutērion* on the west side of the Agora every day except the days of festivals (about 40 a year). The main job of the Council was to set the agenda of the Assembly. Holders of important offices and prominent citizens could suggest the agenda to the Council. Plutarch says that Pericles was seen walking to the *Bouleutērion* almost every day.

Each group of 50 Council members from a *phylē* served as *prytaneis* (presidents; singular, *prytanis*) for one-tenth of the year. This period was called a prytany (*prytaneia*). The *prytaneis* were on duty every day. They made arrangements for meetings of the Council and the Assembly, received envoys and letters addressed to the state, and conducted other day-to-day business. They lived and dined in the circular building called *tholos* next to the *Bouleutērion* every day at public expense. Each day one of the *prytaneis* was picked by lot to be their foreman (*epistatēs*). In the fifth century he was the chairman at any meeting of the Council or Assembly held on this day. Socrates was the chairman on the day the Assembly judged the fate of the six generals recalled from Arginusai (see the section "Classical age" in Chapter 1, "History"). In the fourth century, the chairman's duty was taken over by a Council member (called *proedros*) selected from those who were not *prytaneis*.

Besides setting the agenda of the Assembly, the Council had the following functions (Aristotle, *The Constitution of Athens*, XLVI): (1) supervision and control of the implementation of the Assembly decisions; (2) supervision of internal revenues and expenditures; (3) appointment of ten of its own members as auditors to examine the accounts of all public officers; (4) supervision of the construction of triremes; (5) supervision of public buildings and works; and (6) supervision of festivals.

At the time of the writing of Aristotle's *The Constitution of Athens* (XLII. 3), the payment for a Council member was five obols a day, and a *prytanis* one drachma a day.

Public courts (*Dikastēria*)

There were two kinds of lawsuits called *dikē* and *graphē*. The former was initiated by the injured party or their guardian or relative. The latter involved matters of public concern and could be initiated by anybody. The Athenians were quite litigious. To discourage too many cases of *graphē*, there was an interesting rule called *epōbelia* which stipulated that one-sixth of the damages should be assessed to the plaintiff if he should not get a fifth of the votes cast by the jurors. A pool of 6,000 jurors (*dikastai*; singular, *dikastēs*) was selected every year from citizens over the age of 30 years, 600 from each *phylē*. These jurors were assigned to various courts by lot. The number of jurors in a court ranged from 201 to over 1,000 depending on the nature of the case. The decisions of the court were final; there were no appeals to higher courts. Noncitizens had to be in principle represented by their guardians (*prostatēs*). Isager and Hansen (1975, p. 68), however, cite forensic speeches where metics speak directly as defendants and plaintiffs. The number of court cases increased greatly after the formation of the Athenian League because it stipulated that most of the legal actions occurring in the member states of the League had to be made in the Athenian courts.

One of the important cases deliberated by the courts was the aforementioned *graphē paranomōn*. In the fourth century it was a popular method of attacking prominent politicians. Aristophon (c.435–c.335) is said to have boasted that he had been acquitted of this type of charge 75 times. The most famous example is the prosecution of Ktesiphon by Aeschines for his proposal to confer a gold crown on Demosthenes. The surviving speeches of Aeschines (see "Glossary"), *Against Ktesiphon*, and Demosthenes, *On the Crown*, were written for this trial.

The payment for jurors, two obols a day, was instituted by Pericles in the 450s and was raised to three obols a day in the 420s. Some disputes were handled by arbitrators (60 years old) and were sent to the public courts if the involved parties did not abide by their decisions. In Table 3.1, the characteristics of the three public institutions of classical Athens are given.

Archons

The power of the archons gradually declined through the reforms of Cleisthenes and Ephialtes. The method of selection also gradually changed from election to lot. At the same time, the property qualification became weaker. In the later fifth and fourth centuries, the duties of the archons were mainly religious (including festivals) and judicial. They conducted preliminary inquiries of lawsuits and handed them down to the public courts, which decided the verdict. The role of archon *polemarchos* was gradually replaced by that of generals (*stratēgoi*).

Table 3.1 Characteristics of Athenian institutions

Institution	Qualification	Selection	Place	Sessions	Functions
Assembly	Male citizens over 18	Free attendance	*Pnyx*, holding 6,000	40 a year	Laws and decrees
Council	Male citizens over 30	500, 50 from each *phylē* by lot. Could not serve more than twice	*Bouleutērion*	Every day except 40 festival days	Set the agenda for the Assembly
Courts	Male citizens over 30	6,000, 600 from each *phylē*. First come first served	Various courts	As needs arose, which was quite often	*dikē* and *graphē*

Areopagus

As mentioned earlier, Areopagus was an important institution in Solon's days, but after the reforms of Cleisthenes, its importance diminished in proportion to the decline of the importance of the functions of the archons, with some of its functions being taken over by the Council. Its powers were reduced further by Ephialtes in 462, as most of its judicial powers were transferred to the Council and the public courts. This change signified a gradual shift of power from aristocracy to the common people. The Areopagus retained the right to try cases of homicide, wounding, arson, and also some religious cases.

Officers

There were two kinds of public officers, those chosen by lot and those chosen by election. The latter involved jobs that required skill and expertise. Generals and the treasurers of the Athenian League are examples of this kind of office. Elected officers were allowed to serve continuously, provided they were re-elected. All public officers, about 300 of them, were chosen by the Assembly and watched over by the Council (see Aristotle, *The Constitution of Athens*). In spite of it, there were cases of corruption. Aeschines in *Against Timarchos* (106–107) mentions an instance where governorship of a region was bought for 30 minas.

Military service

MacDowell (1978, p. 159) writes

> Every man between his eighteenth and his sixtieth year, if he was an Athenian citizen or metic resident in Attika, had to turn out for military service when required. He might serve in the cavalry (providing his own horse and equipment) or as a hoplite (a fully armed infantryman, providing his own armour) or as a soldier without full armour (*psilos*) or as a sailor.

Christ (2001, p. 405) states that in the fifth century a man had to be wealthy enough to serve as a hoplite, but in the fourth century hoplite service became more accessible to the less wealthy as they came to use less equipment and the state started providing shield and spear. Conscription of all the categories of military service was done on the basis of the *dēmoi* registry. Note that metics were also registered in the *dēmos* where his citizen guardian resided.

4 Was Athenian democracy a success?

Introduction

We can safely say that Athenian democracy was resilient. Since Cleisthenes laid the foundation of democracy in 510, it lasted until Macedonian general Antipater established oligarchy in 322. During this period there were two brief periods of oligarchy in 411 and 404, but each time democracy was restored within a year. Even after 322 in the Hellenistic age, there were several revivals of democracy as a form of local government. However, only writings critical of democracy remain: Plato, Aristotle, and Old Oligarch (author of *The Constitutions of the Athenians* ascribed to Xenophon). As mentioned in "Trial and execution of Socrates" in the section "Classical age" (Chapter 1, "History"), Socrates himself seemed to support Athenian democracy by obeying its law even if it meant his death.

After the first battle of the war in 431, Athenians gathered for the burial of the dead soldiers and Pericles gave a funeral oration (Thucydides, II. 35). In his speech Pericles glorified Athenian democracy, where people lived good flourishing lives without much external constraint. We will see to what extent his praise of Athenian democracy was justified.

Examples of failure

1 In 428, Mytilene, a *polis* in the southeastern corner of Lesbos, revolted against Athens, being encouraged to do so by the Spartans. In 427 Athenian general Paches commanding a thousand hoplites conquered Lesbos. Acting on the proposal of Cleon, the Assembly at first voted to put the whole adult male population of Mytilene to death. So they sent a trireme to Mytilene with the order for Paches to carry out the decision of the Assembly. The next morning the Athenians repented their decision and opened the Assembly to discuss the issue once more (Thucydides, *The Peloponnesian War*, III. 35–50). See item 2 under the section "Examples of success".
2 In 416, Melos, a Spartan colony, which was at first neutral, became openly hostile toward Athens. Athenian armed forces conquered Melos and their envoys exchanged dialogs with the Melian representatives. The Athenians demanded total subjugation. Their argument was a typical example of the

philosophy of "Might is right": "since you know as well as we do that right, as the world goes, is only in question between equals in power, while the strong do what they can and the weak suffer what they must" (Thucydides, *The Peloponnesian War*, V. 89, trans. Richard Crawley). The Athenians praised an aspect of the Spartans – "they are most conspicuous in considering what is agreeable honorable, and what is expedient just" (V. 105). The Melians surrendered and the Athenians put to death all the grown men, sold the women and children for slaves, and subsequently sent out 500 colonists and settled the place themselves (ibid., V. 116).

3 The Sicilian expedition of 415. Syracuse (Συράκουσαι) was founded by Corinth in the eighth century. Egesta was in dispute with Selinus, which was allied with Syracuse. In 416, an envoy from Egesta arrived in Athens seeking a help and promising a large sum of money if Athens came to their aid. See "Sicilian Expedition" in the section "Classical age" (Chapter 1, "History").

4 The execution of six generals after the battle of Arginusai in 406 (see "Battle of Arginusai' in the section "Classical age" in Chapter 1, "History").

5 The execution of Socrates in 399 (see "Trial and execution of Socrates" in the section "Classical age" in Chapter 1, "History").

Examples of success

1 In 483 the Athenians voted for the proposal of Themistocles to build 200 triremes using the money obtained from silver mines instead of distributing 10 drachmas to each of the adult male citizens.

2 The prompt rescinding of the decision to kill the Mytileneans. Diodotos argued against Cleon and succeeded in convincing the Assembly to rescind the earlier decree. He pointed out that a severe punishment would not necessarily be a deterrent to future revolts, and moreover, a lenient punishment would encourage the more moderate members of the revolting party to break away from the extremists when they realize their attempt was unlikely to succeed.

3 The amnesty given to the participants of the Oligarchy of Thirty in 403.

4 In 339, Demosthenes succeeded in using a surplus in the theoric fund (*theōrika*) to establish a war treasury (for the theoric fund, see the section "Public finance" in Chapter 6, "The Athenian economy of the fifth and fourth century").

5 Lycurgos (see "Glossary") also put a limit on the distribution from the theoric fund and carried out useful public expenditures.

Freedom of speech

We can deduce there was a great deal of freedom of speech, at least in the theater, from the outspoken criticism of politicians by Aristophanes. In the play called *Babylonians* performed at Dionysia in 426 of which only fragments have survived, it is most likely that Aristophanes criticized Cleon harshly, for he indicted Aristophanes for the ostensible reason of denigrating Athens in the presence of foreigners who attended the Dionysia. Aristophanes was brought to the Council but was set free. Cleon could not complain directly that Aristophanes derided him because of the tradition of personal ridicule in comedy. The above facts are known from the following parts of *Acharnians*:

> And I know myself, what Cleon did to me
> because of the comedy I staged last year.
> He dragged me in before the Councillors
> and slandered me, tongue-lashing me with lies,
> a roaring rapids soaking me with abuse;
>
> (Speech of Dicaeopolis, 377–82)

and

> And this time Cleon won't make allegations
> that I slander the *polis* in front of foreigners;
> for we're alone, it's a Lenaean competition,
> the foreigners aren't yet here, nor tribute-money
> nor allied troops from the cities of our empire.
>
> (Speech of Dicaeopolis, 502–6; www.perseus.tufts.edu)

Freedom of speech in the Assembly was called *isēgoria*. It was introduced at the time of Ephialtes' reform. "*Isēgoria* was later considered by the Athenians to be a cornerstone of democracy" (Ober 1989, p. 79). It does not mean that most of the common people spoke at the Assembly. However, it changed the basic mentality of people and made them more serious in listening to various arguments presented in the Assembly and judging their merits.

In the second half of the fifth century, a more general freedom of speech (*parrhēsia*), which implied individual freedom of thought, was recognized (Ober 1989, p. 296). Freedom of speech, either in the sense of *isēgoria* or a more general sense of *parrhēsia*, did not mean that people came to the Assembly and the public courts with diverse ideas that clashed with each other, for the Greeks cherished consensus-building (Ober 1989, p. 297). Demosthenes XIX, *On the Embassy* (298), advises the Athenians as follows:

> The oracle also bids you keep the commonwealth together, that all may be of one mind, and may not gratify the enemy.
>
> (Trans. C. A. Vince and J. H. Vince, Loeb Classical Library)

Was Athenian democracy radical or moderate?

Closely related to the above is the question of whether Athenian democracy was radical or moderate. Besides the above-mentioned tendency for consensus-building, a factor which made Athenian democracy more of a moderate nature than radical was the fact that decrees and laws constituted a certain constraint on the sovereignty of people. We should note, however, that the laws and institutions (such as ostracism) also protected people against the attempt by ambitious politicians to usurp the rights of the people.

From around 410, efforts were made to remove obscurities or inconsistencies from existing laws and to inscribe the revised laws on stone; henceforth, no uninscribed law was to be enforced, and no decree could override a law. From around 403, new decrees were still made by the Assembly, but the making of new laws was handed over to groups of citizens known as *nomothetai* (lawgivers) chosen by lot from 6,000 jurors (see Chapter 3, "Athenian democracy"). By the end of the fifth century, ostracism was replaced by the institution of *graphē paranomōn* (see "Glossary"). Wolin (1994, p. 40) quotes Martin Ostwald (*From Popular Sovereignty to the Sovereignty of Law*) to say, "the end of the fifth century BC" was "the time [when] the principle of the sovereignty of law was given official primacy over the principle of popular sovereignty." Wolin (1994, p. 41) further states, "Thus 403 might be taken as the dividing line between what one historian has called 'the radical democracy' of the fifth century and what another has called 'the constitutional democracy' of the fourth century."

It is argued that experts became "necessary" because of the inhibitions of the *graphē paranomōn* and *eisangelia* (impeachment); that without the experts "there would be few bold and original policy initiatives" (Wolin 1994, p. 44). Strauss (1991, pp. 220–1) writes as follows:

> Athens took a number of steps in the direction of government efficiency and specialization, sometimes at the expense of democracy. The most important changes were in finance. In the fifth century, Athens had a central treasury closely controlled by the Assembly ... By contrast, in the first quarter of the fourth century, a new financial system emerged, in which funds were allocated on a prearranged plan to the various governmental departments. Furthermore, both in the 350s under Eubulos and in the 330s and 320s under Lykurgos, the Athenians entrusted finances to the supervision of one man ... In sum, the government became more efficient by loosening the reins of the Assembly.

How does Athenian democracy compare with American democracy? Alexis de Tocqueville said that nineteenth-century New England enjoyed "a democracy more perfect than antiquity had dared to dream of." Americans had resolved the tension between democracy and constitutionalism, between liberty and law, majority rule and legal limitation on power (Wolin 1994, p. 32).

But how does American democracy today fare? Writing three years after the Persian Gulf War, Wolin criticizes American leaders who hailed the triumph of Desert Storm as a restorative moment for democracy. He goes on to write:

Desert Storm ... demonstrates the futility of seeking democratic renewal by relying on the powers of the modern state. The possibility of renewal draws on a simple fact: that ordinary individuals are capable of creating new cultural patterns of commonality at any moment. Individuals who concert their powers for low-income housing, worker ownership of factories, better schools, better health care, safer water, controls over toxic waste disposals, and a thousand other common concerns of ordinary lives are experiencing a democratic moment and contributing to the discovery, care, and tending of a commonality of shared concerns.

(p. 58)

Issues

The major political issues in classical Athens were the matter of war and peace, income redistribution, form of government, education, and punishment. These are major issues even in present times. The other issues that are important today, such as economic policy, ecology and environment, conditions of minorities, gun control, and abortion, were not as important or nonexistent. Here I will concentrate on the first two issues: war and peace and income redistribution.

War and peace

Both during the Peloponnesian War and the war against Macedonia at a later time, there were people both for and against the war. We can read about the people during the Peloponnesian War in the work of Thucydides and for the latter period in the works of Demosthenes and other orators. For example, Nicias was generally on the side of peace, concluding a peace treaty with Sparta in 421 and arguing against the Sicilian expedition in 415, whereas Alcibiades and Cleon were eager to wage wars. When Cleon argued for the killing of all the adult males in Mytilele, he appealed to the belligerent sentiment of the populace, whereas Diodotos was more rational. Cleon and Alcibiades were typical demagogs in the modern sense of the word. The word is derived from Greek *dēmagōgos*, a people leader, because *dēmos* is a common man and *agō* is to lead. Originally, it was a neutral word but later acquired a derogatory meaning.

The following quote from Raaflaub (1994, pp. 137–8) aptly pinpoints the crux of the issue:

Decisions concerning the empire and the war thus became tools in Athens' domestic power struggle. Inevitably, the prevailing tendency called for activist policies, new involvement, and further expansion because it was such policies, not those of caution and restraint, that offered their sponsors the opportunity to gain success, glory, wealth, and personal power. Thus, to satisfy their ambition, many of the politicians bred by and adapted to the political conditions of the fully developed democracy needed the empire, imperialism, and war; for them, the activism that had become typical of

Athenian politics was almost indispensable. To some extent, this is true already for Pericles, who, despite the restraint he displayed in critical situations, certainly was one of the most ambitious and aggressive imperialists Athens ever had; it is even more true, under the conditions of war, for Cleon and many others, and especially for Alcibiades, whose motives for advocating the Sicilian expedition Thucydides described as "his desire to hold the command and his hopes that it would be through him that Sicily and Carthage would be conquered – success which would at the same time bring him personally both wealth and honor."

A noted pacifist among literary figures was Aristophanes. I have already mentioned his immense dislike of Cleon. *Acharnians*, *Peace*, and *Lysistrata* abound in the themes of peace. Xenophon was a pacifist for an economic reason:

> If, on the other hand, any one supposes that financially war is more profitable to the state than peace, I really do not know how the truth of this can be tested better than by considering once more what has been the experience of our state in the past. He will find that in old days a very great amount of money was paid into the treasury in time of peace, and that the whole of it was spent in time of war; he will conclude on consideration that in our own time the effect of the late war on our revenues was that many of them ceased, while those that came in were exhausted by the multitude of expenses; whereas the cessation of war by sea has been followed by a rise in the revenues, and has allowed the citizens to devote them to any purpose they choose.
> (*Ways and Means*, V. 12, trans. E. C. Marchant, Loeb Classical Library)

In the struggle against Macedonia, Demosthenes and Lycurgos were hardened antagonists, whereas Aeschines was ambivalent and Isocrates distinctly pro-Macedonian.

Income redistribution

Among the most important ways to collect money from the rich were *leitourgia* (contributions to such things as staging dramas and building and manning triremes), *eisphora* (tax), and fines. Redistribution was done through payments for attendance to the Assembly, Council, and courts. There was also more direct remittance called *theōrika* (the theoric fund) or *diōbelia*, both instituted toward the end of the fifth century. The former was the payment of two obols, which enabled poor citizens to buy tickets for the theater, and the latter was a benevolence given to poor citizens. (It is not certain whether these were identical or two separate practices.) I will discuss these in more detail in the section "Public finance" (Chapter 6, "The Athenian economy of the fifth and fourth century").

Elite and mass

Whenever there are issues, we can find two opposing groups adhering to the opposing beliefs. Concerning the matter of war and peace, we find nationalists and pacifists. Concerning income redistribution, we find the rich and the poor. Here we will consider the second conflicting pair in the context of a broader conflict between the elite and the mass, following Ober (1989).

The words "the elite" and "the rich" are not synonymous but there is a high degree of association between them. The elite in classical Greece were characterized by status, wealth, and ability (Ober 1989, p. 13). Status was usually associated with good aristocratic birth, although it was conceivable for a successful general or a rich citizen without an aristocratic background to acquire status by means of military feats or generous contributions. There was no well-defined class of aristocrats in Athens, but we may more or less identify them with a ruling class who held positions of archons until Cleisthenes' and Ephialtes' reforms. There were some well-known aristocratic families such as *Alcmaionidai*. The word means the descendants of Alcmaion, who was born toward the end of the seventh century. Cleisthenes, Pericles, and Alcibiades all belonged to this family. An important descendant of Alcmaion was Megacles, who was archon in 632. He banished the tyrant Cylon who fled to Megara and killed his associates, who took refuge at the altar of Athens – a sacrilegious act. Megacles was banished by Megarians, again later by Peisistratos, and eventually reinstituted by Cleisthenes.

One of the self-applauding terms that were used to denote the aristocrats was *kalos k'agathos*, which means "fine and good." The feelings and attitudes of the Athenian common people toward good birth were analogous to those toward wealth: namely, admiration and malice coexisted. Good birth, as well as wealth, could easily lead to *hybris*, the most odious vice. We might say the public only respected aristocrats with *sōphrosynē* and the rich who were benevolent.

It was customary for a speaker in the court to disparage the *hybris* of the rich to win sympathy from the jurors. For example, the plaintiff in Isocrates' *Against Lochites*, who brought suit for heavy damages against a rich young citizen named Lochites who had struck him, calls himself "a poor man and one of the people" and goes on to say, " the defendant should be required to pay so large a sum that he will in future refrain from his present unbridled wantonness [*hybris*]" (16, trans. La Rue Van Hook, Loeb Classical Library). Lysias in *On the Refusal of a Pension to the Invalid* says, "For insolence [*hybris*] is not likely to be shown by poor men labouring in the utmost indigence, but by those who possess far more than the necessaries of life" (16, trans. W. R. M. Lamb, Loeb Classical Library). Young Demosthenes, who was struck by a rich politician named Meidias at the Great Dionysia, sued him and began his speech by the remark: "The brutality and insolence [*hybris*] with which Meidias treats everyone alike are, I suppose, as well known to you, gentlemen of the jury, as to all other citizens" (XXI, *Against Meidias*, 1, trans. J. H. Vince, Loeb Classical Library).

It seemed permissible and appropriate for a rich man to point out to the jurors that he had generously contributed to various liturgies and thereby expect a return of favor from the public. For example, the rich metic Lysias tells jurors

> I have equipped a warship five times, fought in four sea-battles, contributed to many war levies, and performed my other public services as amply as any citizen. But my purpose in spending more than was enjoined upon me by the city was to raise myself the higher in your opinion, so that if any misfortune should chance to befall me I might defend myself on better terms
> (XXV, *Defense Against a Charge of Subverting the Democracy*, 12–13, trans. W. R. M. Lamb, Loeb Classical Library)

However, boasting too much about one's generosity had a negative effect. Read the following remark of Demosthenes: " though I might speak, men of Athens, of the equipment of war-galleys and of choruses, of money contributions and of the ransom of captives, and of other instances of liberality, I would say not a word of them" (VIII, *On the Cheronese*, 70–71, trans. J. H. Vince, Loeb Classical Library). Also

> If, men of Athens, public service consists in saying to you at all the meetings of the Assembly and on every possible occasion, 'We are the men who perform the public services; we are those who advance your tax-money; we are the capitalists (*plousioi*, rich – my addition)" – if that is all it means, then I confess that Meidias has shown himself the most distinguished citizen of Athens; for he bores us at every Assembly by these tasteless and tactless boasts.
> (XXI, *Against Meidias*, 153)

All I have said above seems to point toward the power of the populace in Athens. The elite politicians vied with each other for the favor of the common people. An orator who gained the support of the jurors in the public courts later found it easier to win votes for his proposals in the Assembly (Ober 1989, p. 148).

Charis

Did the Athenians succeed in keeping the strife between the rich and the poor to a manageable level?

> Athens is rife with lamentations. For some are driven to rehearse and bewail amongst themselves their poverty and privation while others deplore the multitude of duties enjoined upon them by the state – the liturgies and the nuisances connected with the symmories and with exchanges of property; for these are so annoying that those who have the means find life more burdensome than those who are continuously in want.
> (Isocrates, *On the Peace*, 8. 128, trans. George Norlin, Loeb Classical Library)

At all events, they think it right to receive pay for singing, running and dancing, and for sailing in the fleet so that they may have money and the rich may become poorer.

(Pseudo-Xenophon, *The Constitution of Athens,* I. 13, trans. J. M. Moore, University of California Press, 1975)

Aristophanes speaks of the rich trying to avoid liturgies and concealing their money. Concealment of wealth was widely practiced. The Greeks called real property (land and houses) φάνερα οὐσία. οὐσία means property and φάνερα means visible, coming from the word φαίνω meaning "make to appear." (Note φαινόμενον means "what is seen," from which the English word phenomenon is derived.) The other kind of property was called ἀφανής οὐσία, meaning invisible property.

An equilibrium was attained through the notion of *charis* (χάρις). This word signifies a reciprocal relationship, meaning both favor (going from the giver to the taker) and gratitude (going from the taker to the giver). Thus, the rich extended *charis* to the poor and the poor return *charis* to the rich.

The oligarchies in 411 and 404 may be characterized as brief disruptions of the equilibrium in favor of the rich.

Rhetoric

There are different kinds of rhetoric: that which appeals to reason, that appealing to emotion, and that appealing to base human desires. The first was the only kind Socrates recognized as genuine and worthwhile. Examples of the second kind are the rhetoric of nationalism and pseudo-religion. Examples of the third kind are proposals for tax cuts and measures to help business when they are contrary to broader public interests. We have already mentioned Cleon and Alcibiades as examples of orators who appealed to base human emotion and desires.

However, there were good orators who did not always try to please people, but criticized and opposed them (Ober 1989, p. 323). We have mentioned the example of Diodotos. "In Assembly speeches, Demosthenes vigorously denounces both the practice of crowd-pleasing orators and the demos' tendency to listen to them" (Ober 1989, p. 321).

It is natural for orators to present themselves as persons of good characteristics and their opponent as the opposite. How do present politicians try to characterize themselves? As patriots, as pacifists, as good family men and women, as upholders of law and order, as friends of business, as friends of poor people, as supporters of the minorities, as protectors of ecology and environment, etc. Athenian orators tried to characterize themselves as patriots or pacifists, as men of virtue, as friends of the common people, as men of good birth, and as reasonably wealthy. The emphasis on virtue was perhaps more important for Athenian politicians than American politicians because their political role was not completely differentiated from their social role (Ober 1989, p. 126).

The most striking character traits listed above are good birth and wealth. We do not usually hear modern politicians boasting about these. As I mentioned under the section "Elite and mass", good birth and wealth had both positive and negative connotations. Therefore, Athenian orators had to proceed subtly when they presented themselves as possessors of good birth and wealth. They had to walk on a tightrope, so to speak. A prime example of the subtle approach can be found in Demosthenes' Speech LVII, *Against Eublides*. The speaker at first presents himself as quite a poor man to win the jurors' sympathy. And yet later he nonchalantly discloses that he once dedicated shields to the temple of Athena, a deed possible only for a rich man. It was a good tactic to condemn the nouveaux riches who gained money through military ventures or litigation (Ober 1989, p. 234) and the rich who did not contribute to public liturgies. For example, Demosthenes portrayed Aeschines as being born in a poor family and becoming rich by unseemly means whereas he himself was wellborn (XVIII, *On the Crown*). However, depicting oneself as wellborn had to be done tactfully because otherwise it would earn the envy of the public.

Part II
Economy

5 Modernist–primitivist and formalist–substantivist controversy

Part II begins with the discussion of the controversies: the modernist–primitivist and the formalist–substantivist. These two pairs of opposing concepts are closely related to each other, though conceptually different. A modernist believes the Athenian economy was a well-developed market economy differing from a modern capitalist state only in degree and not in quality. A primitivist disagrees. A formalist believes that the Athenian economy can be analyzed by the basic behavioral assumptions of modern economics, namely, utility and profit maximization, whereas a substantivist believes that a different set of behavioral assumptions, such as status maximization, must be substituted. A formalist is more likely to be a modernist, and a substantivist a primitivist, but not necessarily so. For example, one who believes that even the modern American economy should not be explained by utility and profit maximization may be said to be both a modernist and a substantivist with regard to the American economy. Consideration of these problems will, therefore, be relevant not only for the Athenian economy but also for the modern one and will force us to think deeply about the role of economic theory in general.

In 1983, Bücher argued that the ancient Greek economy was primitive – that is, a self-sufficient household economy based on exchange rather than market. Meyer disagreed, saying it was well developed, differing from a modern economy only in a matter of degree. This initiated the modernist–primitivist controversy. Finley, following Weber and Polanyi, suggested that there was no "separate" economy in ancient Greece; it was "embedded" in society. Consequently, Finley argued, ancient Greek economy cannot be analyzed by the methods of modern economics, and one must develop new assumptions and new methods to understand it. He called this idea "substantivism." Thus, we might say, he shifted the emphasis of the debate, from modernist versus primitivist to formalist versus substantivist. Typically, a formalist presupposes the existence of a well-developed market and assumes that consumers and producers seek only selfish interests and all the economic quantities are determined by the market equilibrium that equates the supply and demand. A substantivist, on the other hand, believes that economic decisions are influenced or constrained by sociopolitical considerations and institutions. These two debates are, of course, not identical: the former is concerned with the degree of the development of the economy and the latter with the methods of its analysis. Nevertheless, it is often the case that primitivists are substantivists, as Weber, Polanyi, and Finley were, and modernists tend to be formalists.

It should be pointed out here that what I loosely called "ancient Greek economy" should be more precisely called "the Athenian economy of the fifth and fourth century BC." Thus, "classical Greek economy" might be a better term. The reason why we say Athenian instead of Greek is that we do not know much about the economies of the other city-states of Greece. "Ancient" refers to a long period which could possibly include any time between the sixteenth to the fourth century. Primitivism and substantivism are surely applicable to the earlier part of this long period, but scholars like Polanyi and Finley are primitivists and substantivists concerning the Athenian economy of the fifth and fourth century BC.

The question of primitive or modern is rather relative. What should be asked is: Is the ancient Greek economy more like the present American economy or more like the economy of Papua New Guinea, Africa before the nineteenth century, or America before Columbus? And in what sense are we using the terms primitive and modern? One way in which the modern American economy differs from a primitive one is its abundant material wealth – more food to eat, more variety of food, better housing, better sewage, safer water, better sanitary conditions in general, better health care, electricity and gas and the appliances that use them, better modes of transportation, more extensive education, a greater variety of entertainment, and so on. This was made possible by the development of technology which was due, in considerable degree, to the mentality of people who were driven by desire for more and more profit and more and more efficiency and the desire to excel even at the expense of others. Social institutions, too, are more developed and extensive – laws and legal institutions, better police protection, information networks, etc. But we are not concerned with these matters now. We are primarily concerned with economic institutions – market, currency, and facilities for lending and borrowing.

We define "market" as an institution with the following characteristics:

1   Goods are exchanged for money. Not a barter system.
2   Competition. Many buyers and many sellers.
3   Consumers maximize utility and producers maximize profit. (2 and 3 lead to the state of efficiency called Pareto optimum.)
4   Impersonal. One buys and sells to everybody.

Note that market is not merely a place where people exchange goods for money, but is associated with a certain behavior pattern. This definition of market coincides with Finley's definition of "disembedded economy."

Primitivism-cum-substantivism was popular in the first half of the twentieth century because it was a part of a broader movement called "cultural relativism" propounded by cultural anthropologists such as Ruth Benedict and Margaret Mead. Their belief was contrary to the fundamental tenet that people are essentially the same everywhere in every period. Thus, Mead portrayed a far-fetched picture of Samoan culture and Benedict presented a biased model of Japanese culture. It was partly under the influence of cultural relativism that Finley underestimated the common human desire for profit among the ancient Greeks and substituted in its place the want for status. It is hard to believe that the ancient Greeks desired status more than profit, and such an idea is not substantiated by various writings of the time. Nevertheless, the formalist's idea of explaining economic activities solely by the principle of profit and utility maximization is the other extreme. It is obvious that we cannot explain even the modern economy, let alone the ancient Greek economy, by this principle alone. In this sense, we must say that there is an element of truth in substantivism.

I will present some evidence of substantivism in ancient Greek economy. (1) Condemnation by philosophers of the trading and exchange carried out by professional merchants for profit was shared, generally, by the old ruling class who looked upon the merchants as a threat to social norms and cohesion. (2) Contempt of manual labor – the story of Aristarchos in Xenophon, *Memorabilia*, II. 7. Before talking to Socrates, Aristarchos preferred a hard living with nonworking women to a good living with working women. (3) A unique relationship between the rich and the poor – the rich trying to win the political support of the poor through generous liturgies, as discussed in Chapter 4, "Was Athenian democracy a success?". (4) Another argument for substantivism is the extreme instability and unpredictability of ancient Greek economy which made an elaborate calculation of profit maximization useless and unwise.

In contrast, I should also give evidence for the proposition that the ancient Greeks sought profit. (1) Demosthenes, in a court speech titled *Against Dionysodoros,* speaks of a grain trader who sailed to Egypt in order to import grain into Athens but, upon hearing from his friend who remained in Athens that a large amount of grain-import from Sicily had brought the price of grain down, decided to take the grain to Rhodes instead. I will discuss this speech later in more detail, in the section "Trade" in Chapter 6, "The Athenian economy of the fifth and fourth century". (2) The speaker in Lysias' *Against the Corn-Dealers* indicted grain dealers who sought profit to the detriment of the citizens. This speech too will be discussed in detail in the section "Trade" (Chapter 6, "The Athenian economy of the fifth and fourth century"). (3) In Xenophon's *Oikonomikos*, Ischomachos says that his father increased the value of a farm and sold it for a profit, and Socrates likens it to the grain dealer who buys grain at the lowest possible price and sells it at the highest possible price. Ischomachos is offended by Socrates' remark because, like any other gentleman of the day, he thought it honorable for anyone to gain profit through farming but dishonorable to take profit by manufacturing or trade. Socrates, who was well ahead of his time in this and many other respects, did not see a difference between taking profit in farming and any other way. (4) Xenophon's *Ways and Means* notes that some rich Athenians made a huge profit from silver mines and recommends the state's direct investment into the production of silver.

The fact of the matter, however, is that there is no economy, ancient or modern, which is completely independent of society and politics. What comes closest to it might be the extreme laissez faire economy that Adam Smith envisioned in his invisible hand doctrine – that consumers and producers seeking their self-interests will benefit the society. The present American economy is certainly not. There are many government regulations, the rich do make benevolent contributions, and there are producers who consider other things than pure profit maximization. Even Adam Smith did recognize the necessity of some government interventions. For example, Smith writes, "Division of labour destroys intellectual, social and martial virtues unless the government takes pains to prevent it" (*Wealth of Nations*, p. 839).

There is a greater danger in the formalistic tendency of the typical modern economist, who wants to apply the principle of utility and profit maximization to every aspect of the economy. Some even try to explain the decision of marriage and the number of children a couple will have by the maximization of the discounted sum of a future income stream. A formalist claims that he is only interested in the scientific and objective model that explains the working of the economy, but the normative notion that whatever is determined by the equilibrium of the market is good tends to creep into his mind. Hausman and McPherson (1996, pp. 49–50) write, "It's no wonder that students who take economics courses tend to become more selfish and less willing to cooperate, for they are taught in their courses that selfishness is prudent and that selfishness is always acceptable in economic life."

Other examples of economy embedded in society are as follows:

1. Buying organic food even if it is more expensive. If a person buys organic food not for his own health but for the sake of ecology, it is an example of economy embedded in society.
2. Boycotting a product because the company engages in an unethical conduct (moral constraint).
3. Not eating pork for a religious reason.
4. Producing good products regardless of profit, as Shakers used to do.
5. Making charitable contributions. (This constitutes as an example of economy embedded in society only if they are made for the sake of convictions and principles, and not just to feel good.)
6. Buy a Mercedes, instead of a Toyota, to show off to a neighbor.

So far as the original modernist–primitivist controversy is concerned, we can safely say that the scholarship of the last ten years has decisively supported the modernist's view regarding fifth- and fourth-century Athens. The general consensus now is that the economy of this period was developed in considerable degree in terms of the market, manufacturing process, and financial institutions. I will elaborate this point in detail in sections "Market, prices, and wages" and "Money, lending and borrowing" in Chapter 6, "The Athenian economy of the fifth and fourth century".

Osborne (1991) offers four reasons for Finley's extremely primitivist view of the Athenian economy: (1) the influence of Mickwitz's article which showed that commercial accounting was not well developed at that time; (2) his interpretation of the Athenian *horoi*, inscribed mortgage stones, as the mortgages used for consumption rather than production; (3) the influence of Aristotle's works which degraded manufacturing and trade; and (4) his mistrust of statistics.

Ian Morris writes in the foreword to the updated edition of Finley (1999, xxvii):

> The most common argument has been that Finley consistently underestimated the scale of ancient trade, industry, banking, and other nonagricultural economic activity, so that his substantivism, the idea that economic activities were embedded in other social relations, in fact slid over into crude primitivism, the belief that ancient economies were basically household economies.

Finley (1999, p. 20) quotes Schumpeter: "most statements of fundamental facts acquire importance only by the superstructures they are made to bear and are commonplace in the absence of such superstructures." What does Schumpeter mean by superstructure? It becomes evident later. Finley (1999, p. 132) mentions Gomme's remark as an example of a statement which lacks superstructure. Gomme said, "the Greeks were well aware that imports and exports must in the long run, somehow, balance." This is what I would call an accounting identity. An accounting identity does not need superstructure, and yet it is extremely important. A precise definition of superstructure is not given until p. 182 and p. 194 where it becomes evident that by superstructure Finley means a model of behavioral assumptions. But Finley himself does not offer any model for the Greek economy except for a vague remark about status. A noted economist Thomas C. Shelling, in his commencement address to the Department of Economics, University of California, Berkeley, on 20 May 1994, published in *The American Economist*, 39 (Spring 1995), 20–22, said that five candidates for things he learned in economics that are true, important, and not obvious are all accounting identities.

6 The Athenian economy of the fifth and fourth century

Introduction

In this chapter, I will examine various aspects of the Athenian economy – market, agriculture, trade, public finance, and money; then, I will incorporate these facts into a model of the Athenian economy.

The main sources from which we can learn about the Athenian economy may be classified as follows:

Historian:	Herodotos, Thucydides, Xenophon.
Philosopher:	Plato, Aristotle, Theophrastos.
Orator:	Demosthenes, Lysias, Aeschines, Isocrates, Isaios, Andocides.
Comedy poet:	Aristophanes.
Epigraph:	Inscriptiones Graecae.

The numbers pertaining to economic activities that appear in the literature are often unreliable. For example, Demosthenes in Speech XX, *Against Leptines* (31–2), states that Athens annually imports 400,000 *medimnoi* of grain from the Black Sea area and about an equal amount from the rest of the world. It is not clear, however, how much credence we can put to the quoted number as the reliability of Demosthenes' source is debatable; also, we should keep in mind that orators may sometimes distort facts to bring out a point. Aristophanes often mentions the prices of everyday goods in his comedies, and they are believed to be generally accurate. It is conceivable, however, that he should sometimes exaggerate in order to enhance the comic effect.

The numbers that appear in epigraphs are likely to be more accurate. The problem with epigraphs, however, is that many of them have not survived to this day and those which have survived contain many passages or words which are undecipherable.

Even if we make use of all available written documents and the existing epigraphs, therefore, it is impossible to arrive at the accurate quantification of the economic phenomena. At best, we can hope to specify the upper and lower limits of very wide ranges of possible values. If we use a system of accounting identities, however, we may hope to narrow down these ranges by making all the variables satisfy the system of equations. For example, let A be the population, B the per capita consumption of grain, C the area of cultivated land, D agricultural productivity, E the grain import, then we must have $A \times B = C \times D + E$ and certain values of these five variables will be incompatible with the equation and can consequently be eliminated from consideration. The model I will present later consists of several of such accounting identities.

My model lacks what Finley calls superstructure, that is, behavioral assumptions. In that sense it is beyond the formalist–substantivist controversy. The modern economist may give the impression that he believes that every consumer maximizes utility and every producer maximizes profit, but he is actually much more pragmatic. Every applied econometric work does start with the ritual of observing the tenets of utility and profit maximization but quickly moves on to a more realistic statistical model that simply purports to fit the data well. A purist will try to estimate a so-called structural model that is derived from theoretical behavioral assumptions, but most econometricians are content with estimating statistical models called reduced form. This latter majority of econometricians would be just as comfortable with the Athenian economy as with the modern industrialized economy, aside from the problem of the lack of data in the former. Even the purist, however, cannot completely rely on his theoretical assumptions. Take a demand and supply model, for example. Utility maximization under the budget constraint tells the economist that the demand will depend on the income and the prices – the prices of all the goods, not just the goods in question. A practical necessity will force the economist to select only a few prices as well as a functional form, usually linear, about which economic theory can tell nothing. To quote Blaug (1992, p. 144),

> In their authoritative survey of empirical research on demand relationships since World War II, Brown and Deaton (1972) noted that much empirical work on demand had been purely "pragmatic" and carried out with very little reference to any theory of consumer behavior.
>
> (pp. 1150–2)

In Athens during this period, no significant progress in technology was apparent except in the military and agriculture. Abundance of slaves may have weakened the incentive for innovation. There is no evidence of economic growth in Athens during the fifth and fourth century. This can be attributed to Athens spending nearly half of the time on war and the resulting population decrease. On the other hand, looking at a longer period of time, it has been estimated from human bones and house remains that consumption per capita increased nearly double in all of Greece from 800 to 300 BC This is equal to 0.14 percent increase per year. Let us compare this number to modern data: between 1580 and 1820, annual per capita consumption increase in the Netherlands was 0.2 percent (Ian Morris 2004).

Regarding agriculture, Pomeroy (1994, p. 47) observes, quoting *Hellenica Oxyrhynchia* (written in the fourth century BC), that the Athenians improved the methods of cultivation in the first half of the fourth century through such means as increased employment of slaves, short fallow, application of liquid manure, and reclamation of underproductive land.

Market, prices, and wages

Market

Osborne (1991, pp. 133–5) believes that in fourth-century Athens, there was a high degree of monetization and a well-developed market for both agricultural and manufactured goods. In the story of a rich farmer named Phainippos told in Demosthenes XLII, *Against Phainippos*, the speaker challenges Phainippos in *antidosis* (see "Glossary"). The speaker claims that Phainippos owns land whose circumference is 40 stades (στάδια), earns 12 drachmas a day by selling wood, produces 1,000 *medimnoi* of barley (5,000 drachmas at 5 drachma per *medimnos*), and earns 9,600 drachmas from sale of wine. Osborne argues that, even if we must discount for the numbers because the speaker is exaggerating the wealth of Phainippos, the speech shows that the need for *eisphora* (see "Glossary") and liturgies creates a rich man's demand for cash. Cohen (1992, p. 6) corroborates Osborne's account by saying, "But by the fourth century, agricultural products were increasingly raised for cash sale; consumer items were now often produced by commercial workshops." In the footnotes on this page, Cohen substantiates his claim by citing several original sources. Already in the fifth century, according to Plutarch, Pericles sold all the proceeds of his farm and bought everything he needed in the market (*Pericles*, XVI.4).

The fact that the speaker gave the circumference of Phainippos' land is an indication that he is trying to impress the jurors of the size of his land. If Phainippos' estate consisted of a single piece of land and its shape were a perfect circle, a circumference of 40 stades would imply the maximum possible area of 436 hectares. If his estate consisted of more than one piece of land and/or the shapes were irregular, the area could be much less. Ste Croix (1966) states that even if the size of Phainippos' land were as little as 100 acres (approximately 40 hectares), it would still be the largest known Athenian estate (see the section "Agriculture").

A few decades ago a prevalent theory was that for a long time after gold-silver coins were minted in Lydia in the seventh century and silver coins minted in Greek cities in the sixth century, coins were used only in large denominations in the transactions involving states. This theory was based on the fact that until recently archaeologists had discovered hordes containing coins of only large denominations. The picture has changed as, in the last two or three decades, they have discovered hordes containing coins of many small denominations, sometimes as small as one-tenth of a gram, and many small-weight silver chips before the use of coins (see Kim 2001). This indicates the development of the moneyed economy at a fairly early date. The use of small coins increased rapidly in the middle of the fifth century as state pay was instituted. Davies (1981, p. 55) states, "the fifth- and fourth-century rents were almost universally paid and reckoned in coin."

In Athens silver was used as money before coins were minted as early as Solon's time. A discovery of small silver chips has proved that they were capable of measuring the weight of silver remarkably accurately.

Burke (1992, pp. 200–1) thinks that the market economy developed rapidly in the period 355 to 325 and gives the following reasons for this development:

1 development of trade;
2 an increase of payment to the public; and
3 a reduction of dependence on agriculture as a result of Pericles' policy at the beginning of the Peloponnesian War.

Harris (2002) has compiled a list of all the occupations that he found in the original sources including written works and inscriptions. After eliminating similar occupations, they numbered about 170. Manufacturers of just about everything one can think of are included in the list. Fischer-Hansen (2000, p. 92) notes that considerable evidence for workshops in the western Greek world seriously undermines Finley's view that the Greek *polis* was a consumer city. These workshops are too numerous to have served just local consumers, but were clearly aimed at generating exports.

Garlan (1988, p. 65) points out that the general mentality toward the manufacturing sector changed between the fifth and fourth century. In Old Comedy the "new politicians" such as the tanners Cleon and Anytos, the lamp-maker Hyperbolos, and the lyre-maker Cleophon, who had increased their fortunes through manufacturing, were ridiculed as nouveaux riches, but by the fourth century this attitude seems to have disappeared. The family of Demosthenes, whose wealth came from workshops and moneylending, suffered no ridicule.

Assuming the number of metics in fourth-century Athens to be 20,000, Harris (2002, p. 70) conjectures that 19,000 of them worked in these shops. Now we know that out of the workers on the Erechtheion in the years 409–6 whose status is known, there were 24 citizens, 42 metics, and 20 slaves (Austin and Vidal-Naquet 1980, p. 276). In the account of Eleusinian sanctuaries in the year 329, the ratio was 20 citizens, 44 metics, and 20 slaves (IG ii/iii^2 1672). From this, Harris conjectures that the number of citizens working in shops was approximately 10,000. This seems to me to be a rather high estimate if we believe that only 5,000 citizens did not own land in 403 (Austin and Vidal-Naquet 1980, p. 266), for some of these 5,000 must have worked on rented land.

Note that Socrates in Xenophon, *Memorabilia* (III. 7. 6), speaks as follows:

> The wisest do not make you bashful, and the strongest do not make you timid; yet you are ashamed to address an audience of mere dunces and weaklings. Who are they that make you ashamed? The fullers or the cobblers or the builders or the smiths or the farmers or the merchants, or the traffickers in the market-place who think of nothing but buying cheap and selling dear? For these are the people who make up the Assembly.
> (Trans. E. C. Marchant, Loeb Classical Library)

In the section "Slavery" in Chapter 2, "Society and culture", I have mentioned that the value of the sword factory of Demosthenes Senior was 190 minas and that of his bed factory 230 minas, including the value of slaves and the inventory. The size of the factory owned by Pasion and Lysias, respectively, seems to be double or triple that of the factories owned by Demosthenes Senior, so their values should be commensurably greater. Pantainetos sold his workshop in the mining district for three talents and 2,600 drachmas (Demosthenes XXXVII. 31). Epicrates bought a perfume shop for 40 minas (Hyperides, *Against Athenogenes*, 18). Harris (2002, p. 81) reports the amounts of the loans secured by the property recorded on the *horoi* placed next to the workshops. There were eight of them, and the two highest amounts were one talent, the next highest 1,700 drachmas, and the rest were 800, 750, 700, 500, and 500 drachmas. (In order to get the value of a workshop, one should double these numbers.) These small loans were well within reach of many Athenians, not necessarily very rich.

In his attempt to convince Aristarchos that he should let his female relatives earn money by processing wool to produce clothes, Socrates mentions a few successful artisans: Nausicydes who manufactured groats, Cyrebus who baked bread, Demeas who made capes, and Menon who made cloaks (Xenophon, *Memorabilia*, II. 7. 6).

The excavation of the Athenian Agora started in the 1930s and continues to this day. They have excavated thousands of amphoras, pitchers, and cups from the sites of wine shops and taverns. From the shape of the ware and the composition of clay, one can determine where the wines came from. Most popular were the wines from Mende, Chios, Lesbos, Thasos, and Corinth. They also excavated the remains of the house and shop of a shoemaker. From this site they found a cup with the name of Simon inscribed on it. This is believed to be the cobbler's house mentioned by Diogenes Laertios (who lived in the third century AD and wrote about Greek philosophers) as the place Pericles visited and Socrates frequented to teach young pupils (see Camp 1992).

The Athenian Agora was frequented by both the rich and poor, citizens and noncitizens. When addressing a court made up of rich and poor alike, a client of Lysias (XXIV, 20) observes that "each of you is in the habit of paying a call at either a perfumer's or a barber's or a shoemaker's shop" (trans. W. R. M. Lamb, Loeb Classical Library). Metics could trade in the Agora if they paid the tax *metoikion* (Demosthenes LVII, 31) and foreigners could trade there if they paid *xenika*.

Harris (2002, p. 75) notes

> The market in Athens was so large that it was divided into several different sections. Parts of the Agora were named after the goods sold there. Xenophon (*Oikonomikos*, 8.22) did not worry about his slave knowing where to go in the Agora to buy goods because they were all kept in an assigned place.

Isager and Hansen (1975, p. 51) state, "at least half the population of Attica were engaged in trade, which presupposes the existence of a 'market economy'."

Theophrastos (*c*.371–*c*.287) was a pupil of Aristotle and his successor as head of the Peripatetic school of philosophy. He wrote on many subjects, of which the most famous are his treatises about trees, and the work called *Characters* (Loeb Classical Library, Harvard University Press, 1993), which consists of 30 brief humorous descriptions of various unsavory characters. It is a good source to learn about the everyday life in Athens:

> *Obnoxiousness:* "When the Agora is crowded he goes to the stands for walnuts, myrtleberries, and fruits, and stands there nibbling on them while talking with the vendor."
> *Lack of generosity:* "Even though his wife brought him a dowry, he doesn't buy her a slave-girl, but rents from the women's market a slave to go along when she leaves the house."
> *Boorishness:* "And when he is going into town, he asks anyone he meets about the price of hides and salt fish."
> *Sponging:* "If anyone makes a purchase at a bargain price, he asks to be given a share too."
> *Pennypinching:* "When someone has bought goods for him at a bargain price and presents his bill, he says they are too expensive, and rejects them."
> *Bad timing:* "He is apt to bring in to a man who has already completed a sale a buyer who will pay more."
> *Grouchiness:* "If he is selling something, he doesn't tell customers how much he would sell it for, but asks 'What will it fetch?'"
> *Griping:* "If he buys a slave at a good price, after much haggling with the seller, he says 'I wonder how sound the merchandise can be if I get it so cheap.'"

Aristophanes, *Acharnians* (880), lists the goods Athenians used to buy from Boeotia before the war (www.perseus.tufts.edu/):

Theban	All the goods Boeotia boasts.
	Got marjoram, pennyroyal, rush-mats, wicks for lamps,
	got ducks and jackdaws, francolins and coots,
	got wrens and grebes –
Dicaeopolis	You've hit my market-place
	just like an autumn storm with its foul winds.
Theban	Got geese, got rabbits, got some foxes too,
	got moles and hedgehogs, kitty-cats and badgers,
	got martens, otters, eel from Lake Copais.

Copaic eels were a Boeotian delicacy much prized at Athens.

There were laws regulating the market and public officers enforcing them: *agoranomoi* (market officers) who controlled the quality of goods sold at the market, *metronomoi* (weight controllers), *dokimastai* (coin assayers), *sitophylakes* (grain inspectors) who controlled the fair price of unground grain, ground grain, and bread (the millers to sell barley meal in accordance with the price paid for the unground barley, and the bread-sellers to sell bread of the prescribed weight in accordance with the price paid for the wheat), and *emporiou epimelētai* (trade supervisors) who supervised the import and export trade at the Athenian port of Peiraieus. (There was no price control in products other than grain and grain products.) See Aristotle, *The Constitution of Athens*, LI, for a list and a description of these and other public officers.

The market seemed to be working efficiently. Harris (2002, p. 76) gives many examples of how the prices fluctuated with supply and demand taken from various sources.

Prices

Wheat (cf. Pritchett and Pippin (1956, p. 197). Prices of wheat and barley fluctuated a lot within a single year.)

415	Sale of confiscated properties, $6-6\frac{1}{2}$ drachmas
E 4c	6 drachmas per *medimnos* (IG II^2 1356).
392	Blepyrus in Aristophanes, *Ecclesiazusae* (545), talks of $\frac{1}{6}$ *medimnoi* of wheat lost as a result of not attending the Assembly, which would have brought 3 obols. This implies 3 drachmas per *medimnos*. However, this may be a characteristic comedy exaggeration.
335	Normal price, 5 drachmas per *medimnos*; earlier it advanced to 16 drachmas per *medimnos* (Demosthenes XXXIV, 39).
340–30	9 drachmas per *medimnos* (IG II^2 408).
332–23	Cleomenes of Egypt bought wheat at 10 drachmas per *medimnos* and sold it at 32 drachmas per *medimnos* (Pseudo-Aristotle, *Oikonomikos*, 1352B14–20).
330	Demosthenes proposes that Heraclidas of Cyprus be made *proxenos* (see "Glossary") for selling 3,000 *medimnoi* of wheat at 5 drachmas per *medimnos* (SIG^3 304).
329	5–6 drachmas per *medimnos* (IG II^2 1672).
324	5 drachmas per *medimnos* (IG II^2 360).
300?	Dion moves that Agathocles of Rhodes be granted citizenship for selling wheat at a price lower than the Agora rate of 6 drachmas (SIG^3 354).

Barley

4c	3–5 drachmas per *medimnos* (Osborne, p. 125).
4c	Phainippos sold barley for 18 drachmas per *medimnos*, three times the former price (Demosthenes XLII, 20). This is an overestimate because the speaker is trying to exaggerate the wealth of Phainippos.
330	5 drachmas per *medimnos* (IG II^2 408).

329   3 drachmas to 3 drachmas and 5 obols per *medimnos* (IG II^2 1672. 282–283, 298).

Bread

L 4c   Loaf of wheat bread, 1 obol (Demosthenes XXXIV, 37).

Olive trees

4c   1,000 olive trees worth 2 talents (Demosthenes XLIII, 69).

Olives

L 5c   2 drachmas per *medimnos* (Plutarch, quoted in Pritchett and Pippin 1956, p. 184).

Olive oil

E 4c $\frac{1}{2}$ obol per *kotylē* (Pritchett and Pippin 1956, p. 184). Daily cost, $\frac{1}{16}$ obol (Markle 1985, p. 281).
L 4c $1\frac{1}{2}$ obol per *kotylē* (*Aristotle, Oikonomikos*, 1347A).
4c   In Delos, $2\frac{1}{3}$ obols per *kotylē* (Pritchett and Pippin 1956, p. 184).
250   In Delos, $\frac{2}{3}-\frac{3}{4}$ obols per *kotylē* (ibid.).

Honey

E 4c   3 obols per *kotylē*. Daily cost, $\frac{1}{2}$ obol (Markle 1985, p. 280).

Wine

5c   Chian wine (high quality), 2 drachmas per *chous* (Amyx 1958, p. 176).
5c   Ordinary wine, 4 obols per *chous* (ibid.).
4c   12 drachmas per *metrētēs* (= 10 gallons) in Phainippos' farm (Demosthenes, ILII). This is an overestimate because the speaker is trying to exaggerate the wealth of Phainippos.
4c   3 or 4 drachmas per *metrērēs* (Markle 1985, p. 281).
4c   10 obols per *chous* (a fragment of Alexis quoted by Davidson 1998, p. 191).
L 4c   2 drachmas per *chous* (Menander's Arbitration quoted op. cit.).

Dried figs

L 3c   2 drachmas per *medimnos* (Pritchett and Pippin 1956, p. 191).

Livestock

L 5c   Piglet, 3 drachmas (Aristophanes, *Peace*, 374).
L 5c   Full grown pigs, 20–40 drachmas (Jameson 1988, p. 98).
L 5c   An ox-hide, 6–8 drachmas (Jameson 1988, p. 111).
415   Sale of cattle from confiscated properties, 35–50 drachmas.
410   Cow: 5,114 drachmas were given for a hecatomb in the Great Panathenaea, which implies 51 drachmas for a cow (Pritchett and Pippin 1956, p. 255).
375   109 oxen, costing 8,419 drachmas, were purchased for sacrifice at the festival for Apollo at Delos. This implies 77 drachmas a piece (Pritchett and Pippin 1956, p. 255).
400–350   90 drachmas for a cow or ox (Pritchett and Pippin 1956, p. 255).
4c   Goat, 12 drachmas (Pritchett and Pippin 1956, p. 258).
363   Goat, 10 drachmas (Pritchett and Pippin 1956, p. 258).
M 4c   Mules, 800 and 550 drachmas (Isaios VI, 33).
4c   The average price of a cavalryman's horse, 408 drachmas (Pomeroy 1994, p. 219).
4c   A riding horse, 1,200 drachmas (Pritchett and Pippin 1956, p. 258).
403   Sheep, 12, 15, or 17 drachmas (Pritchett and Pippin 1956, p. 259).
400   A lamb to be offered in sacrifice, 16 drachmas (Lysias XXXII, 21).
4c   Sheep, approx. 19 drachmas (Demosthenes XLVII, 57 and 64).

Fish

425   Eel of Lake Copaia in Boeotia (highest quality), 3 drachmas (Aristophanes, *Acharnians*, 962). Davidson (1998, p. 187) states that the prices quoted in Aristophanes' comedies are generally trustworthy.
4c   An octopus 4 obols, a barracuda 8 obols, a mullet 5 obols, a sea bass 10 obols (Davidson 1998, p. 187).

Clothes

L 5c   Woolen garment, 20 drachmas (Pritchett and Pippin 1956, p. 204).
392   A pauper who appeared at the Pnyx unclad announces himself in need of 16 drachmas for an outer garment (Aristophanes, *Ecclesiazusae*, 413).
388   A young man asks the old lady he was pretending to woo for a cloak worth 20 drachmas (Aristophanes, *Plutos*, 982–3).
329   A coat for a slave, 10 drachmas and 3 obols (Pritchett and Pippin 1956, p. 206).

327 Tunics bought for the Eleusinian public slaves, 7 drachmas and 3 obols. Cloaks, 18½ drachmas. Leather jerkins (coats), 2½–4½ drachmas (Pritchett and Pippin 1956, p. 206).

L 4c A dress worn by common people, 10 drachmas (Boeckh 1842, p. 105).

Shoes

388 8 drachmas (Aristophanes, *Plutos*, 982–3) – "on the high side" (Boeckh 1842, p. 106).

327 Shoes for the Eleusinian public slaves, 6 drachmas a pair. Needs a pair every other year (Pritchett and Pippin 1956, p. 204).

Ointment

L 4c A *kotylē* of fine ointment, 5–10 minas according to Menander (Boeckh 1842, p. 106).

Land and house

414 In the prices of the confiscated properties of the *Hermokopidai* and Profaners of the Mysteries, the cheapest recorded price of a house at an unattractive location was 105 drachmas and most were well above 1,000 drachmas (Pritchett and Pippin 1956, pp. 260–71). The median value of seven houses sold in Athens was 410 drachmas (Pritchett and Pippin 1956, p. 275).

4c The prices of the properties mentioned by the Attic orators were as follows: House, 300–5,000 drachmas (average of 12 being 2,600); house and land, 5,000 drachmas; multiple-dwelling house, 10,000 and 1,600 drachmas; farm land, 6,000–15,000 drachmas (average of four being 10,000); land, 1,000–7,000 drachmas (average of six being 4,000) (Pritchett and Pippin 1956, pp. 271–2).

388 Aristophanes (not the playwright) bought 70 acres of land and a house (worth 50 minas) for five talents (Lysias XIX, 29 and 42).

362 The house bequeathed to Demosthenes, 30 minas (Demosthenes, *Against Aphobus I*, 6).

360 A cottage, 300 drachmas (Davies 1981, p. 50).

4c Many plots are in the range of 2,000–3,000 drachmas, occupying 3.6–5.4 hectares (Jameson 1977/1978, p. 125).

L 4c 2 out of 3 Athenians had property worth at least 2,000 drachmas (Jameson 1977–1978, p. 125).

4c House rent, 36 drachmas a year – 12 percent of 3 minas (Boeckh 1842, p. 109).

4c Hoepfner and Schwandner (1994, p. 150) suggest that a typical house cost approximately 3,000 drachmas in mid-fourth century.

Furniture

5c Chair with a back, 2–6 drachmas; bench, 1–5 drachmas; chest, 21 drachmas; couch, 6–8 drachmas; simple bed, 2 obols; wooden lamp stand, 1 obol; table, 4 drachmas. Greek furniture was not expensive. The price of furniture including dishes and utensils rarely exceeded 500 drachmas. A very large town house with a family of four adults, three children, and 15 slaves containing furniture, dishes, and utensils worth 650 drachmas (Pritchett and Pippin 1956, pp. 210ff.).

Vases

L5c Panathenaic painted amphoras (more than 100 sold from an estate, possibly Alcibiades'), about 3 obols a piece (Amyx 1958, p. 178).

Hetairai

4c "the girls who play the flute, the harp or the lyre," not more than 2 drachmas (Aristotle, *The Constitution of Athens*, L. 2).

Voyage

4c Aigina to Peiraeus, 2 obols. Egypt or Pontos to Peiraeus, 2 drachmas (*Gorgias*, 511D–511E).

Funeral

400 A wealthy woman left 300 drachmas for her funeral (Lysias XXXI, 21). Pomeroy (1977, p. 118) states that the average price of a funeral was about 30 drachmas.

4c 1,000 drachmas (Demosthenes IL, 52).

Wages

(According to Loomis (1998, p. 253), before 432 most attested wages were 4 obols per day; in the period 432–12, 1 drachma per day; after 412 wages were different depending on the kind of work done by workers.)

Payment for attending public meetings

Assembly

403 1 obol per session.
392 3 obols (*Ecclesiazusae*, 290).
330 1 drachma per regular session and 1 drachma per main session.

Council

4c 5 obols per day and for *prytanis* 1 drachma per day.

Courts

450s 2 obols per session.
420s 3 obols per session (*Wasps*, 690).

Theater

4c Theoric fund, 2 obols per person for attending the theater.

Other public officers

450 Administrative official (*epistatēs*), 4 obols – 1 talent every day of the year (Loomis 1998, p. 10).
422 Public prosecutor (*synēgoros*), 1 drachma per day (Aristophanes, *Wasps*, 482).
L 4c Archons, 4 obols per day (Aristotle, *The Constitution of Athens*, LXII. 2).
343 Undersecretary (*hypogrammateus*, probably not a high position because Demosthenes is trying to deprecate Aischines), 2–3 drachmas per month (Demosthenes XIX, 200).
4c Scythian policemen, 3 obols a day (Andreades 1933, p. 215).

Welfare

4c 2 obols a day for citizens possessing less than 3 minas and unable to work (Aristotle, *The Constitution of Athens*, XLIX. 4).

Temples

408 Account of Erechtheion, $1–1\frac{1}{2}$ drachmas per day for citizens, metics, and slaves (Austin and Vidal-Naquet 1980, p. 276).
328 Eleusinian accounts, slaves 3 obols, unskilled labor $1\frac{1}{2}$ drachmas, skilled labor $2–2\frac{1}{2}$ drachmas (IG II–III^2. 1672–1673).

Military

428 A hoplite got 2 drachmas a day, 1 for himself and 1 for his slave (Thucydides, III. 17. 4). Austin and Vidal-Naquet (1980, p. 303) state this was a special case and the pay was usually $\frac{1}{2}$–1 drachma.
422 Soldier paid 2 obols a day (Aristophanes, *Wasps*, 1185).

74 *Economy and Economics of Ancient Greece*

351   2 obols a day for soldiers (Demosthenes IV, 28). This is an underestimate because he is trying to show that a military campaign can be financed cheaply.

330s   *Ephēbos* got 4 obols a day for military training (Aristotle, *The Constitution of Athens*, XLII. 3).

Agriculture

Grain output

I will present three recent estimates of Athenian grain production in Table 6.1. Earlier estimates tended to be on the low side because they were based on an Athenian inscription recording the First Fruits offered to Demeter at Eleusis in 329 (IG II^2 1672). Assuming that the contribution amounted to 1/600 in the case of barley and 1/1,200 in the case of wheat – the proportions reported in an inscription in the late fifth century, Jardé (*Les Céréales dans l'antiquité grecque*, Paris, 1925) calculates the total production as 27,500 *medimnoi* of wheat and 340,500 *medimnoi* of barley. Theses figures are not reliable because it is not certain whether farmers contributed according to the set proportions as well as because we do not know whether 329 was a full-harvest year or not.

An average household holds land of about 3 hectares in modern Greece (Gallant 1991, p. 42). Jameson (1977/1978, p. 131) says it was 3–5 hectares in ancient Greece. If I use 5 hectares per family, 240,000 hectares of arable land suggests 48,000 as the number of citizens owning land. If we add 5,000 who did not own land (see the section

Table 6.1 Estimates of grain production

	Whithy (1998)	Garnsey (1998)	Scheidel (1998)
Available for grain	30%	30%	30%
Actual with fallow	10%	15%	17.5%
Area for grain (ha)	24,000	36,000	42,000
Wheat/barley ratio	1/4	1/4	1/4
Area for wheat (ha)	4,800	7,200	8,400
productivity (hl/ha)	6	6	8
Gross wheat (*med.*)	55,598	83,398	129,730
Seed/output ratio	1/4	1/4	1/4.8
Net wheat (*med.*)	41,699	62,548	102,703
Area for barley (ha)	19,200	28,800	33,600
Productivity (hl/ha)	12	12	12
Gross barley (*med.*)	444,787	667,181	778,378
Seed/output ratio	1/4	1/4	1/6
Net barley (*med.*)	333,590	500,386	648,648

1 *medimnos* = 51.8 lt, 1 hl = 100 lt, 1 hl = 1.9305 *med.*, 1 *med.* of wheat = 40 kg, 1 *med.* of barley = 33.3 kg, 1 ha = 2.471 acres, 100 ha = 1km^2.
Arable land in Attica amounts to nearly 240,000 ha.

"Market, prices, and wages"), it would imply 53,000 as the total number of citizen population. This is close to the upper bounds of an estimate of citizen population given in Table 2.2 in Chapter 2, "Society and culture". However, we should bear in mind that the presence of a few large landowners will tend to increase the average inordinately, as well as the fact that some land was owned by the state and the temples. It has been suggested that a household needed to possess approximately 5 hectares for the use of an oxen to be feasible and such a household would qualify for the hoplites class (Hodkinson 1988, p. 39). Some owned a much bigger plot. Alcibiades is said to have owned a farm of 300 plethra or 29 hectares (Plato, *Alcibiades*, I. 123C). Only citizens were allowed to own farmland. Some metics were allowed to own real property by the decree of *enktēsis* (see "Glossary") but not farmland.

Biological need for grain

Foxhall and Forbes (1982, pp. 41–90) give the following tabulations.

Calorie contents

Wheat. 3,340 calories per kg.
Barley. 2,158 calories per kg.

Food and Agriculture Organization (FAO) estimates of daily calories

Adult male, 62 kg, 20–39 years, very active: 3,337 (2,836).
The average height of ancient Attic males was 162.2 cm based on 61 skeletons
    (Foxhall and Forbes 1982, p. 47).
Adult female, 52 kg, 20–39 years, very active: 2,434 (2,069).
Average child: 2,600 (2,210).

Amount of wheat or barley needed for a family of four

Assumptions

1   Considering that in 1948 in Crete an average calorie intake of an adult male living in rural areas was 2,565, the FAO estimates can be reduced by 15 percent. The reduced estimates are given in the parentheses above. A point to note is that more recent estimates of the required calorie intake are generally lower than the FAO estimates.
2   A person takes 70 percent of calories from grain. (At present less than 60 percent, Foxhall and Forbes 1982, p. 56.) Gallant (1991, p. 66) states that this ratio was 85–90 percent among Cypriots in the 1920s.
3   A family consists of a male, a female, and two children. Gallant (1991, p. 23) states, "Raepsaet (1973) tabulated the total number of individuals by age set in

the speeches of Isaios, Demosthenes, and Lysias, then divided by the number of families and produced a figure of 2.14 children per family."

Total calories needed per day, 9,325; per person, 2,331; times 0.7, 1,632; 4.46 *medimnoi* of wheat per person per year; and 8.29 *medimnoi* of barley per person per year.

Daily food cost for a family of four (in obols)

Cost of wheat	1.76	(assuming price of wheat is 6 drachmas per *medimnos*)
Cost of barley	1.64	(assuming 3 drachmas per *medimnos*)
Honey	0.5	
Olive oil	0.0625	(Assuming 0.5 obols per *kotylē*, it amounts to 0.125 *kotylē*. According to Foxhall and Forbes, in Methana in 1972–1975, 0.36 *kotylē* was consumed per person per year (p. 68). Foxhall and Forbes give reasons why ancients consumed less olive oil (p. 69).)
Wine	0.5	(at 4 obols per *chous*, this amounts to 3.3 ounces)
Pulses	0.2	
Opson	1.0	(see below for the definition of *opson*)
Total	4.0225 obols	

The figures for honey, oil, and wine have been taken from Markle (1985, p. 280). Gallant (1991, p. 104) says 65 percent of the calories came from cereals, 25 percent from vegetables, and 10 percent from olive oil and wine. The figure for pulses is a wild guess. However, "it does seem legitimate to infer from Theophrastos that pulses were grown on a considerable scale for human food. This message is corroborated by other sources, for example, comic poets" (Scheidel 1998, p. 211). Gallant (1991, p. 40) also quotes Theophrastos (*Historic Plantarum*) saying barley, wheat, pulses, vines, and olives were grown in intercropping. Boeckh (1842, p. 103) quotes Timocles (comedy poet of the late fourth century) as saying that eight pods of beans were sold for an obol and thinks it is an exaggeration. Theophrastos gives a long list of vegetables: asparagus, beans, beets, cabbage, celery, chickpeas, cucumbers, gourds, leeks, lettuce, lentils, onions, radishes, and turnips. He also mentions fruits such as apples, almonds, dates, figs, pears, plums, pomegranates, and quinces, and relishes and herbs such as garlic, horseradish, mint, parsley, rue, sage, savory, and shallot (Michell 1957, p. 58).

A definion of *opson* given by Liddel and Scott is "everything eaten with bread or food, to give it flavor and relish." Another definition given by them is "at Athens, mostly fish, the chief dainty of the Athenians." An expensive item like eels from Lake Copais was indeed dainty, but there was cheap fish which was the main *opson* of the poor people. When Socrates describes a simple idyllic life, where people enjoy loaves of barley and wheat with wine (*Republic* 372), Glaucon interrupts saying these people are feasting without *opson*. Then, Socrates adds salt, olives, cheese, onions, greens, figs, pulses and beans, myrtle berries, and acorns. When Markle (1985, p. 296) mentions a daily allowance of 0.2 obols for *opson* for a slave, it is not clear whether he includes in it other items like honey and oil as well. Boeckh (1842, pp. 101–3) cites various instances of daily allowances for *opson*: (1) One obol of cabbage and a little fish for an old man. (2) According to Theophrastos (*Character* 28), nobody but a contemptible miser would allow his wife only three *chalkoi* for *opson* (eight *chalkoi* are worth one obol). (3) Three obols are sufficient for a few moderate persons to buy *opson* uncooked. (4) Lysias thought that a guardian's charge of three obols for the *opson* of two boys and a little girl was excessive. (5) Four small pieces of dressed meat cost one obol according to Antiphanes (comedy poet of the early fourth century). (6) A piece of meat, prepared for eating and of a reasonable size cost one obol, according to Aristophanes. (7) Anchovy cost a half obol. (8) Pickled fish cost one obol.

Jameson (1988, p. 105) conjectures that only about 2 kg of meat per person per year was consumed in classical Athens, mainly at the time of a sacrificial ritual. An average annual consumption of meat in modern America is about 37 kg.

In 422, a family of three could feed itself for three obols a day (Aristophanes, *Wasps*, 300).

Jones (1986, p. 143) reports that in the Eleusinian accounts (IG II–III^2, 1672) of 329, the state paid three obols a day as food allowance to the public slaves. It is possible, however, that Eleusinian slaves were generously paid.

The above figure indicates that 44 percent of the total food cost is spent on wheat. According to Clark (1957) the corresponding proportions (wheat and barley) for various countries at various times are as follows:

52 percent in Turkey in 1935 (p. 84)
39 percent in Greece in 1934–38 (pp. 428–9)
27 percent in Germany in 1929 (p. 80)
25 percent in Russia in 1952 (p. 241)
20 percent in France in 1932 (p. 79)
10 percent in the U.S. in 1935 (p. 85).

Other living costs

Clothes. A tunic for a slave 3.5 obols and a cloak for a slave 10.5 drachmas (Markle 1985, p. 296). If we assume that a tunic lasts a year and a cloak three years, one needs 16 drachmas a year for a family of four.
Shoes. An Eleusinian public slave needed 3 drachmas per year for shoes (Pritchett and Pippin 1956, p. 204).
Clothes and shoes. The most moderate person needed at least 15 drachmas per year (Boeckh 1842, p. 109).
House rent. 36 drachmas (12 percent of 3 minas) (Boeckh 1842, p. 109).

Total living costs

Using the slave figures for clothes and shoes, the living costs come to 307 drachmas a year for a family of four. Under this assumption, the food cost amounts to 80 percent of the total expenditure. It will be 336 drachmas a year if Boeckh's figure for the most moderate person is used. Here the food cost is roughly 70 percent. In contrast, the figure is 77.5 percent for Indian rural wage workers in 1939 (Clark 1957, p. 470), 77 percent in Rome in AD 301 (p. 664), and 34 percent in Japan in 1934 (p. 83). The annual total living costs increase to 355 and 396 respectively if the cost of *opson* is increased from 1 to 2 obols a day. The other expenditures for Indian rural wage earners in 1939 was housing 0.8 percent, clothing 11.7 percent, and other 10 percent.

Lysias XXXII, 28 (year 400) says 1,000 drachmas a year are needed for two girls and a boy with a male nurse and a maid. Demosthenes XXVII, 36 (year 363) says 700 drachmas a year for himself, his sister, and mother during his minority (rent not included).

The plaintiff of (Pseudo) Demosthenes (XLII, *Against Phainippos*, 22) who challenged Phainippos in *antidosis*, said, "Yet my father left to each of us, my brother and myself, an estate of forty-five minae merely, on which it is not easy to live" (trans. A. T. Murray, Loeb Classical Library). At 12 percent per annum, this amount would produce an annual income of 540 drachmas.

A disabled citizen who could not work and owned less than three minas as given one obol a day in the early fourth century and two obols a day in the late fourth century (Aristotle, *The Constitution of Athens*, 49. 4).

Markle (1985, p. 295) states that 4 obols a day would be sufficient for a family to live quite comfortably.

Historical record (Foxhall and Forbes)

Herodotos (VII. 187. 2)

Normal soldier's ration – 1 *choinix* a day (48 *choinikes* = 1 *medimnos*). It means 7.6 *medimnoi* a year.

Rations of Spartans at Sphacteria (Thucydides, IV. 16. 1)

2 *choinikes* of *alphita* a day. *Alphita* is 60–70 percent ground barley containing 3,320 calories per kg. Therefore, two *choinikes* of *alphita* is approximately worth 3 *choinikes* of barley, which is equivalent to 22.8 *medimnoi* of barley a year. Slaves were given half of this ration.

Athenian prisoners at Syracusae (Thucydides, VII. 87. 2)

0.5 *choinix* of barley a day, which is 3.8 *medimnoi* per year.

Animal husbandry

Hodkinson (1988) gives a good discussion of the state of animal husbandry in ancient Greece. Much of what is stated below is based on his study.

That some rich Attic farmers owned a considerable number of animals is attested to by Attic orators and historians. For example, Euctemon, who had a farm in a place about seven miles northeast of Athens, sold some goats with the goatherd for eight minas (Isaios VI, 33). Theophon left land at Eleusis worth two talents, 60 sheep, 100 goats, and a horse he rode when he was a cavalry commander (Isaios XI, 41). The plaintiff of Demosthenes (XLXII, 52) claims that Theophemus seized fifty soft-wooled sheep that were grazing near his home and the shepherd. The confiscated property of one of the *Hermokopidai* (those who were accused of destroying Hermes' statues in 415) included 84 sheep, 67 goats, two work oxen, and six further cattle (Hodkinson 1988, p. 62). Xenophon's *Memorabilia* (II. 3. 9 and II. 7. 13) mentions the dogs that guard sheep and in IV. 3. 10 Socrates says

> For what creature reaps so many benefits as man from goats and sheep and horses and oxen and asses and the other animals? He owes more to them, in my opinion, than to the fruits of the earth. At the least they are not less valuable to him for food and commerce.

Memorabilia (II. 7. 6) mentions Nausicydes who owned large herds of swine and cattle. In a conversation with Critobulos, Socrates says, "the art of breeding stock I closely linked with husbandry" (Xenophon, *Oikonomikos*, V. 3). Importance of husbandry in combination with farming is further mentioned in *Oikonomikos* (VII. 20 and XX. 23) and sheep grazing, in particular, in I. 9 and V. 6.

All the examples above concern rich farmers, but grazing sheep and cattle was also important for common farmers. Thucydides (II. 14) states that when the Athenian citizens were advised by Pericles to abandon farms and move to the city at the beginning of the Peloponnesian War, they sent their sheep and cattle to Euboea and the adjacent islands. Also, when Decelea was occupied by the Spartans in 413, more than 20,000 slaves deserted and all their sheep and beasts of burden were lost (VII. 27. 5). The ordinary farmer Strepsiades in Aristophanes' *Clouds* had a lot of sheep on his farm and grazed goats in mountains (40–74). Theophrastos in his treatises on plants (*De causis plantarum* and *Historia plantarum*) goes into great detail about the use of manure, including animal dung, suitable for various plants and crops.

Socrates points out the risk involved in animal husbandry due to unusual weather (Xenophon, *Oikonomikos*, V. 18). Cattle are less prone than sheep and goats to disease and drought, but they breed and mature at a slower rate. Therefore, farmers of many countries raise both kinds of animals to minimize risk (Hodkinson 1988, p. 60). Hodkinson conjectures that owning a few small livestock "may often have made a critical difference in enabling a family to achieve its regular subsistence; or, in the case of somewhat better-off households, to create a small surplus sufficient for the maintenance of hoplite status" (p. 61). Hodkinson (1988, p. 62) believes that due to the limited availability of wetland grazing, there were many more sheep and goats than cattle even on wealthy Athenian farms.

Hodkinson (1988, p. 64) believes that rich farmers maintaining a fairly large size of flocks (mean size 50–70 sheep) made considerable profit from the sale of high-quality wool. Milk and cheese were important products as well. Making clothes from wool is mentioned often in the literature (see, for example, Xenophon, *Oikonomikos*, VII. 6. 21, and 36). Jameson (1988, p. 103) states that the production of milk and wool was the prime goal of the owners of flocks of sheep or goats. He believes that the Athenian demand for sheep and goats were more or less satisfied by local Attic pastoralism, although no doubt sheep and goats, as well as pigs and cattle, were brought to market from neighboring areas (pp. 103–104).

Trade

Introduction

Athens engaged in active foreign trade throughout the classical period. Much of the trade took place on the Aegean Sea. Trade over land routes existed but at a much lower rate. There are several reasons for Athenian foreign trade to be so prosperous: (1) A shortage of domestic grain production necessitated trade. (2) The wide circulation of Athenian silver coins over the Greek world and adjacent countries facilitated trade. (3) The dominance of the Athenian navy over the Aegean Sea made the voyages of Athenian merchants safer. (4) Peiraieus provided excellent port facilities. (5) In Athens and Peiraieus there were bankers who extended maritime loans and money-changers dealing with foreign currency exchange and testing. (6) As I will explain further under the section titled "Bottomry loans", there was an efficient legal system dealing with trade disputes. (7) In Athens and Peiraieus there was the office of *proxenos*, much like the modern consul, who looked after the needs of foreign merchants.

Amount of grain import

Grain was mainly imported from Pontos, Sicily, Cyprus, Thrace, and Egypt. It seems Athens imported grain also from Euboea, but the quantity is uncertain (Michell 1957, p. 261). Aristophanes tells of a demagog promising 50 *medimnoi* of barley brought from Euboea distributed to each citizen (*Wasps*, 715). When the Spartans took Euboea from Athens in 411, Thucydides writes, "a panic ensued such as they had never before known. Neither the disaster in Sicily, great as it seemed at the time, nor any other, had ever so much alarmed them" (VIII.96).

445   King Psammetichus of Egypt presented the Athenians with 40,000 *medimnoi* of grain which were distributed gratis among the citizens (Isager and Hansen 1975, p. 24).

355   Leucon sent 2,100,000 *medimnoi* of grain from Theodosia in the Bosporus to Athens (Strabo, 7.4.6). Earlier in 438 Spartocus, a

The Athenian economy of the fifth and fourth century 81

Thracian noble, became a tyrant of Bosporos and the succeeding rulers including Leucon were friendly to Athens (Isager and Hansen 1975, p. 21).

Strabo was born c.64 BC in Pontos. This figure is uninformative because it does not specify the period – whether one year or 40 years when Leucon was the king of the Bosporus.

355 400,000 *medimnoi* of grain (σῖτος) were imported from the Bosporus, which equal the total import of grain from all the other regions combined (Demosthenes XX, 31–2). Isager and Hansen (1975, p. 18) point out that the grain mentioned here includes both wheat and barley.

We do not know how reliable these figures are.

340 Philip of Macedonia detained about 200 Athenian ships in the Bosporus. If each ship was carrying 120 tons, it would have been carrying 600,000 *medimnoi* of grain. If 160 tons, 800,000 *medimnoi* (Whitby 1998, p. 124–5). The sale of the spoils amounted to 700 talents (Sealey 1993, p. 188). This amount would mean 700,000 *medimnoi* at 6 drachmas per *medimnos*.

335 Chrysippus claims he imported more than 10,000 *medimnoi* of wheat (πυρός) and sold them at a normal price of 5 drachmas per *medimnos* (Demosthenes XXXIV, 39).

330 Cypriot Heraclides of Salamis sold 3,000 *medimnoi* of wheat at five drachmas per *medimnos*, way below the current market price and was later awarded the title of *proxenos* (see "Glossary") (Isager and Hansen 1975, p. 201).

325–317 Cyrene made gifts of 805,000 *medimnoi* of grain including 150,000 to Athens (Isager and Hansen 1975, pp. 24–5).

307 Antigonus, Macedonian satrap governing the Levant, granted a large grain shipment of 150,000 *medimnoi* to Athens (Isager and Hansen 1975, p. 25).

Lysias XXII, Against the Corn Dealers

According to the introduction by Lamb in Loeb Classical Library, this speech was written about the end of the Corinthian War (387), when Athens suffered from a shortage of grain, partly as a result of Cyprus coming under the control of Persia. Corn dealers (σιτοπωλαί) were accused of buying more than 50 *phormoi* in a violation of the law. The corn dealers argued that they did so at the suggestion of grain-controllers (σιτοφύλακες), but a controller maintained that he advised them to buy in unison in order to keep the price of grain down. The speaker points out a fallacy of the corn dealers' defense saying that if their intention were to keep the price of grain down, it would contradict the fact that they violated another law, which prohibited adding more than an obol to the price of grain, by sometimes adding even a drachma to the price. The corn dealers insisted that they acted to help citizens, but the speaker proclaimed it to be a lie, saying corn dealers are the kind of people who gain when citizens suffer. (Note that corn dealers themselves were metics.) The speaker says, "so much profit do they make by it that they choose rather to risk death every day than to cease making illicit gain out of you" (20). It is interesting to note that the speaker is not only defending citizens but also traders (ἔμποροι) and importers (ἐισπλέοντες) against corn dealers, saying that buying in bulk to keep the price down would hurt traders and importers.

Demosthenes LVI, Against Dionysodoros

Dareios (speaker) and Panphilos extended a maritime loan of 3,000 drachmas to Dionysodoros and Parmeniskos and stipulated that the ship should go from Athens to Egypt, and back to Athens. Both principal and interest were to be paid on the ship's return to Peiraieus, and the ship was given as security for the principal of the loan. If the ship should be lost the borrowers were to be free from all liability, but in the event of their failing to keep their contract they were to pay double the amount of the loan. After Dionysodoros sailed for Egypt, Parmeniskos, who remained in Athens, sent a letter to Dionysodoros telling him of a sudden decline in the price of grain as a result of a great amount of import from Sicily. Thus, Dionysodoros decided not to bring grain from Egypt back to Athens and instead unloaded the grain at Rhodes. He did not return to Athens for two years, sailing between Rhodes and Egypt. The plaintiffs rejected the offer of the defendants to pay the principal and the interest up to Rhodes. The defendants claimed that the ship was damaged and therefore could not sail back to Athens. The plaintiffs rightly discredit the defense argument, however, by pointing out that, if the ship had been damaged, it could not have sailed back and forth between Egypt and Rhodes, and that their excuse contradicted their offer to pay interest up to Rhodes.

The speaker denounces the defendants as pawns of Cleomenes of Egypt, Alexander's satrap who monopolized grain trade in Egypt thereby making an enormous profit. The speaker refers to Cleomenes as a former ruler of Egypt. Since Cleomenes was executed in 323, Murray (Loeb Classical Library) doubts that this speech was written by Demosthenes, who was executed in 322.

Regulations concerning grain import

1. Solon forbad the export of any crop except olives.
2. If you buy more than 50 *phormoi* (same as *medimnoi* according to Pritchett and Pippin (1956, p. 194)) of grain, you will be executed (Lysias XXII, 5).
3. You can add no more than an obol per *medimnos* to the price (Lysias XXII, 8).
4. The severest penalties should be imposed if anyone resident at Athens should transport grain to any other place than the Athenian market (Demosthenes XXXIV, 37).
5. "It shall be unlawful for any Athenian or any alien residing at Athens or any person over whom they have control, to lend money on any vessel which is not going to bring to Athens grain or the other articles specifically mentioned" (Demosthenes XXXV, 51, trans. A. T. Murray, Loeb Classical Library).

6 Two-thirds of the grain imported must be brought to Athens (Aristotle, *The Constitution of Athens*, LI. 4).
7 Women cannot go into contract about more than one *medimnos* of grain (Aristophanes, *Ecclesiazusae*, 1025).

Other imports

Athens had to import timber (mainly, pine, fir, and cedar) from Macedonia for house construction and shipbuilding, and charcoal required for silver smelting. It also imported copper from Cyprus; gold from Thrace and Siphonos; iron from Thrace, the islands and from the west; and tin (to be used with copper in the manufacture of bronze for armor, statues, containers, etc.) from Phoenicia, Britain, and Gaul (J.A.C.T. 1984, pp. 65–66 and Isager and Hansen 1975, pp. 29–31). (Bronze consists of 90 percent copper and 10 percent tin.)

The other materials for shipbuilding Athens needed to import were pitch, hemp, and flax (Jones 1986, p. 93).

Pericles in his funeral oration (Thucydides, II. 38) boasts of Athens as follows: "the magnitude of our city draws the produce of the world into our harbor, so that to the Athenian the fruits of other countries are as familiar a luxury as those of his own" (trans. Richard Crawley).

A fragment from Hermippos' comedy (*c.*430) lists the following items of Athenian import (quoted in Harris 2002, p. 79).

> From Cyrene stalks of silphium, and ox-hides, from the Hellespont mackerel and all sorts of dried fish, from Thessaly pudding, and ribs of beef, ... the Syracusans bring pigs and cheese ... From Egypt masts with sails and papyrus. From Syria frankincense, beautiful Crete supplies cypress for the gods, Libya much ivory for sale, Rhodes raisins and dried figs for sweet dreams. Slaves come from Phrygia, mercenaries from Arcadia, Pagasae sends slaves and branded scoundrels. The Paphlagonians send Zeus' acorns and shining almonds (these are what adorn a feast). Phoenicia for its paert fruit of palm and semodalin, Carthage carpets and richly coloured pillows.

Jameson (1988, p. 108) observes, "Despite the heavy slaughter of cattle in fourth century Athens the demand for hides remained high and it was profitable to import them in large quantities." Michell (1957, p. 287) observes, "Exports of dried or pickled fish from Pontus and Propontis were of great importance, for these were the fishing grounds for tunny and sturgeon."

As mentioned in the section "Animal husbandry", much of the demand for wool must have been satisfied by domestic production. Since there were many regions outside Attica that were known for better quality wool, notably Miletus, Athens must have imported some amount of wool (Michell 1957, p. 292). Hopper (1979, p. 98) observes that wool export, if it existed, must have been inconsequential.

See the section "Athenian slave import" for an estimate of the slave import.

The total value of import excluding grain

Andokides (I, 134) tells that in 399 he put in a bid of 36 talents and won the contract to collect the import–export tax (2 percent each for the export and import) and gained a profit of 2 talents. This implies 1,900 talents of trade (export plus import). Isager and Hansen (1975, p. 52) think this is an underestimate and suggest 2,300 talents. The imported grain was subject to a different tax (Harris 2002, p. 87).

Export

Silver

The main export of Egypt was grain and the main import silver. As noted in the section "Slavery" (Chapter 2, "Society and culture"), Isager and Hansen (1975, p. 43) estimate the number of slaves working in the silver mines at the end of the fifth century to be 30,000. J.A.C.T. (1984, p. 185) estimates the number of slaves at as many as 40,000 at the peak, whereas Osborne (1991, p. 134) gives a low figure of 10,000.

The Spartan occupation of Decelea (413–4) crippled mining operations. More than 20,000 slaves were said to have fled to the Spartans (Thucydides, VII.27.5). The Athenians started minting copper coins at that time. By 390, however, they were again replaced by silver coins. Lysias (XIX, 11) suggests that in 389 there was still a shortage of silver in Athens. By the middle of the fourth century, silver production rose to the level of the fifth century. The above incident of minting copper coins and a later restoration of silver coins is mentioned by Aristophanes in the following quotations from *Frogs* staged in 405 and *Ecclesiazusae* staged in 392.

> Many times it seems to us the city has done
> the same thing with the best and the brightest of its citizens
> as with the old coinage and the new gold currency.
> For these, not counterfeit at all,
> but the finest it seems of all coins,
> and the only ones of the proper stamp, of resounding metal
> amongst Greeks and foreigners everywhere,
> we never use, but the inferior bronze ones instead,
> minted just yesterday or the day before with the basest stamp.
>
> (*Frogs*, 720, www.perseus.tufts.edu)

> Ah! that cursed money did me enough harm. I had sold my grapes and had my mouth stuffed with pieces of copper; indeed I was going to the market to buy flour, and was in the act of holding out my bag wide open, when the herald started shouting, "Let none in future accept pieces of copper; those of silver are alone current."
>
> (*Ecclesiazusae*, 815, www.perseus.tufts.edu)

Isager and Hansen (p. 45) estimate the total silver production in about 340 to be about 1,000 talents.

Stele (in year 342) described in Crosby (1950, p. 203) lists leases ranging between 20, 150, and 6,100 drachmas. There is a dispute, however, about the period of the lease because these small numbers do not match the higher figures of 9,000 drachmas and 2,000 drachmas mentioned respectively in Demosthenes XXXVII, 22 and XL, 52. It may be a year, three years, or a *prytany* (35–39 days) (see Austin and Vidal-Naquet 1980, pp. 310–15). If it were a year, the state revenue would have been 16 talents. If it were a *prytany*, the total amount would have been 160 talents. Andreades (1933, p. 272) believes that the state received 50–100 talents a year from the leasing of the mines and that they constituted an important revenue source in the days of Lycurgos.

Generally, metics were not allowed to participate in the leasing of silver mines. Only two foreigners from Siphonos appear as lessees in the inscriptions preserved with us (Isager and Hansen 1975, p. 67).

Scholars agree that the mining rights belonged solely to the state, but there have been disputes as to who owned the land above a mine. Some argued that it was owned by the state, others opined that it was owned privately, yet some others say that a part was owned by the state and some privately (see Ito 1981, pp. 68–97). Osborne (1985, p. 117) states that the men well known to have made large amounts of money from the mines generally owned property in the mining region. He believes that the owner must have extracted some payment from the lessee who leased the mine that was situated below the owned land (Osborne 1985, p. 118).

Olive oil

A great part of the oil export went to the Black Sea regions, which did not grow olives.

Painted vases

A great deal of Attic red-figure vases have been excavated from Spina in Italy. In Beazley (1963), 1,022 vases from Spina are cataloged, of which 736 are of the fifth century and 286 of the fourth century (Isager and Hansen 1975, p. 27). They were exported as artifacts rather than containers of other goods (Isager and Hansen 1975, p. 38).

Athenian vase production and export diminished considerably in the fourth century (Isager and Hansen 1975, p. 41). Even in its heyday, however, only about 500 people worked in the production at a time (Isager and Hansen 1975, p. 41).

Marble

Speaking of Athens, Xenophon wrote, "Nature has put in her abundance of stone, from which are fashioned lovely temples and lovely altars, and goodly statues for the gods. Many Greeks and barbarians alike have need of it" (*Ways and Means*,

I.4). Michell (1957, p. 290), however, states that Attic marble was not of the finest quality. Marble from Paros, Thasos, Lesbos, and Chios better known. Then, Attic export of marble, if there was any, must have been insignificant.

Wine

Isager and Hansen (1975, p. 35) state that they could not find a single piece of evidence for the Athenian export of wine. They believe that wine should be classified as an import item rather than export (Isager and Hansen 1975, p. 36). Demosthenes (XXXV, 35) indicates that wines exported to the Pontus did not originate in Athens, but rather in the states around Athens such as Kos, Thasos, and Mende. Some other scholars, however, think that wine was an important export item for Athens.

Manufactured goods

Isager and Hansen (1975, p. 42) state as follows:

> How did Athens pay for her imports in the years around 400 when many of the olive trees had been cut down and the silver mines were not being worked? All reserves were exhausted and Athens had no other natural resources or crops to sell. The only possible answer is that Athens paid for her imports with the export of her manufactured goods.

Osborne (1991, p. 133) also thinks "that manufacture did in fact play a significant part in the creation of wealth at Athens." The graves of South Russia belonging to the ruling classes indicate that a great variety of manufactured articles in bronze and ivory, furniture and weapons, engraved gems and personal ornaments in various metals, were imported, and Athens must have had a large share of such items (Hopper 1979, p. 98). I have mentioned Demosthenes Senior's bed and sword factories, Lysias' and Pasion's shield factories, Cleophon's lyre factory. I should add to this list flute-producing factories owned by the father of Isocrates (Hopper 1979, p. 102). No doubt a part of these products must have been exported.

Bottomry loans

(Pseudo) Demosthenes has written five court speeches concerning the disputes that arose as the borrowers of the bottomry loans did not return the capital and/or the interests. They are XXXII, XXXIII, XXXIV, XXXV, and LVI (*Against Dionysodoros*). All of these loans concerned the import of grain. The suppliers of wheat were Sicily (XXXII), the Pontus (XXXIV and XXXV), and Egypt (LVI). The discussion of this section owes much to Ito (1981) and Isager and Hansen (1975).

The loans were extended to *emporos* (trader) or *nauklēros* (shipowner) for the outfitting of a ship or the purchase of wares. Although the distinction is not absolutely clear, roughly the former means the trader who does not own a ship, and the latter, the owner of a ship. Most shipowners had only one ship. An exception was Phomion, who owned several ships (Isager and Hansen 1975, p. 73). In these five speeches, 13 *emporoi* or *nauklēroi* appear, of which one is an Athenian citizen, one (Lampis in XXXIV) is a slave, and the remaining 11 are foreigners. Of the 13, five also acted as lenders. This must be an underestimate because fewer disputes are likely to arise when lenders and traders are the same (Isager and Hansen 1975, p. 73). In all the forensic speeches, however, 14 are metics or foreigners and 15 are citizens (Isager and Hansen 1975, p. 72, with all the sources).

Lampis was an *oiketēs* (home slave) of Dion (XXXIV, 5). He was called a *naiklēros* but probably used the ship that belonged to Dion (XXXIV, 36). He advanced a loan of 1,000 drachmas (6), and lived in Athens with a wife and children (XXXIV, 37).

Of the 10 lenders appearing in these speeches, two are Athenian citizens, one is a slave (Lampis), one is unknown, and the remaining six are foreigners. The nine borrowers, on the other hand, were all foreigners. In all the forensic speeches, 12 lenders are metics or foreigners and 7 are citizens (Isager and Hansen 1975, p. 72).

The bottomry loans were made with the ship and/or the cargo as the security. The value of the security was generally twice the amount of the loan (XXXIV, 6–7 and XXXV, 18). The lender was entitled to receive the capital and the interest only when the ship safely returned to Athens. Thus, in the event of a shipwreck or a pirate attack, the lender could recover neither the capital nor the interest. Because of this risk, the interest rates on the bottomry loans were considerably higher than the other kinds of loans. A loan of 2,000 drachmas carried an interest of 600 drachmas, or the rate of 30 percent (XXXIV, 23), and a loan of 3,000 drachmas carried an interest of 675 drachmas, or the rate of 22.5 percent (XXXV, 10). The lender in XXXV demands an interest rate of 22.5 percent if the ship were to sail through the Bosporos Strait before mid-September but requires 30 percent after that date. Since a journey to and from Bosporus took no more than two or three months, the 30 percent interest, if calculated on an annual basis, would amount to from 120 to 180 percent. In contrast, in the case of loans on the security of real property, the interest rate was normally 12 percent per annum (but 8 percent in Isaios XI, 42). A contract on maritime loans was always written, one copy to be kept by the lender, another by a third party, usually a banker (Isager and Hansen 1975, p. 78).

The disputes involving overseas trade were tried under the special court rules called *dikai emporikai* (trials concerning overseas trades). They had the following special features: (1) the trials were concluded within one month, and (2) foreigners could initiate suits without citizen guardians. The aforementioned Lampis also exercised this right.

Athenian slave import

In order to estimate the number of slaves Athens had to import every year, we have to make many assumptions such as the total number of slaves, their age distribution, and the proportion of slaves who are bred at home. The validity of any of these assumptions cannot be easily ascertained; therefore, the resulting estimate of slave import is necessarily inaccurate. The purpose of this exercise is not to obtain any accurate estimate of the slave import, but rather, to show what number of slave import is logically consistent with the initial assumptions.

Initially, the total number of slaves and the proportion of the home-bred slaves are denoted by N and r respectively, and later, numbers will be inserted into them. We must make some assumption about the age distribution. For this purpose age distributions of various countries in various periods depicted in the figure in Jones (1986, p. 82) have been used. In this figure the distribution for England and Wales in 1946 is parabolic, whereas the distributions for Carthage in AD 1–250, Rural Africa in AD 1–250, and India in 1901–1910 are more or less linearly declining. Jones believes the distribution for fourth century Athens should have a pattern closer to the latter. Isager and Hansen (1975, p. 13) reproduce Jones' figure and agree with Jones' conclusion.

As a preliminary to this discussion, we need to define age distribution, survival function, and hazard function and establish their relationship clearly. Let $N(t)$ be the number of people at age t and $N(0)$ be the number of births. We consider a stationary model and therefore these numbers do not depend on calendar years. We call $N(t)$ the age distribution. The survival function $S(t)$ is defined as the proportion of people still alive at age t. Clearly, $N(t) = S(t)N(0)$. Thus, if the age distribution is linear, so is the survival function. The hazard function $H(t)$ is defined as the proportion of people who die from the period t to $t + 1$. The survival function and the hazard function are related to each other in the following manner:

$$S(1) = 1 - H(1)$$
$$S(2) = [1 - H(1)] [1 - H(2)]$$
$$\vdots$$
$$S(t) = [1 - H(1)] [1 - H(2)] \ldots [1 - H(t)]$$

To specify the stationary model of Athenian slave import, I make the following simplifying assumptions: (1) No slaves live beyond the age of 40. (2) The unit of period t is a decade rather than a year. (3) The survival function declines linearly. (4) K slaves of age interval (10, 20) and G slaves of age interval (20, 30) are imported every decade, and no slaves of the other age interval are imported. Given the assumptions above, the hazard function and the survival function for the four age intervals are given as follows:

	Hazard function	Survival function
(0, 10)	1/4	3/4
(10, 20)	1/3	(3/4)(2/3) = 1/2
(20, 30)	1/2	(3/4)(2/3)(1/2) = 1/4
(30, 40)	1	0

Let A, B, C, and D be the stationary number of slaves in each of the four age intervals. Note that A is the number of slaves born at home in every decade. Then, these variables must satisfy the following equations:

$$A+B+C+D = N \tag{1}$$

$$B = (3/4)A + K \tag{2}$$

$$C = (2/3)B + G \tag{3}$$

$$D = (1/2)C \tag{4}$$

Since the number of slaves who were born at home should be equal to $A + (3/4)A + (1/2)A + (1/4)A$, which is the r proportion of the total number of slaves, we have

$$A = (2r/5)N \tag{5}$$

Inserting equation 5 into 2, we obtain

$$B = (3r/10)N + K \tag{6}$$

Inserting (6) into (3), we obtain

$$C = (r/5)N + (2/3)K + G \tag{7}$$

Inserting (5)–(7) into (1), we obtain

$$2K + (3/2)G = (1 - r)N \tag{8}$$

From (8) we learn that K and G, and hence their sum $S(\equiv K + G)$, cannot be uniquely determined by our model. A modern economist would probably determine K and G by maximizing the net revenue as a function of K and G subject to (8), by considering the productivity of slaves in the age intervals (10, 20) and (20, 30) and their costs. But such an exercise would not be worthwhile because data on the productivity and the cost by age group are not available.

Then, how do we determine K and G? First, we note that S is minimized by setting $G = 0$ and maximized by setting $K = 0$. To see this, write S as a function of K and N by using (8) as

$$S = [2(1 - r)/3]N - (1/3)K \tag{9}$$

Since the coefficient on K is negative, S is minimized by taking K to be the maximum possible value subject to (8), or equivalently, by taking G to 0. This is also intuitively obvious because the slaves imported at age interval (10, 20) are going to remain in the population longer than those imported at age interval (20,

30). The above consideration is useful because the values of S corresponding to $K = 0$ and $G = 0$ give its upper and lower limits. Next, we will determine K and G by making the arbitrary assumption $K = G$. Then, (5) remains the same as before, but (6), (7), and (8) become

$$B = [(20 + r)/70]N \qquad (6)^*$$

$$C = [(50 - 29r)/105]N \qquad (7)^*$$

$$K = G = [2(1 - r)/7]N \qquad (8)^*$$

Our remaining task is to evaluate the values of the variables under the three different schemes of $K = 0$, $G = 0$, and $K = G$ for representative values of N and r. Unfortunately, however, there is no consensus among scholars about the reasonable estimates of N and r. As for N in the fourth century, J.A.C.T. (1984, p. 157) gives a low figure of 50,000, whereas Hansen (1991, p. 93) believes that the number could be as high as 150,000. We take 100,000 as our rough estimate. As for r, there are only two inscriptions which have bearings on this question. One is the record of manumission found at Delphi, which shows that 217 out of 841, or roughly 25 percent, were born at home (Pritchett and Pippin 1956, p. 281). Pritchett believes, however, that this figure is upward-biased because the slaves born at home are more likely to be manumitted than others. A more reliable figure can perhaps be obtained from the inscription recording the sale of slaves from the confiscated properties of the *Hermokopidai* in 414 BC. In this record, three out of 40 slaves (the rate of 0.075) were born at home (Pritchett and Pippin 1956, pp. 280–281). In the following calculations, I will choose three possible values of r: 0.25, 0.15, and 0.075. The results are given by Table 6.2.

Note that the numbers in the table are for a decade. Therefore, if, for example, $r = 0.25$ and $K = 0$, it means that 5,000 slaves must be imported annually.

Isager and Hansen (1975, pp. 15–32) assume $N = 150,000$ and $r = 1/15$ and conclude that at least 6,000 slaves must be replaced annually, out of which more than half must be imported. Let us see if this result is consistent with the

Table 6.2 Slave import under varying assumptions

	$r = 0.25$			$r = 0.15$			$r = 0.075$		
	$K = 0$	$K = G$	$G = 0$	$K = 0$	$K = G$	$G = 0$	$K = 0$	$K = G$	$G = 0$
A	10,000	10,000	10,000	6,000	6,000	6,000	3,000	3,000	3,000
B	7,500	28,929	45,000	4,500	28,786	47,000	2,250	28,679	50,750
C	55,000	40,714	30,000	59,667	43,476	31,334	63,167	45,548	30,834
D	27,500	20,357	15,000	29,833	21,738	15,667	31,583	22,774	15,417
S	50,000	42,857	37,500	56,667	48,571	42,500	61,667	52,857	48,500

Table 6.3 Slave import under the Isager-Hansen assumptions

	$K = 0$	$K = G$	$G = 0$
A	4,000	4,000	4,000
B	3,000	43,000	73,000
C	95,333	68,667	51,666
D	47,667	34,333	25,833
S	93,333	80,000	70,000

assumption of a linear survival function. The values of the variables under their assumptions are given by Table 6.3.

Thus, even under the most favorable condition of $G = 0$, the annual replacement is 7,400, most of which must be imported. As we can see from Table 6.2, if $N = 100,000$ and $r = 0.25$ and $K = 0$, we also arrive at 6,000 as the number of the annual replacement, but even in this case five-sixths must be imported.

Public finance

Introduction

According to an authoritative treatise on ancient Greek public finance written by Andreades (1933), the Athenians did not have a comprehensive annual budget found in modern developed countries, which tries to match revenues and expenditures. The Assembly voted on each item of expenditure and allocated a specific revenue for it (Andreades 1933, p. 366). To some extent the Athenians must have tried to foresee their expenditures and revenues and strike a balance between them, but this was not done in any systematic way. The actual administration of the budget, receiving revenues and dispensing them, was handled by the Council. The lack of a comprehensive budget gave rise to a tendency toward extravagance. A surplus was deposited in the treasury of Athena and managed by ten treasurers each chosen from ten tribes. Later, at the time of Eubulos (355–42), the surplus went into the theoric fund.

Starting at the time of Eubulos and later Lycurgos (338–25), the administration of the state budget began to concentrate on the responsibility of a single person. It is not clear what kind of office Eubulos and Lycurgos had, but they succeeded in improving the financial situation of Athens considerably. It is said that Eubulos increased the state revenues from 130 to 400 talents, and Lycurgos increased the revenues to 1,200 talents. They also expanded various public expenditures. Eubulos, as head of the theoric fund, spent surplus money generously on theaters, rituals, and festivals but at the same time built roads, shipyard, and arsenal. Lycurgos was responsible for making the Athenian fleet bigger than at any time before, built docks, arsenal, temples, and public buildings. Andreades says that most ancient buildings still seen in the center of Athens were built either by Pericles or Lycurgos. One way by which Eubulos and Lycurgos achieved an increase in revenues was by being watchful over delinquencies in payments and misuses of public funds and imposing strict penalties on wrongdoing.

Revenues

Tributes

478	Tribute fixed at 460 talents (Thucydides, I. 96. 2).
454–33	Approx. 370 talents per year (Andreades 1933, p. 309).
431	600 talents (Thucydides, II. 13. 3).
425	776 talents (Andreades 1933, p. 309).
405–378	Tribute abolished.
377–57	200–350 talents for war contributions (Andreades 1933, p. 314).
357–38	46–60 talents for war contributions (Hopper 1979, p. 101).
343	60 talents a year (Aischines, *On the Embassy*, 71).

Total revenues and wealth

450	Athenian treasury possessed 9,700 talents of silver. Dropped to 6,000 by 431 as the nine-month siege of Samos cost 1,200 talents (van Wees 2000, p. 107).
433–22	Borrowed a total of 5,598 talents from the treasurers of Athena and the other gods (Loomis 1998, p. 243).
431	Internal and external revenues 1,000 talents (J.A.C.T. 1984, p. 227).
431	Reserve fund of 6,000 talents, public and private offerings of 500 talents, and treasures of the other temples (Thucydides, II. 13. 3–5, Pericles' speech).
422	State revenues (tribute, direct taxes, one-percents, court fees, revenues from mines, market, harbor, rents, confiscations) 2,000 talents (Aristophanes, *Wasps*, 655–663). One-percents here probably refer to indirect taxes (see Andreades 1933, p. 347).
411	Used the 1,000 talents reserve for the first time (Thucydides, VIII. 15).
407	Nike's gold statues melted down.
340	Not a long time ago, the revenue did not exceed 130 talents but now it is 400 talents (Demosthenes X, 37–38).
338–26	Lycurgos controlled the state finances and raised the revenue to 1,200 talents a year (Buchanan 1962, pp. 75–79). "All our authorities are agreed that he was the commanding genius in the financial administration for twelve years, but it is impossible to determine precisely in what capacity or through what department he worked" (Johnson 1915, p. 429).

Wealth distribution

5c	Oinias owned land worth more than 81 talents (Davies 1981, p. 59).
5c	Ischomachos had 70 talents (10 at his death), Stephanos 50 (11 at his death), Nicias 100 (his son 14), Callias inherited 200 (now has 2) (Lysias XIX, 46–48).
420	400 people could afford a drain on their income of 1 talent a year, which is the upper bound of the cost of *trierarchia* (Davies 1981, p. 17).
4c	300 people could afford a drain on their income of 3,000 drachmas a year (Davies 1981, p. 24).
4c	Men whose property was less than 3 talents were free from liturgies. Men with a property over 4 talents could not avoid liturgies (Davies 1981, p. 28).
4c	About 300 whose property was worth more than 3 or 4 talents, about 1,200 worth 1 talent (Davies 1981, p. 34).
380	Demosthenes' father left him a property worth 13 talents 46 minas (Demosthenes XXVII, *Against Aphobus I*, 9–11).
370	Pasiōn bequeathed landed estates worth 20 talents, 50 talents of cash, and a shield factory employing 60 slaves, probably worth 5 talents (Demosthenes XXXVI, 5).
345	Timarchos' father left him a house south of the Acropolis (worth 20 minas), a large suburban estate, a piece of land about 2 km away from the city wall (worth 2,000 drachmas), about ten slaves, a woman skilled in flax-working, a man skilled in embroidery, and money loaned to people (30 minas to one person). (Aeschines, *Against Timarchos*, 97–99).
320s	It was not easy to live off a property worth 4,500 drachmas (Demosthenes XLII, 22).
320s	Income of a skilled workman is 700 drachmas a year (Davies 1981, p. 28).
322	When Antipater imposed a property qualification for citizenship – property worth more than 2,000 drachmas – 9,000 out of 21,000 citizens qualified (Diodotus XVIII, 18. 4–5). This latter figure is based on the census taken by Demetrius of Phalerum (317–7). Thus, Jones (1986, p. 9) states that there were 9,000 hoplites and 12,000 *thētes*.

Liturgies

LYSIAS XXI, 1–5

Speaker in the age group 18–26 spent 10.5 talents for various liturgies (including *eisphora*). He says he should have spent only one-quarter of it.

Tragedy	3,000 drachmas
	2,000
War dances	800
Chorus and tripod	5,000
Chorus	300

Warships (7 years)	36,000
Eisphora	3,000
	4,000
Torch races	1,200
Children's chorus	1,500
Comedy	1,600
War dances	1,500
Religious services	3,000
Total	**63,600**

LYSIAS XIX, 42–3

Aristophanes performed the following liturgies. The period in which these were done is not specified.

Dramas	5,000 drachmas
Warship	8,000
Eisphora	4,000
Sicilian expedition	10,000
Infantry and arms	30,000

Festivals

355   97 festival liturgies (118 in a Panathenaic year) (Davies 1981, p. 27).
4c   100,000 drachmas by 100 citizens every year (a conservative estimate). 120,000 drachmas by 120 men every fourth year in Panathenaic (Osborne 1991, p. 130).
4c   300 of the richest voluntarily contributed to the festival liturgies (Davies 1981, p. 27). They are probably identical to the class of trierarchs (see the next section).

Trierarchy

A standard trireme was manned by 200 men – 170 oarsmen, 16 petty officers, 10 hoplites, and 4 archers (Gabrielsen 1994, p. 106). The length of a trierarch's normal term of service was 12 months (p. 78). "Generally, the construction of new ships and the proper upkeep of existing ones was to a fairly large degree the responsibility of the state. However, a significant part of that responsibility was in practice allocated to the trierarchs" (p. 126). A trierarch was expected to keep his ship in good, seaworthy condition (p. 137). *Syntriērarchia* started at the end of fifth century. First, two people shared the burden, soon three and more, up to ten (p. 175). The practice of absent trierarchs gradually increased (p. 181).

350   1 talent (Demosthenes XXI, 155).

	4,000–6,000 drachmas (Davies 1981, p. 82).
342–325	3,000 drachmas per trierarchy on average (Gabrielsen 1994, p. 222).
340	Demosthenes' Naval Board (originally proposed in 354 – see Demosthenes XIV below) stipulates that the trierarchs are to be chosen according to the assessment of 10 talents (Demosthenes XVIII, 106). Its aim was to make the richer pay more and the less rich not as much (Gabrielsen 1994, p. 209).

Demosthenes XIV, On the Navy-Boards

At the end of the Social War in 355, some Athenians perceived the danger of Persian invasion and made jingoistic speeches in the Assembly arguing for a declaration of war against Persia. Demosthenes, who was 30 at that time, gave his first speech in the Assembly calling for restraint in a most statesmanlike manner. He argued, however, that Athens should be prepared for a war against Persia by building up its fleet, which would have a deterrent effect. The following two passages from his speech offer sound advice to any nation at any age.

> From this state of things I conclude that it is to your interest to be careful that your grounds for entering on war shall be equitable and just, but to proceed with all the necessary preparations, making that the foundation of your policy. For I believe, Athenians, that if there were clear and unmistakable signs of the King's hostile intentions, the other Greeks would join us, and would be deeply grateful to those who would stand up for them and with them against his attacks; but if we force on a war, while his aims are still obscure, I am afraid, men of Athens, that we shall be obliged to encounter, not only the King, but also those whom we are minded to protect.
>
> (3–5, trans. J. H. Vince, Loeb Classical Library)

> To your rash advisers, who are so eager to hurry you into war, I have this to say, that it is not difficult, when deliberation is needed, to gain a reputation for courage, nor when danger is at hand, to display skill in oratory; but there is something that is both difficult and essential – to display courage in the face of danger, and in deliberation to offer sounder advice than one's fellows.
>
> (Ibid., 8)

A detailed plan to build up the fleet follows. First, choose 1,200 of the richest citizens and divide them into 20 boards (συμμορίαι); subdivide each board into five groups (μέρη) each consisting of 12 men. Each group is to pay for three ships, so that the total number of ships to be built is 300. There should be 10 dockyards, supervised by 10 *phylai*, and each dockyard is assigned to two boards. This proposal was not put into effect until 340.

Other liturgies

336	Demosthenes contributed 3 talents for the repair of the fortifications and 100 minas for sacrifices (Demosthenes XVIII, 118).
330–320	During the grain shortage, the rich contributed to the purchase of grain. Demosthenes gave 1 talent (Isager and Hansen 1975, p. 207).

Total

388	Speaker's father paid in his lifetime 9 talents 20 minas (Lysias XIX, 59).
L 4c	At least 100 talents by 1,000 citizens (Osborne 1991, p. 131). This figure seems too small.

Eisphora

The first epigraphical record of *eisphora* appears in 434. Thucydides mentions levy in 428 (III. 19), but we have no details about the fifth-century tax. In the fourth century it was a proportional levy, imposed when the Assembly chose and at the rate it decided. The class of *eisphora* payers was probably larger than the class of liturgy-performers. Metics were liable. (According to Andreades 1933, p. 329, one-sixth of the *eisphora* was borne by metics.) "The levying of *eisphora* was irregular, rare, and unpredictable" (Davies 1981, p. 82).

Demosthenes (XIV, *On the Navy-Boards*, 19) says the total assessment (*timēma*) of Athens was 6,000 talents. There is a dispute among scholars about the meaning of the assessment. (Andreades 1933, p. 346, estimates the Athenian assessment as 10,000 talents including the hidden asset and the asset of the men whose property did not qualify for the *eisphora*.)

In 378 those liable were organized in 100 *symmoriai* and, shortly afterwards, the richest three members of each *symmoria* were given the duty of advancing the whole sum due from their *symmoria* as a *proeisphora*, and left to reimburse themselves from the other members (*Oxford Classical Dictionary*). Gabrielsen (1994, p. 183) poses the question: Were the symmories into which the trierarchy was organized in 358 the same as those established in 378 for the *eisphora*? He agrees with Rhodes who says that the class of men liable for the *eisphora* was wider than the class liable for the trierarchy (Rhodes 1982, pp. 5–11). *Proeisphora* was a liturgy in the 320s (Davies 1981, p. 17).

See also the section "Trierarchy" earlier. "By the 320's, probably indeed by Demosthenes' law, the panel of the 300 men liable to the trierarchy and the panel of the 300 men liable to the *proeisphora* were effectively identical" (Davies 1981, p. 19).

428	*Eisphora* 200 talents (Thucydides III. 19. 1).
390s	Payment of *eisphora* by two men totaling 4,000 drachmas (Lysias XIX, 3).
392	*Eisphora* 0.2 percent (*Ecclesiazusae*, 1007).

378	Those with less than 25 minas of property were excluded from *eisphora* (Jones 1986, p. 29).
377–357	Eisphora 15 talents per year, which means 0.25 percent of 6,000 talents (Demosthenes XXII, 44).
4c	50 talents were expected from *eisphora* (Davies 1981, p. 23).

Metoikion

12 drachmas a year for men and 6 drachmas for women. $12 \times 30{,}000 + 6 \times 15{,}000 = 75$ talents (J.A.C.T. 1984, p. 188).
There might have been three-obols tax on every slave owned (Boeckh 1842, p. 332).
There were taxes on prostitutes (Boeckh 1842, p. 333).

Export–import tax

413	In the latter part of the Peloponnesian War, when the tributes declined, Athens imposed 5 percent import–export tax in the ports of the allies (IGII^2 28, Boeckh 1842, p. 325).
399	36 talents (Andokides, *On the Mysteries*, 133–4). This year was soon after the Athenian defeat; therefore, the trade was at a low point (Hopper 1979, p. 100; Boeckh 1842, p. 318).
390	Thrasybulos took Byzantium and imposed a 10 percent toll on all goods shipped through the Bosporos strait (Isager and Hansen 1975, p. 23).
5c–4c	2 percent import and export and 1–2 percent per head tax for slaves raised 38 talents. Slaves who accompanied visitors were also levied (Andreades 1933, pp. 282–83).
4c	2 percent import tax on grain would have raised 8–16 talents a year.
4c	There were harbor dues charged for the use of docking privileges at Peiraieus (Michell 1957, p. 257). Xenophon in *Ways and Means* proposed improving the dock facilities at Peiraieus, presumably to increase revenues.

Leases on silver mines

Hopper (1953, pp. 200–54) thinks that the state revenue from the leasing of the silver mines in 342 was 160 talents. In the section "Trade', it was mentioned that Andreades (1933, p. 272) believed that the state received 50–100 talents a year from the leasing of the mines. Mattingly (1968, pp. 170–472) believes that in addition to the leases, the miners had to pay 10 percent of their total silver output to the state. Goldsmith (1987, p. 260) thinks the total output from Laureion might have been about 1,000 talents. If so, 10 percent would yield 100 talents a year.

Rents from public land

No numerical figures.

Epidosis

Epidosis is a private contribution made according to a public decree.

Theophrastos, *Characters* 22, "Lack of Generosity" (3): "When emergency contributions (*epidosis*) are announced in an Assembly, he either remains silent or gets up and leaves in the midst" (Loeb Classical Library, 1993, p. 129).

Demosthenes gave 8 talents toward the campaign against Euboea and Chersonesus. Aristophanes gave 5 talents toward the campaign against Cyprus (Andreades 1933, p. 349).

Court fees (Boeckh 1842, pp. 354 and 379)

PRYTANEIA (IN PRIVATE SUIT)

Paid by both the plaintiff and the defendant: 3 drachmas for 100–1,000 drachmas and 30 drachmas for 1,001–10,000 drachmas

EPŌBELIA (IN PUBLIC SUITS)

1,000 drachmas

Fines

Fines imposed by *boulē* on *eisangelia* were 50 drachmas. If higher fines were suitable, cases were sent to public courts (Boeckh 1842, p. 382).

479 Miltiades paid 50 talents. Pericles paid 50 talents. (Andreades 1933, p. 275).
345 When a formal summons to testify in court was refused, a fine of 1,000 drachmas had to be paid to the state (Aeschines, *Against Timarchus*, 46).
345 An official who stole money to be used for the payment of mercenary troops was fined 1 talent if he did not confess, a half talent if he confessed (ibid., 113).

Confiscations

404 The confiscated property of Lysias and Polemarchos was 70 talents.
4c   Lycurgos indicted Diphilos for an illegal gain from a silver mine, which led to the confiscation of his property worth 160 talents (Plutarch, *Moralia*, 843D).

Sale of ox-hides

For the year 334, the income recorded for the sale of the ox-hides from state sacrifices amounted to over 10,000 drachmas (Jameson 1988, p. 96).

Spoils

407   Alcibiades raised 100 talents raiding the coast of Caria (Pomeroy, *et al.* 2004, p. 220).
360s   Timotheus' conquest of Cotys brought 1,200 talents (Andreades 1933, p. 319).

Expenditures

State pay

Assembly	1 drachma after 370 (1.5 drachmas for the main session). $(30 \times 1 + 10 \times 1.5) \times 6000 = 45$ talents a year.
Council	5 obols a day (1 drachma for a prytanis). $(5/6 \times 450 + 50) \times 325 = 23$ talents a year.
Courts	100 talents a year (Andreades 1933, p. 253). 150 (Aristophanes, *Wasps*, 660).

Domestic public officials (4 obols a day) 28 talents
Foreign public officials (1 drachma a day) 42 (Andreades 1933, p. 252).
Total   238 talents (Goldsmith 1987, p. 31 estimates this amount to be 250 talents).

Diōbelia

410–405   20 talents per year (Buchanan 1962, pp. 43–46). Buchanan thinks that the *diōbelia* covered two-obol payments to those jurors who, on any given day, applied for but failed to receive a court appointment (Buchanan 1962, p. 46).

Theoric fund (Payment of two obols, four obols, and a drachma to people who attended theaters, festivals, and rituals.)

354   Eubulos became the head of the theoric fund. Passed the law that all the annual surpluses from the city's various treasuries should be diverted to, and put at the disposal of, the theoric board (Buchanan 1962, p. 58).
349   Demosthenes hints at a criticism of this law (*First Olynthiac*).
349   Demosthenes criticizes it more strongly (*Third Olynthiac*).

343	War treasury becomes more important than theoric fund.
354–43	25–90 talents a year (Buchanan 1962, p. 88).
339	Lycurgos assumes the position of the head of the war treasury (στρατιωτικά).
335	Theoric fund practically ended.

Pension for the disabled

According to Aristotle (*The Constitution of Athens*, 49. 4), if the Council determines that a person has property less than three minas and cannot be engaged in work because of disability, he should be given two obols a day. It seems there was a specific public fund allocated for this purpose and a treasurer selected by lot. Aristotle was writing sometime between 328 and 322. Lysias, in *On the Refusal of a Pension to the Invalid*, written around 403, defended a person on the disability list who was challenged by someone. At that time the pension was one obol a day. The defendant had a business but had a hard time attending to it because of his trouble walking. The speech does not say how much income the speaker obtained from his business.

The maintenance of orphans

The children of those who fell fighting for their country were supported and educated by the state up to their eighteenth year.

Military expense

TRIREMES

480	180 ships at Salamis (Herodotos, VIII. 44).
L 5th	Approx. 15 talents for state ships Paralos and Salaminia (Andreades 1933, p. 231).
440	During the nine-month siege of Samos, the treasury of Athena paid 1,276 talents for 60 ships (Gabrielsen 1994, p. 115).
431	Athens had 300 triremes (Thucydides, II. 13. 8).
428	250 ships employed in one summer (Thucydides, III. 17. 2).
406	110 ships at Arginusae (Xenophon, *Hellenica*, I. 6. 24).
405	180 ships at Aegosopotami (Xenophon, *Hellenica*, II. 1. 20), of which 40 are allied ships (Davies 1981, p. 21).
357–22	250–380 ships (Gabrielsen 1994, pp. 127–129). Some argue that 10–20 ships were built annually, but it is not certain (Gabrielsen 1994, p. 135).
356	60 talents to maintain 120 ships – conservative estimate (Osborne 1991, p. 130).
326	A new ship cost 5,000 drachmas (Isager and Hansen 1975, p. 202). 7,200–9,100 drachmas (Gabrielsen 1994, p. 222).

322   85 talents to maintain 170 ships. The number of ships at sea was far less than the total number of ships – 120 in 356 and 170 in 322, whereas the total number was 283 in 357 and 412 in 325 (Osborne 1991, pp. 130–131).

Estimates of annual expenditure on triremes (G stands for Gabrielsen (1994))

COST OF BUILDING A NEW TRIREME

Hull 5000 drachmas (G 221).
Equipment (oars, flax, pitch, ruddle, masts, ropes, rudder, anchor) 2200 drachmas in 345 and 4100 drachmas in 323 (G 152).
10–20 ships built annually (G 135).
A "significant" part was borne by trierarchs (G 126).
My estimate: 10 talents by trierarchs and 10 talents by the state.

REPAIR

Roughly 2000 drachmas on the average (deduced from G 142).
60 triremes repaired in 356 (G 142).
Done both by state and trierarchs but more by the latter (G 136).
My estimate: 16 talents by trierarchs and 4 talents by the state.

MANNING

State paid $\frac{1}{2}$–1 talent and trierarchs paid $\frac{1}{2}$ talent (G 124–5 and 215).
Ships at sea: 120 in 356 and 170 in 322 (Osborne 1991, p. 131).
My estimate: 70 talents by trierarchs and 105 talents by the state.

TOTAL

Trierarchs 96.
State 134 (above plus 15 talents for Paralus and Salaminia).

Cavalry

365   40 talents per year (Xenophon, *Hiparchikos*, I. 19).
        40–80 talents a year (Andreades 1933, p. 219).

Cost of armed forces in 420 (time of peace of Nicias)

Sailors	70 talents
Hoplites	100
Cavalry	60

Archers	60 (4 obols a day)
Soldiers	20 (3 obols a day)*
Total	310 (Andreades 1933, p. 220)

* Aristophanes, *Wasps* (staged in 422), 1189, quotes 2 obols as a soldier's daily allowance.

Costs by periods and events (Andreades 1933, pp. 222–3)

440 Siege of Samos	At least 1,275 talents
431 Siege of Potidaia	2,000
431–425 (seven years)	5,000–9,000
Sicilian expedition	4,500–5,000
378–369 (nine years)	3,400–3,900 (Considerable part of it was covered by rich spoils.)
357–355	Mercenaries 1,000

Demosthenes IV, First Philippic, 47–8

2 obols a day × 200 sailors per ship × 10 ships = 40 talents a year.
2 obols a day × 2,000 hoplites = 40 talents a year.
6 obols a day × 200 cavalry = 12 talents a year.
(He says he is proposing a half of the normal pay.)

Total expenditure

900 talents (Goldsmith, p. 31).
1,000 talents (Xenophon, *Anabasis*, VII. 1. 27).

Money, lending and borrowing

Interest rate

In a speech delivered in 384, Lysias (X, 18) refers to the Athenian law that stipulates that money shall be loaned at whatever rate the lender may choose.

Davies (1981, p. 63) cites the following examples of moneylending at interest in years between 399 and 346.

1,600 drachmas at 25 percent.
6,000 drachmas at 12 percent.
1,600 drachmas at 16 percent.
4,000 drachmas at 18 percent.
3,000 drachmas at 18 percent.
4,500 drachmas at 12 percent.

The state, however, was able to borrow money from Athena's treasury at 1.2 percent (IG I² 324). Davies (1981, p. 64) attributes these high rates to a generally insufficient liquidity. Thus, those with liquid capital to spare were able to make a high profit, and many borrowers detested them. However, the speaker of Demosthenes (XXXVII, 53–4) defends the moneylender as follows:

> I, for my part, do not regard a moneylender as a wrongdoer, although certain of the class may justly be detested by you, seeing that they make a trade of it, and have no thought of pity or of anything else, except gain. Since I have myself often borrowed money, and not merely lent it to the plaintiff, I know these people well; and I do not like them either; but, by Zeus, I do not defraud them, nor bring malicious charges against them. But if a man has done business as I have, going to sea on perilous journeys, and from his small profits has made these loans, wishing not only to confer favors, but to prevent his money from slipping through his fingers without knowing it, why should one set him down in that class? – unless you mean this, that anyone who lends money to you ought to be detested by the public.
> (Trans. A. T. Murray, Loeb Classical Library)

Similarly, in 355 Isocrates (VII, *Areopagiticos*, 35) wrote:

> the wealthy were better pleased to see men borrowing money than paying it back; for they thus experienced the double satisfaction – which should appeal to all right-minded men – of helping their fellow-citizens and at the same time making their own property productive for themselves.
> (Trans. George Norlin, Loeb Classical Library)

As mentioned in the section "Trade", maritime loans required much higher interest rates, which included insurance against defaults due to shipwrecks and pirate attacks. The rates of return on investment varied greatly with the types of investment. The return on land was as low as 8–12 percent, whereas the return in the factories of Demosthenes Senior was earlier calculated to be 15–16 percent. The highest return occurred in silver mines, where the return could have been as high as 30 percent (Casson 1976, p. 39).

Profit–output ratio

Earlier on in this chapter, the rate of return on the worth of slaves in Demosthenes' father's two factories was calculated. Here I will estimate the profit–output ratio as the ratio of net profit over total output in the bed factory. Total output is defined to be net profit plus total cost. The earlier estimate of the net profit in the bed factory was 12 minas per year. The items of the total cost are estimated as shown in the table overleaf:

Cost of maintaining a slave	65 drachmas per year (Markle 1985, p. 296)
Cost of maintaining 22 slaves	1,430
Replacement cost on 22 slaves	727 (assuming two slaves die every year)
Ivory	2,400 (see paragraph 31 of *Against Aphobos I*.)
Other material cost	2,400
Total cost	7,022

Therefore, profit–output ratio is equal to $1200 \div 8222 \cong 0.15$.

Banking

The Greek word for "bank" is τράπεζα, which means table. The word was used because banks started as moneychangers and they operated on moneychangers' tables.

Demosthenes LII, 4, describes the practice of a bank regarding a deposit and an order to pay:

> It is the custom of all bankers, when a private person deposits money and directs that it be paid to a given person, to write down first the name of the person making the deposit and the amount deposited, and then to write on the margin "to be paid to so-and-so"; and if they know the face of the person to whom payment is to be made, they merely do this, write down whom they are to pay; but, if they do not know it, it is their custom to write on the margin the name also of him who is to introduce and point out the person who is to receive the money.
>
> (Trans. A. T. Murray, Loeb Classical Library)

Theophrastos, *Character* 23, Pretentiousness, (1) and (2):

> The fraud is the sort who stands on the breakwater and tells strangers how much of his money is invested in shipping; he goes into detail about the extent of his moneylending business, and the size of his profits and losses; and while he exaggerates these, he sends his slave to the bank because a drachma is on deposit for him there.
>
> (Loeb Classical Library)

Temple treasuries acted like banks lending money at interest. A stele from the Athenian demos of Rhamnous records the summary accounts of the monies of their goddess Nemesis. About 4 talents of capital was lent at about 7 percent interest and grew to about 5.7 talents in seven years (Davies 2001, pp. 117–128).

Cohen, Athenian Economy and Society

Cohen's book starts with the following quotations from Austin and Vidal-Naquet (1980, p. 8) and Finley (1999):

The very concept of "the economy" in the modern sense is untranslatable in Greek, because it simply did not exist.

(Austin and Vidal-Naquet 1980)

The banker was little more than a moneychanger and pawnbroker.

(Finley 1999)

Cohen bluntly characterizes these remarks as "This denial presently is as fashionable as it is false" (p. 3). He admits that Athenian bankers did serve as moneychangers (but not as pawnbrokers) but asserts that accepting deposits and extending loans were much more important activities, and thereby Athenian banks played the role of creating money supply like modern banks. There were moneychangers (ἀργυραμοιβοί) besides τράπεζαι.

Demosthenes (XXXVI, 11) characterizes the bank as "a business operation producing risk-laden revenues from other people's money" (p. 10). The other activities of a banker were "providing sureties, negotiating claims, offering guarantees and personal advice to important customers" (p. 21), as well as witnessing transactions (Demosthenes XXXV, 10), safekeeping documents (Demosthenes XXXIV, 6 and LVI, 15), and accepting valuables for safekeeping (Demosthenes ILIX, 31–2). When someone looks for the banker Pasion, he finds him not at the table but in the city (Demosthenes LII, 8). Banking became important in the fourth century because the rich transferred the visible property (land) to the invisible (ἀφανής) property to conceal their wealth (p. 191). Blepyros in Aristophanes' *Ecclesiazusae* (600) says, "And how about the man who has no land, but only gold and silver coins, that cannot be seen (ἀφανή)?" (www.perseus.tufts.edu).

The names of 30 bankers are known in Athens in the fourth century (p. 31). This fact obviously did not discourage Finley because he said, "not thirty Athenian are known from the whole of the fourth century who are specifically identified as bankers, a reflection of the rarity of the occupation" (Finley 1981, p. 73). Athens did not license banks (p. 31); a bank and a banker were indistinguishable. Thus, they would say, either "I have a deposit at Pasion's bank" or "I have a deposit with Pasion" (p. 64).

There was a prevailing belief that Athenian bankers did not take part in maritime loans. This belief came from the assumption that the four people mentioned in Demosthenes XXVII, *Against Aphobos I*, 11, Xouthos, Pasion, Pylades, and Demomeles, are all individual lenders and not bankers. Cohen convincingly shows from grammatical and other evidences that all the four people mentioned here are bankers (pp. 121–2). Many overseas traders (ἔμποροι) had business with Pasion (Demosthenes LII, 3). Phormion also engaged in maritime loans (Demosthenes XLV, 64).

Cohen gives several examples of banks making loans for business operations (p. 15): (1) Banks provided funding for the ongoing operations of retail fragrance businesses (Lysias, frag., 38. 1). (2) Banks provided loans to purchase mining concessions and processing mills (Demosthenes XXXVII). (3) To establish a clothmaking operation (Xenophon, *Memorabilia*, 2. 7). (4) To finance the import of lumber (Demosthenes ILIX, 35–6). There were no regulations concerning bank loans. Only a particular contract mattered (p. 42). There was no restriction on a banker's handling of money on deposit (p. 113).

Demosthenes (ILIX, 23) tells the following story: In 374, Athenian general Timotheos failed to collect enough funds to pay for a navy operation against Sparta and, on account of it, was recalled to Athens and tried. One day, two people who defended him in the court came to visit Timotheos in his home. Timotheos sent his slave to the house of Pasion and borrowed mattresses, cloaks, and two silver bowls (p. 66). This story might have led Finley to remark that an Athenian banker was little more than a pawnbroker. Cohen, on the other hand, uses this story as evidence that an Athenian banker was a respectable businessman, being a friend of even a general.

It was commonly believed that the banking business was carried on by slaves and metics. In order to give the banking business certain credibility, Cohen cites evidences that some of the bankers were Athenian citizens (p. 70). Slaves who managed banks were often manumitted to the state of a metic so that they could bring a suit. As a metic, Pasion conducted his own case against one of his clients (Isager and Hansen 1975, p. 89).

There was no paper money in classical Athens, but there was an equivalent of bank checks. When Stratokles needed funds available at the distant Black Sea, he did not take his money with him; instead, he carried a bank guarantee of payment issued by Pasion's bank, where Stratokles had a deposit (Isocrates XVII, 35–7) (p. 16). "When the merchant Lykon was leaving Athens and wanted to make payment of 1,640 drachmas to a business colleague, he directed that funds on deposit at Pasion's bank be paid at a future time to Kephisiades (Demosthenes LII, 3)" (p. 16). Athenians called this kind of cashless settlement *diagraphē* (p. 17). (The verb *diagraphō* means "cross out.")

Cohen disagrees with Millett's (1990) contention that credit sale did not exist in classical Athens. Cohen argues that, even though it was illegal, it existed *de facto* (p. 14). The fact that Plato prohibits credit sales in the *Laws* suggests that credit sales actually existed (Cohen 1992, p. 14). Banks extended consumer credit, too.

The model of Athenian economy of the fourth century BC

Introduction

The purpose of this chapter is to get a rough idea of the magnitudes of the economic activities in Athens in the latter half of the fourth century. Since there are few accurate data, I am not as interested in obtaining the point estimates of economic variables as understanding their inter-relatedness. Ideally one should try to obtain interval estimates, but that is a topic of future study.

Starting with the population estimates (see the section "Population" in Chapter 2, "Society and culture"), people (citizens, metics, and slaves) are divided into three sectors – "Poor," "Rich," and "Mfg." "Poor" means poor farmers cultivating their own land, "Rich" means rich farmers who own workshops and other business in the "Mfg" sector. "Mfg" is an all-inclusive term including manufacturing, service, and trade. I also consider the "Government" sector but its sole function is the transfer of money among the Athenian residents and between Athens and foreign countries. The construction of warships and public buildings are assumed to be done in the "Mfg" sector. The model consists of five accounting identities, balancing the revenue and the expenditure in "Poor," "Rich," "Mfg," "Gov," and "Import and Export Account" sectors. The revenue equals the expenditure in "Poor," "Gov," and "Import and Export," but there are small savings in "Rich" and "Mfg." The savings would diminish if the prices of grain were higher than what I assumed – 3 drachmas per *medimnos* for barley and 6 drachmas per *medimnos* for wheat. The prices of grain fluctuated widely year to year. For example, Demosthenes (XXXIV, 39), writing in 335, says that the price of wheat earlier advanced to 16 drachmas per *medimnoi*, and in 330 the price of barley was 5 drachmas per *medimnoi* (IG II² 408).

The consumption of grain is determined by estimating the calorie needs (see the section "Agriculture") and the percentage of the calories taken from grain (see Appendices 1 and 2). The consumption of the other food is determined by estimating the grain–other food ratio (see Appendix 6.1). The consumption of the other goods is determined by estimating the food–other expenditure ratio (see Appendix 6.1). Next, the amount of the domestic agricultural production is estimated using Scheidel's estimates (see the section "Agriculture"). The production in the "Mfg" sector is determined by the number of labor force in the "Mfg" sector, the wage rate, how many days they work in a year, the percentage of the labor cost, and the profit rate. From the above, the import and the export of these items are determined.

The estimates of the revenues and expenditures of the government have been gathered from the studies of various authors. For transfer payment, see Appendix 6.3.

Model

The population estimates adopted in this model are as follows (see the section "Population" in Chapter 2, "Society and culture"):

adult male citizens	25,000
with family (×4)	**100,000**
Metics	20,000
with family (×1.5)	**30,000**
Slaves	**90,000**
home slaves	30,000
mine slaves	30,000[1]
mfg slaves	30,000

"*Poor*" 48,000 citizens (including families)[2]

They own 10,000 slaves and together grow and consume 497,620 *medimnoi* of barley,[3] which is worth 249 talents assuming that the price of barley is 3 drachmas per *medimnos*. They produce other farm products worth 149 talents. They receive 261 talents from the state for civil, welfare, and military payments[4] and with it they buy 100 talents of other food, spend 15 talents for the replacement of slaves,[5] and 146 talents for other expenditures (20 of which is for agricultural investment).

Revenues		Expenditures	
State pay	261	Other food	100
		Other expenditure	146
		Slave replacement	15
Total	261	Total	261

"Rich" 32,000 citizens[6]
10,000 metics (single male 2,000, married male 2,000, wives 2,000, children 4,000)

They own 20,000 home slaves. They grow 151,028 *medimnoi* of barley,[7] and they need 199,400 *medimnoi* of barley to feed the home slaves. They own 30,000 mine slaves, for whom they need additional 388,800 *medimnoi* of barley. The total barley they have to import, therefore, is 437,172 *medimnoi*, worth 219 talents. They grow 102,703 *medimnoi* of wheat,[8] citizens consume 122,240 *medimnoi* of wheat or 122 talents worth at 6 drachmas per *medimnos*, and metics consume 39,860 *medimnoi* of wheat or 40 talents' worth. Therefore, they need to import 59,397 *medimnoi* of wheat or 59 talents' worth. They also grow other agricultural products worth 285 talents. They own manufacturing and trade shops, from which they receive proceeds of 1071 talents a year. They receive 230 talents from the state and pay to the state 584 talents in various forms of contributions (see the details in the table below). In addition, they spend 393 talents for food other than grain, 386 for other expenditures (including 25 for agricultural investment), and 116 for slave import.[9]

Revenues		Expenditures	
Silver	1,000[10]	Wheat import	59
Farm product	285	Barley import	219
State pay	230	Other food	393
Receipts from Mfg	1,071	Other expenditure	386
		Slave import	116
		Contributions	584*
		Raw material import	700
Total	2,586	Total	2,457

* The details are as follows: *Eisphora* 50 (Davies 1981, p. 23); *metoikion* 8 (12 drachmas a year for men and 6 drachmas for unmarried women); festival liturgies 18 (Osborne 1991, p. 130); trierarchy 96 (see the section "Public finance"); mining fees 175[11]; fees, fines, and confiscations 100; *epidosis* 40; slave tax 20; and grain and trade tax 77.[12]

Mfg & trade

Population:	Citizens	20,000 (with families)
	Metics	20,000 (single male 7,000, married male 3,000, single female 1,000, wives 3,000, children 6,000)
	Slaves	30,000
Labor force:[13]	Citizens	5,000
	Metics	11,000
	Slaves	30,000

Citizens and metics work for 200 days a year[14] and earn 1 drachma a day,[15] and slaves earn 2 obols a day. Thus, the total wages are 867 talents. Let x be the value of the total output. Then assuming that the other cost is 50 percent of the output[16] and the profit rate is 15 percent,[17] x must satisfy the equation

$$x - 0.5x - 867 = 0.15x$$

Therefore, the value of the total output is 2,477 talents. Of the other cost of 1,239, I assume 1,115 (415 purchased domestically and 700 imported) is the raw material and 124 (5 percent of the total output) is the depreciation and maintenance.[18] Of the remaining 1,938 (2477 − 415 − 124), 1,466 talents is exported. They receive 197 talents from the state for the civil, welfare, and military payments. Citizens eat 89,200 *medimnoi* of wheat per year or worth 89 talents, and metics 95,420 *medimnoi* of wheat per year or worth 95 talents; therefore, the Mfg sector needs to import 184,620 *medimnoi* of wheat per year, or 184 talents worth. Slaves eat 299,100 *medimnoi* of barley, or worth 150 talents. The people in this sector spend 329 talents for other food and 285 talents for other expenditures. The metics pay to the state 20 talents of the *metoikion* and 50 talents of the market tax.

Revenues		*Expenditures*	
Wages	867	Wheat import	184
State pay	197	Barley import	150
		Other food	329
		Other expenditure	285
		Metoikion	20
		Market tax	50
Total	1,064	Total	1,018

Government account

Revenues		Expenditures[19]	
War contributions and spoils	369	State pay	238
Taxes from "Rich"	584	Theoric fund	60
Taxes from "Mfg"	70	Trierarchy	230
Total taxes	654	Military	160
		Other military exp	335[20]
Total	1023[21]	Total	1023

Import–export account

Imports		Exports	
Wheat[22]	244	War contributions and spoils	369
Barley[22]	368		
Other food	637*	Silver	825
Other exp	345#	Mfg goods[23]	1,466#
Raw material	700	Farm products	100
Military exp	335		
Slaves	131		
Total	2,760	Total	2,760

Total taxable trade (including grain but excluding military exp, slaves, war contributions and spoils, and silver): $3{,}860 \times 0.02 = 77$[24]

* This number is calculated as follows:

Domestic output	434
Export	100
Available for domestic consumption	334
Consumption by the Mfg sector	329
Consumption by the "Rich"	393
Consumption by the "Poor"	434
Total consumption	1,256
Import	1256 − 334 = 637

\# The following table shows where the output of the Mfg sector goes and how many Mfg goods are exported and imported:

	Expenditure	Domestic	Foreign
Available for consumption		1,938	
Mfg sector	285	140	145
"Rich"	386	186	200
"Poor"	146	146	
Export		1,466	
Import			345

GDP

Gross wheat	130
Gross barley	389
Farm products	434
Silver	1,000
Manufacturing	2,477
Total	4,430[25]

Notes

1. Isager and Hansen (1975, p. 43) estimate the number of slaves working in the silver mines at the end of the fifth century to be 30,000 (see the section "Slavery", Chapter 2, "Society and culture").
2. Jones (1986, p. 9) says 12,000 *thētes* in 322. I multiplied it by 4 to include family members. See Gallant (1991, pp. 23–4) for the discussion of the appropriate multiple to get at the family figure.
3. See Appendix 6.2.
4. See Appendix 6.3.
5. See the section "Athenian slave import".
6. Jones (1986, p. 9) says 9,000 hoplites in 322. I decreased it to 8,000 and multiplied it by 4.
7. See the section "Agriculture".
8. See the section "Agriculture".
9. See the section "Athenian slave import".
10. Isager and Hansen (1975, p. 45) estimate the total silver production in about 340 to be about 1,000 talents.
11. Andreades (1933 p. 272) believed that the state received 50–100 talents a year from the leasing of the mines. Mattingly (1968, pp. 170–72) believes that in addition to the leases, the miners had to pay 10 percent of their total silver output to the state.
12. See import–export account below.
13. According to the Erectheion account of the years 409–406 (IG I² 372-4), 24 citizens, 42 metics, and 20 slaves have been identified. According to the Eleusinian account of the year 329 (IG II/III² 1672), 20 citizens, 44 metics, and 20 slaves have been identified. In both cases, the ratio of citizens, metics, and slaves is roughly 1 : 2 : 1. My figures for citizens and metics roughly reflect this ratio. As for slaves, however, I did not follow the ratio because I expected more slaves working in private workshops and trade than in temples.
14. The consensus of the ancient historians concerning the number of days workers worked in classical Athens is in the range of 200–250.
15. In the aforementioned Erechtheion account, the wage rate was $1-1\frac{1}{2}$ drachmas per day for citizens, metics, and slaves. In the Eleusinian account, slaves received 3 obols,

unskilled labor 1 drachma, and skilled labor $2-2\frac{1}{2}$ drachmas So my estimate is on the low side.
16 Using certain assumptions I calculated the other cost in the bed factory of Demosthenes Senior in Demosthenes' *Against Aphobos I* to be 57 percent of the output.
17 Using certain assumptions I calculated the profit rate in the bed factory of Demosthenes Senior in Demosthenes' *Against Aphobos I* to be 14 percent of the output. I expect the profit rate in his sword factory to be higher.
18 This rate is 5–6 percent in modern nations (Clark 1957, pp. 228–30).
19 See the section "Public finance" and Appendix 6.3.
20 This is the military expenditure on foreign soldiers or on foreign soil; therefore, it will also appear as an import item below.
21 Isager and Hansen (1975, p. 54) state that in Lycurgos' time (338–326), the state revenues were 1,200 talents.
22 These numbers mean that 244,017 *medimnoi* of wheat and 736,272 *medimnoi* of barley are imported, or a total of 980,289 *medimnoi* of grain. This amount is slightly larger than the 800,000 *medimnoi* indicated by Demosthenes XX and Whitby (1998, pp. 124–5). The import of wheat and barley amounts to 612 talents. Compare it to the 700 talents estimated by Adams (1994, p. 92).
23 Osborne (1991, p. 133) criticizes Finley for arguing that silver was the main Athenian export and emphasizes the significant part manufacture played in the creation of wealth. Fischer-Hansen (2000, p. 92) notes that the considerable evidence for workshops undermines Finley's view that the Greek *polis* was a consumer city. Workshops were too numerous to have served just local consumers but were clearly aimed at generating exports. See Harris for the extent of the development of the Athenian Agora.
24 The sum of three import items (other food, other expenditure, and raw material) and three export items (mfg goods and farm products) amounts to 3,248 talents. The 2 percent of it is 65 talents. This is more than the 38 talents given by Andokides but the time of Andokides' tax collection was soon after the end of the Peloponnesian War when the volume of trade was at its low point.
25 Adams (1994, p. 91) estimates GDP to be 6,000 talents.

Appendix 6.1: Calorie percentage in grain, grain–other food ratio, food–expenditure ratio

	Calorie %	Grain/food	Food/exp.
Rich citizen & metic	0.6	0.4	0.6
Mfg citizen & metic	0.7	0.5	0.65
Poor citizen	0.7	0.5	0.7
Home & Mfg slave	0.8	0.6	0.8
Mine slave	0.9	0.7	0.85

Historical records of G/F and F/E ratios are as follows:

G/F

62.5 percent in Lyon in 1550 (Cipolla 1993, p. 24)
62 percent in Antwerp in 1600 (p. 24)
52 percent in Turkey in 1935 (Clark 1957, p. 84)
39 percent in Greece in 1934–38 (pp. 428–429)
27 percent in Germany in 1929 (p. 80)
25 percent in Russia in 1952 (p. 241)
20 percent in France in 1932 (p. 79)
10 percent in U.S. in 1935 (p. 85)

F/E

80 percent in Lyon in 1550 and Antwerp in 1600 (Cipolla 1993, p. 24)
77.5 percent for Indian rural wage workers (Clark 1957, p. 470)
77 percent in Rome in AD301 (p. 664)
34 percent in Japan in 1934 (p. 83)

Appendix 6.2: Annual consumption of grain

Rich citizen (family average)	3.82 *med. of wheat*
Rich metic (adult male)	4.65 *med. of wheat*
(adult female)	3.39 *med. of wheat*
(child)	3.62 *med. of wheat*
Mfg citizen (family average)	4.46 *med. of wheat*
Mfg metic (adult male)	5.42 *med. of wheat*
(adult female)	3.96 *med. of wheat*
(child)	4.23 *med. of wheat*
Poor citizen (family average)	8.29 *med. of barley*
Home & Mfg slave (family average)	9.97 *med. of barley*
Mine slave	12.96 *med. of barley*

med. = *medimnoi*

In calculating these numbers a drastic assumption was made that "poor" citizens and slaves eat barley and the rest eat wheat.

Appendix 6.3: Transfer payment by the government (only adult male)

	Poor	*Rich*	*Mfg*	*Total*
Citizens	12,000	8,000	5,000	25,000
Metics		4,000	9,000	13,000
Civic pay (only citizens)	111 (talents)	76	48	238
Hoplites		50		50
Cavalry		30		30
Trireme	81	55	94	230
Theoric (only citizens)	29	19	12	60
Soldiers	37		43 (all)	80
Total	261	230	197	688

See the section "Public finance" for these numbers.

Part III

Economics

7 Xenophon's economics

In this part we will first discuss Xenophon's two works, *Oikonomikos* and *Ways and Means*. These two works and Aristotle's *Nicomachean Ethics*, Book V, to be discussed later, contain in large measure discussions that belong to the category of modern economics. When I say economics or economic ideas in this book, however, I include contents beyond the boundary of modern economics: namely, contents that would be considered part of ethics today. Why should we consider both the narrow and broad sense of economics, so to speak? It is because modern economics considers only how people do behave and not how people should behave in economic activities involving production, consumption, and distribution. Modern economics has tried to acquire the status of science by excluding the ethical aspect of human behavior. As a result of this, however, it has unwittingly fallen into the trap of thinking that maximization of profit and maximization of utility, hypotheses adopted to explain human behavior, were a good thing. Hausman and McPherson (1996) mention that because economists hypothesize that men constantly pursue selfish motives, people who study economics tend to become egoistic.

Plato and Aristotle discussed much about the broad sense of economics. For them, economics was a part of ethics. Therefore, we must first understand their ethical theories. After discussing Xenophon's economics, Plato's and Aristotle's ethics, Plato's economics, and Aristotle's economics, will be mulled over in that order. Utilitarianism, which has become the philosophical foundation of modern economics, will be deliberated upon at the end and will be compared with Plato's and Aristotle's ethics

Oikonomikos

The English word "economy" is derived from the Greek word *oikonomia*. This is a compound word made from *oikos* (house) and *nomos* (custom, law). Therefore, the literal translation of *oikonomia* is "household management." One of Xenophon's works is called *Oikonomikos*. It is an adjective meaning "experienced in the art of household management"; hence it may be translated as a treatise on the subject. In the beginning of the work, Socrates argues that household management is a science or art like medicine or carpentry.

This work has two parts: the first part is a conversation between Socrates and Critobulos while the second one is a conversation between Socrates and Ischomachos. In the first part, Xenophon develops a strikingly original theory of values through the mouth of Socrates. Goods have use values and exchange values. A flute does not have any use value to a person who does not play the flute, but because it can be exchanged for money at the market, it has an exchange value. If the person misused the money he obtained at the market, however, it would become worthless. Thus, what Socrates calls wealth or property (κτῆσις) here is more like the good (ἀγαθός) rather than material wealth as considered by modern economists. That is why Socrates includes knowledge and friends in a list of a person's wealth. The definition of property (κτῆσις) appears in vi. 4: it is what is useful (ὠφέλιμον) for life (βίος). Finley (1999, p. 19) writes, "In Xenophon, however, there is not one sentence that expresses an economic principle or offers any economic analysis, nothing on efficiency of production, 'rational' choice, the marketing of crops." In the passage mentioned earlier, however, Xenophon shows an understanding of value much more profound than what one can learn from a college course on the principles of economics. Even in terms of more mundane economic analysis, Xenophon has demonstrated his familiarity with it in the work called *Ways and Means*, which I will discuss below.

In the second part, Xenophon expounds upon farm management in general as well as recounts how a rich landlord, Ischomachos, educated his young wife to become a capable house manager. It seems that Xenophon highly valued a wife's contribution to the household economy. In the first part, Socrates tells Critobulos that "the wife who is a good partner in the household contributes just as much as her husband to its good" (iii. 15, trans. E. C. Marchant, Loeb Classical Library). Xenophon makes Ischomachos say that a wife is an equal partner to her husband and even that her contribution is greater than that of her husband's (vii. 13–14). In terms of certain virtues, men and women are equal: Ischomachos says that they have equal powers of memory and care and equal ability to practice self-control (vii. 26). In this respect we can say that Xenophon was more progressive than the average intellectual of the time. Plato, as we will mention later, was also progressive in this way; he included women among philosopher-kings. Aristotle, on the other hand, slighted women's intellectual abilities and regarded a wife not as her husband's equal partner, but as a being who should merely follow her husband's orders. Xenophon's attitude toward slaves was also more liberal than that of Aristotle, who maintained that most slaves lacked reason and, therefore, were slaves by nature. Xenophon, on the other hand, seems to treat slaves as being capable of reasoning. For example, Ischomachos says, "I treat him like a free man by making him rich; and not only so, but I honour him as a gentleman" (xiv. 9).

In the latter half of the second part in *Oikonomikos*, Xenophon describes how Ischomachos' father bought a bad piece of farmland at a cheap price, improved it to raise its value, and sold it for a large profit. This passage is valuable for understanding people's economic ideas at the time. Upon hearing this, Socrates asked Ischomachos if what his father did was similar to a grain trader buying grain when cheap and selling it at a higher price. Socrates was teasing Ischomachos because it was generally considered dishonorable to gain profit from trade, but honorable if the profit came from farming. The second part contains a rather commonsensical discussion of agricultural techniques: what to grow, how to grow, and when to cultivate, seed, and sow. In regarding agriculture as a most virtuous activity, Xenophon shared a common view with the rest of the Athenian aristocracy.

Ways and Means

This work, called Πόροι (ways) in Greek, was written in 355, the year in which the Social War ended and the Second Athenian League was dissolved. It was intended to support the financial policy of Eubulos (see "Glossary"). It suggests various measures to strengthen the Athenian economy and procure revenues for the state. Some of these measures were carried out by Eubulos and then later by Lycurgos (338–25). According to Plutarch, the state revenue in the days of Lycurgos went up to 1,200 talents a year. The bulk of it came from the silver mines, but 1/3–1/4 came from Peiraieus (Burke 1992, p. 203).

One way by which Xenophon planned to accomplish the above objectives was to attract more metics to Athens. For this purpose he proposed to:

1 exempt metics from the duty of serving in the infantry;
2 allow them to serve in the cavalry;
3 build houses in vacant lots and let metics live in them (this was not the same as giving them the right to own land and houses); and
4 give benefits to citizens who served as guardians of many metics.

The following were the measures to promote trade in Peiraieus:

1 offer prizes to the magistrates of trade for the just and prompt settlement of disputes;
2 reserve front seats in the theater for merchants and shipowners;
3 encourage citizens to contribute to the capital fund;
4 build more lodgings and markets in Athens and Peiraieus; and
5 have the state acquire a fleet of public merchant vessels and lease them under securities.

Xenophon believed that unlike gold whose value goes down when there is too much of it, the production of silver was at a stage where profitability would not go down with more production. Thus, he recommended that the state should possess slaves and lease them to the miners, starting with 1,200 slaves and increasing to 6,000 after five years.

8 Plato's ethics

Introduction

Plato was born in 427, so he was 28 when Socrates died. Plato was one of Socrates' pupils and was greatly influenced by him. As socrates did not leave any written work, Plato's writings constitute the only source from which we can find out about the philosophy of Socrates. Xenophon also wrote about Socrates but mentioned little about his philosophy.

Since Vlastos' convincing argument (see Vlastos 1991), most philosophers now believe that Plato's early dialogs represent Socratic philosophy fairly accurately. In these dialogs Socrates engages in conversations with real people, both known and unknown, including famous Sophists like Gorgias and Protagoras. Socrates interrogates his opponents in the method called ἔλεγχος (cross-examination) and exposes the fallacies of their arguments but does not give his own answers. He claims he does not know anything and the only thing he knows is the fact that he does not know anything. In this regard, he is the wisest of all. Socrates' idea of education was not instilling knowledge into the minds of students but making them think for themselves by asking questions, such as "What is courage?" (*Laches*), "What is piety?" (*Euthyphro*), "What is virtue?" (*Protagoras*), "What is pleasure?" (*Gorgias*), and "What is justice?" (*Republic*). Students first think they know the answers to these questions but after Socrates' interrogations, they realize they really did not know anything. Socrates is only interested in people and not in stars, only in ethics and not in metaphysics. His primary concern is the question, "How should a man live?" In the early dialogs Plato presents his arguments in the same way Socrates did: namely, through dialogs (διαλεκτική) rather than through discourses.

In all but one (the *Laws*) of the middle and late dialogs, Socrates still appears as the main speaker but he engages in long monologs more and more, extending his topics toward metaphysical questions. These works seem to reflect more of Plato's own thinking. It is in these works that Plato presents his central metaphysical theory of forms (ἰδέα or εἶδος). See the chronology of Plato's works at the end of this chapter.

The theory of forms serves two purposes. Its first purpose is to explain the relationship between reality and appearance. "What really exists?" is the question philosophers have asked since the days of Thales. A simple-minded materialistic view is that a desk exists and appears to me here. But this view has many deficiencies. First, I have no real understanding of this thing called a desk. Second, it disappears when I close my eyes. Third, it also disappears when I burn it up. Democritos said a desk consists of many atoms, but that is no help because I do not understand atoms any more than I do a desk. Berkeley said that a desk or any other matter does not exist, and what exists is my mind that sees a desk. This is at least more satisfactory than the materialistic view, but I still feel uneasy because not only do I see the desk here but so do other people. Then there may be something here more objective than my simple subjective notion. Plato's theory of forms tries to solve this difficulty by saying there exists the form of a desk and its image that appears here (see Fujisawa 1980). The form of a desk resides in heaven and what appears here is a rather imperfect image of it. The form of a desk that resides in heaven may be understood as its idealized functional property – in other words, what an ideal desk should be.

Its second purpose is to refute the relativistic philosophy of sophists by providing a firm foundation for absolute human values such as goodness, justice, and beauty. Forms of good (goodness), justice, and beauty reside in heaven, and when we were in heaven before we came to this world (note that Plato believed in reincarnation, influenced by Pythagoras), we saw these forms clearly. The reason we can recognize, for example, beautiful things in this world is because we remember the form of beauty we saw in heaven, though only vaguely. The purpose of education is to make one recollect forms through illustration and analogy and grasp them by the eye of the mind.

What is the form of beauty? There are many individual beautiful things in this world: a beautiful woman, a beautiful picture, and a beautiful (noble) action. All these are imperfect and deficient not only in the sense that no beautiful woman is a perfect 10, but in the sense that all these concepts are qualified or conditional – that is, a beautiful something. Plato says there exists the form of beauty that is perfect and unconditional. Individual beautiful things "partake" of the form of beauty. How does form differ from universal? Universal is a common element in things such as beautiful woman, beautiful picture, and beautiful action. Nobody would object to the statement that the word beautiful is common in all these terms, but to argue that a universal exists is another matter. There are two interpretations of a universal. A nominalist says that a universal is just a name and does not really exist. A realist says it exists. Aristotle is a realist. He says, substance (οὐσία) = matter (ὕλη) + form (ἶ δος), and form does exist, but it exists always combined with matter and does not exist separately. Plato says that form exists separately and independently of matter.

The form of the good is the most important form and it encompasses all the other forms under a unified order. This idea is closely related to Socrates' (and Plato's) famous theory of unity of virtues (see the section "Protagoras"). The meaning of this theory is that we can understand individual virtues only by understanding all the virtues. For Plato, true understanding is possible only with the holistic grasp of the subject (see *Laws* 965B).

In Book VII of the *Republic*, Plato presents his famous analogy of the cave. People in a cave can look only at the shadows of the puppets projected on a wall by the light of a lamp behind the puppets and they think these shadows are reality. The true reality (form) exists under the bright sun outside of the cave. If the people in the cave look around and look toward the lamp, they will come closer to reality but still it is not the real thing. As they come out of the cave and their eyes become gradually accustomed to the bright sunlight, they will eventually see the sun, which is the form of the good. Honor and fame in this world are worthless like the shadows in the cave.

The sun does not merely represent knowledge. Turning your eyes toward the sun does not mean studying hard to increase knowledge. The goal is not knowledge but the total development of the human soul. The form of the good integrates all the virtues – wisdom, justice, temperance, and courage. In the *Symposium* Plato uses the word love (ἔρως) to refer to this action of turning your eyes toward the sun. Love means total devotion to an object. Simone Weil (1987, p. 134) writes as follows:

> The principal image which Plato uses in the *Republic*, notably in the passage about the cave, the image of the sun and of sight, shows exactly what love is in man. One would make a complete mistake in believing that the metaphor of the cave relates to knowledge and that sight signifies the intelligence. The sun is the good. Sight is then the faculty which is in relationship with the good. Plato, in the *Symposium*, says as definitely as possible that this faculty is love. By the eyes, by sight, Plato means love.

The purpose of education is to make a man turn toward the sun. Earlier I characterized it by saying, "The purpose of education is to make one recollect forms through illustration and analogy and grasp them by the eye of the mind." The Greeks emphasized the importance of seeing. Both ἰδέα and εἶδος contain the root ιδ, which means "to see." Latin *video* is derived from this root. You can tell this also from words such as θεωρέω, which originally meant "to look at" but is also used to mean "to contemplate." The noun is θεωρία (contemplation), what Aristotle calls the highest kind of human activity. The word νόησις (intuition) comes from the verb νοέω (perceive). A man perceives the form of the good with νόησις. According to Kant, a man can grasp "Ding an sich (thing in itself)" by intuition. This mode of attainment is like the enlightenment of Zen Buddhism. This last point is emphasized by Simone Weil (1987) in the following two passages:

> Absolute beauty is something as concrete as sensible objects, something which one sees, but sees by supernatural sight. After a long spiritual preparation one has access to it by a sort of revelation, of rending: "suddenly he shall perceive a species of miraculous beauty".
>
> (p. 147)

> To him who lovingly contemplates the order of the world, there shall come a certain day and moment when suddenly he shall contemplate another thing, a miraculous sort of beauty.
>
> (p. 148)

These metaphysical discussions are interesting but will not lead to a whole understanding of Plato's forms. We should understand Plato's forms in connection with his ethical theory, that is, what Plato regards as the aim of human life, what in life is truly valuable, and how a man should live. Plato is a moral philosopher before he is a metaphysical philosopher. "According to Plato, the right aim for human life is to understand the order and harmony that characterizes the most fundamental part of reality and embody this also in our lives" (Moravcsik 2000, p. 98). Here, Plato's metaphysics and his ethics are united. That is why Plato does not try to define a whole list of forms and instead gives us only "a relatively small set of privileged elements that combine to give order, harmony, and intelligibility to reality" (Moravcsik 2000, p. 58). Those who have seen the sun and yet have decided to go back to the cave and govern the people as philosopher-kings are the embodiment of this union of metaphysics and ethics.

The fundamental characteristics of Plato's ethics are that (1) goodness is a function of the soul in terms of aim and character and it is not a function of the act in terms of its consequence (see *Laws*, 864A) and (2) pleasure and goodness are distinct and man should seek only goodness. (Here, pleasure is not restricted to physical pleasure.) In both respects it is fundamentally incompatible with utilitarianism. Aristotle more or less subscribes to the same two principles as will be evident when his ethics are discussed later on.

Generally speaking, modern ethics may be said to focus on action, while ancient ethics focused on people. What concerned Plato and Aristotle most was how a man can live an ideal, worthwhile life. Such an ideal life is called *eudaimonia* in Greek. If this word is translated as "happiness," Plato and Aristotle's ethics may be categorized as utilitarianism, which is inappropriate. Happiness can be used to describe a state in a short period, such as "I am happy now." *Eudaimonia*, on the other hand, describes the whole life of a man. Therefore, we do not know if a person is *eudaimōn* (adjective of *eudaimonia*) until his life is completed. In an extreme case, we may not know it even after a person's death. If one's son were to become a thief, one's life could not be said to be *eudaimōn*. Therefore, "truly valuable" or "worthwhile" is a better translation; "*eudaimōn*" is a more objective notion than "happy."

An ideal, worthwhile life is a life in which virtues such as wisdom, justice, moderation, and courage are fully developed. Education's highest goal is to produce an excellent human being who can lead such a life. Once an excellent person is created, excellent action will naturally flow from him. This is the state Confucius attained at age 70. He said, "At seventy, I could follow the dictates of my own heart; for what I desired no longer overstepped the boundaries of right" (the *Analects*, trans. Arthur Waley).

This is the sort of education that Plato described in detail in the *Republic* for the education of philosopher-kings. Plato regarded this kind of education as making people turn toward God. Aristotle also says in *Nicomachean Ethics* that the best life is the life of looking toward God. In contrast, utilitarianism only focuses on the good and evil consequences of actions. Even if a motive is bad, as long as the consequence is good, an action is considered good. A good action for Plato and Aristotle is an action which is carried out with a good motive and after rational deliberation.

Both Plato and Aristotle considered pleasure and good to be different, with good taking priority over pleasure. Unlike stoics, they do not say that pleasure should be avoided. Unlike utilitarians, however, they do not use pleasure as a criterion for action. Right action is taken because it is right. Although pleasure (mental) may often accompany action, we should not choose the action for the sake of pleasure.

Republic

Even though the title of the book is the *Republic*, it is not purely a book on political science. Plato is really concerned with individual persons and is interested in a state to the extent it affects individuals. An ideal state for Plato is the state in which the individual can live the most meaningful life. Thus, the *Republic* is as much a book on ethics as it is on political science. Plato's ideal nation was extremely unpopular in the West right after World War II and Plato was compared to even Stalin and Hitler, but this was due to a complete misunderstanding. This view was even shared by Popper (1963), who should have known better. When Plato says a state is more important than an individual, he is not expounding a totalitarian philosophy; he is simply saying all the individuals that comprise a state are more important than a single individual. We should not forget the fact that for Plato the purpose of a nation is to let its citizens live most virtuous lives. It is true that Plato valued the fostering of public spirit (*Laws*, 875A and 923B); however, that should not be mistaken for totalitarianism. In Books VIII and IX of the *Republic*, Plato ranks tyranny, such as under Stalin or Hitler, as the worst form of government.

Republic I

Socrates successively refutes the definitions of justice given by Polemarchos and Thrasymachos. First, Polemarchos presents Simonides' definition: "It is just to give to each what is owed." Socrates criticizes this definition saying that justice would then mean "helping friends and harming enemies," a popular morality of the day. Socrates argues that a harmed person would become more unjust and therefore that cannot be the definition of justice just as the task of a musician should not be to make men more unmusical. Then, Thrasymachos defines justice as "the advantage of the stronger," by which he means that justice is what a tyrant imposes on the public to his own advantage.

By Socrates' cross-examination, Thrasymachos realizes that he has in fact defined injustice rather than justice. Socrates does not yet give his own definition.

For Kephalos, Polemarchos, and Thrasymachos, justice refers to external duties. For Socrates it is the internal morality of man.

Republic II

The part of Book II that is concerned with the division of labor and how a state is formed will be discussed in Chapter 10, "Plato's economics".

Socrates classifies good into three kinds: (1) good by itself with no other end, (2) good by itself which serves a good end, and (3) not good by itself but with a good end. He states that justice belongs to (2). Annas (1981, pp. 60–64) points out that in modern moral theory (1) corresponds to deontology and (3) to consequentialism including utilitarianism but (2) is not included as a valid alternative. Plato characterizes justice as (2) because in the case of justice, being good by itself and serving a good end are inseparable. Socrates contrasts a perfectly just man who looks unjust and therefore is condemned by society with a perfectly unjust man who looks just and therefore praised by society. Then he asserts that the former is more *eudaimōn* than the latter. It seems that in the mind of Socrates, "just," "good," and "*eudaimōn*" are synonymous (361). He does not say justice is valuable because it brings *eudaimonia*. If he did, he would become a consequentialist. Another clue that Plato is a nonconsequentialist can be found in the following passage:

> The domination of passion and fear and pleasure and pain and envies and desires in the soul, whether they do any injury or not, I term generally "injustice"; but the belief in the highest good – in whatsoever way either States or individuals think they can attain it, – if this prevails in their souls and regulates every man, even if some damage be done, we must assert that everything thus done is just.
> (*Laws*, trans. R. G. Bury, Loeb Classical Library, 863E)

For Simone Weil the archetype of a just man who looks unjust is Christ on the cross, as she says,

> In short, only the penitent thief has seen justice as Plato conceived it, naked and perfect, veiled beneath the appearance of a criminal. Plato, in going as far as to suppose that the perfectly just man is not recognized even by the gods, had premonition of the most piercing words of the gospel: "My God, my God, why hast thou forsaken me?"
> (p. 143)

Republic III

The important role of music in education is discussed. The guardians (philosopher-kings) are mentioned for the first time. Later, they are further divided into overseers (ἐπιστάτης) and assistants (ἐπίκουρος). Only the former may be regarded as the narrow and true sense of guardians (philosopher-kings). They are to possess no private property or money. Wives and children are also communally owned.

Republic IV

Socrates successively defines σοφία (wisdom), ἀνδρεία (courage), σωφροσύνη (moderation), and δικαιοσύνη (justice). He defines these virtues both for an individual and a state using the notion of the tripartition of soul and state. The tripartition of soul and state and the corresponding virtues are arranged as follows:

Man:	Reason	Spiritedness	Desire
State:	Guardians	Warriors	Workers
Virtues:	Wisdom	Courage	———

The state is wise if it is so structured that the wise people rule. Plato defines courage as the right belief about what should and should not be feared, accompanied by the ability to stick to that belief in the face of temptation and coercion. Moderation is not just an ability to control your desires but refers to having a correct idea of who you are and what is due to and appropriate for your position. Moderation in a state is a harmony among the three parts. Finally, justice, like moderation, is also a harmony among the three states, but it goes beyond moderation in the sense that it describes the person or the state in which wisdom, courage, and moderation all exist. Annas (1981, p. 11) states that the Greek *dikaiosynē* is broader than the English justice and is almost synonymous with righteousness. If guardians control workers as reason controls desire, it is hard to know if workers are expected to have any of the virtues at all. In fact, Plato likens the worker to the slave who is ruled by the master (590D).

Spiritedness (θυμός) is difficult to understand. Plato includes shame and love of honor and winning into this category. Also, the analogy between the individual and the state sometimes becomes too stretched. Plato is compelled to treat, for example, the justice of man and the justice of the state homogeneously because of his theory of form.

Hume said that reason is the slave of the passions.

> Unlike "Humean" reason, which takes the goals of the other parts of the soul as given and merely tries to achieve them in an efficient and organized way, reason (λογιστικόν) as Plato conceives it will decide for the whole soul in a way that does not take the ends of the other parts as given but may involve suppressing or restraining them.
>
> (Annas 1981, p. 134)

Plato's λογιστικόν is different from the economist's narrow definition of rationality. In 443C–D, we can see that Plato's moral theory is person-centered rather than action-centered, the point I made earlier.

Gorgias

Gorgias was a celebrated sophist well known for his techniques of rhetoric. In the beginning of this work, Socrates and Gorgias discuss what rhetoric is. Gorgias asserts that rhetoric is the greatest of human affairs and the best. Socrates, on the other hand, would not give it the status of true *technē*, which must aim at something true and good. For Socrates, examples of true *technē* are mathematics, medicine, music, and ethics (see Moravcsik 2000, pp. 14–17). In contrast, the rhetoric practiced by Gorgias and other sophists is merely an art of persuasion and is comparable to cosmetics and gourmet cooking. Gorgias retires in shame and his disciples Polos and Callicles continue conversations with Socrates. Both of them are outright hedonists.

Plato's view of pleasure is presented most clearly in this work. In it, Socrates tells Polos and Callicles that because there are good pleasures and bad pleasures, pleasure cannot be a rule of conduct, and a person should seek justice for justice's sake, regardless of whether it is accompanied by pleasure. Socrates tells Polos that rhetoric aims at the pleasant (ἡδύ) and not at the good (ἀγαθόν). But for a hedonist like Polos, the pleasant and the good are equivalent. Thus, Socrates' statement that if you do wrong, you will be happier (= better) if you are caught and punished for it than if you go free (472E) is unintelligible to Polos. In 470E Socrates surprises Polos by saying that he does not know whether the Persian King is happy or not until he learns what kind of education he had and how he stood with justice. The right kind of education Socrates has in mind here is the kind that the philosopher-kings go through in order to see the form of the good. In 494C Socrates derides Callicles saying that the happiest life for Callicles must be that of continuously scratching a never-ceasing itch. Plato does recognize that some pleasant things are good but others, like scratching an itch, are not worthwhile (495A).

In 504D Socrates says justice and moderation are to the soul as health is to the body. (Recall that for Plato justice and moderation are almost synonymous.) Reading *Gorgias* (pp. 466f), we learn that for Plato, just (*dikaios*), good (*agathos* or *kalos*), and *eudaimōn* are synonymous. As mentioned above, the same theme appears also in the *Republic*, Book II. See 472E, 479E, 496B, and 507C for the equality of good and happy and 470C for the equality of good and just.

A modern reader after Christianity wonders why Plato does not include love of neighbors as one of the virtues. The answer is that it is covered by justice and moderation. In 507E–508A, Socrates states that without justice and moderation one cannot have love of neighbors and friendship, saying "heaven and earth and gods and men are held together by love of neighbors (κοινωνία) and friendship (φιλία), by orderliness, moderation, and justice."

Protagoras

Protagoras was the most famous sophist of his day. His famous saying "Man is the measure of all things" is an indication of his relativistic philosophy, which Plato emphatically criticized.

The first question Socrates puts to Protagoras is "Is virtue teachable?" Protagoras says yes and Socrates says no. "Teachable" here means "teachable in the sense of teaching a person how to build a house." If "teachable" meant "attainable after a right kind of education," Socrates would have of course said yes because the philosopher-kings of the *Republic* are taught virtues in this way (see 323C). By saying yes to the question in the first sense of "teachable," Protagoras revealed that his notion of virtue was a superficial one. As mentioned earlier, for Socrates (and Plato), virtues are things that must be comprehended as a whole after a long training of the right sort. Thus, the first question is closely related to the second question Socrates puts to Protagoras: "Do different virtues constitute a whole as different parts of a face constitute a face, or as different parts of gold constitute gold?" Protagoras chooses the first and Socrates the second. For Protagoras, wisdom, courage, moderation, and justice are separate virtues that can be taught individually in exactly the same way the technique of building a house can be taught.

In paragraph 357, Socrates presents a model of pleasure maximization that could have been written by Bentham. Why did Protagoras have to swallow such a preposterous idea even though he was not a shameless hedonist like Polos and Callicles? It was an inevitable consequence of his shallow understanding of virtues. He did not comprehend virtues such as wisdom, justice, and moderation as absolute values unified by the form of the good. Instead, he perceived them superficially as useful skills one can learn just as one learns how to build a house. Since usefulness is synonymous with utility, a superficial understanding of virtues leads to utilitarianism.

> For there is no doubt that there Protagoras ought to be forced into a radical hedonism as the true consequence of his concept of knowledge. Precisely by decking himself out in another garb and thereby evading this radical consequence, he makes clear negatively that it is a conclusion he would have to draw.
> (Gadamer 1986, p. 48)

Gadamer calls this model of utility maximization "the caricature of an art of living that would amount to technical knowledge of how to get the greatest amount of pleasure possible" (p. 49).

Scholars who took this doctrine of hedonic calculus as Plato's own idea apparently did not understand Socratic irony. As shown above, Plato in *Gorgias* clearly distinguishes goodness from pleasure. More pertinently, Plato in *Phaedo* (68E) criticizes exactly this kind of hedonic calculus. There, Plato says most people's (including Protagoras') idea of moderation is to "keep away from some pleasures because they are overcome by others." Frede (1992) understood this passage correctly as she writes, "Plato very likely never accepted such an intellectual hedonism for himself" (p. 434).

Next I will quote some passages from three relevant sections from Annas (1999) with my commentaries because I regard this book as the best representation of the essence of Plato's ethics.

Julia Annas, *Platonic Ethics, Old and New*

Transforming your life: virtue and happiness

In the *Republic* Plato says "a just man is happy," instead of saying simply "a man must be just." Annas calls this idea "eudaimonist." But in many passages of Plato's dialogs Annas finds Kantian-like deontological views. For example, "we should not consider the consequences of our actions at all, even death, but only the issue of whether the action is just or not (*Apology*, 28B-D)" (p. 33).

Plato's "a just man is happy" is really equivalent to "a man should be just." But then why did Plato not simply say the latter? Urmson (1988, pp. 1–2) provides an answer. Deeply ingrained in the ancient Greeks was the idea that "to be good was to be enviable; to be righteous was to be praiseworthy." Had Plato been free from this cultural constraint, he would have said, "Never mind about being happy and living the good life; never mind about your personal wellbeing; it is more important to be righteous."

We should also remember the difference between the Greek word εὐδαίμων and the English word happy, as mentioned earlier. Thus, to say "a just man is εὐδαίμων" does not sound as strange as to say "a just man is happy."

In the following passage Kant criticized eudaimonism, which he believed characterized all the ancient ethics:

> When a thoughtful man has overcome the incentives to vice and is aware of having done his often bitter duty, he finds himself in a state of peace of soul and contentment, a state that could well be called happiness, in which virtue is its own reward. Now the eudaemonist says: this delight, this happiness is the true motive for his virtuous action. The concept of duty does not determine his will *immediately*; rather he is moved to do this duty *by means of* the prospect of happiness.
> (*The Metaphysics of Morals*, trans. Mary Gregor, Cambridge University Press, 1991, 377)

It is clear, however, that this criticism does not apply to Platonic ethics (see Irwin 1996).

Elemental pleasures: enjoyment and the good in Plato

Some passages of Plato's works contain what seem like hedonism (for example, *Laws*, 662E8–B6). It is true that Plato was more sympathetic to pleasure than the stoics were. However, for Plato pleasure is never the purpose of life and at best it is something which "supervenes." By supervention Annas means the idea that "pleasure must accompany the virtuous life but is not the goal of the virtuous person" (p. 146). "The best pleasure comes only to those who don't seek it" (p. 147). The purpose must always be virtue. Pleasure must be ordered by reason in order for it to become good.

"*Gorgias* appears hostile to pleasure, and is often regarded as anti-hedonistic, whereas *Philebus* is more sympathetic to the extensive discussion of pleasure, and finds it a place in the good life" (p. 155). However, "virtue at the end of the day does not seem itself to involve pleasure." "Many have thought, not surprisingly, that the conclusion of the *Philebus* makes a disappointingly minimal concession to pleasure. It does not in the end recommend a life which seems by ordinary standards markedly more enjoyable than that recommended in the *Gorgias*" (p. 155).

Hedonism in the Protagoras

Finally, is hedonism Socrates' own position? On the one hand, it is introduced as a position which Socrates unsuccessfully tries to get Protagoras to accept, and which is rejected by many. Socrates is the only one discussing it, and at 351C4 it is marked as what Socrates says. As soon as Protagoras starts treating it as Socrates' own position in the argument, however, Socrates drops it abruptly and tries a different tack. We thus have unambiguous indications both that Socrates introduces the position and that it is not his position in the argument.

(p. 170)

Plato's true interest is to "transform pleasure by reason," not to "turn reason into an instrumental means to achieve pleasure as an unquestioned goal" (p. 171).

Chronology of Plato's works (Kraut 1992, pp. 1–50)

Early dialogs	Middle dialogs	Late dialogs
Apology	Meno	Timaeus
Charimides	Catylus	Critius
Crito	Phaedo	Sophist
Euthyphro	Symposium	Statesman
Ion	Republic	Philebus
Laches	Phaedrus	Laws
Protagoras	Parmenides	
Euthydemus	Theaetetus	
Gorgias		
Hippias Major		
Lysis		
Menexenus		
Republic I		

9 Aristotle's ethics

Introduction

Aristotle (384–22) was born in Stagira in Chalcidice (in northeastern Greece) so he is sometimes called the Stagirite. His father was a court physician of Macedonian King Amyntas, father of Philip and grandfather of Alexander. Aristotle went to Athens when he was 17 years old and became a student at Plato's academy. He lived in Athens as a metic (resident alien) until Plato's death (348). Afterward, he did research in biology in Asia Minor, taught young Alexander in a school he built in Macedonia, and then came back to Athens in 335 to open a school in the Lyceum (Λύκειον). His school in Athens was called Peripatetic because he taught while walking in the colonnade (περίπατος) of the Lyceum. He was expelled from Athens in 323 and died in Chalcis in 322.

Aristotle left comprehensive writings on such diverse subjects as logic, metaphysics, psychology, ethics, politics, biology, and astronomy and had a tremendous effect on Western thought. Aristotelian works were first translated into Arabic for the purpose of providing the theological foundation of Islam, and then translated from Arabic to Latin in the thirteenth century. After this, Aristotelian philosophy was systematically studied by scholastic philosophers such as Albert the Great and Thomas Aquinas and became the philosophical basis of the Catholic theology.

In the beginning of the twentieth century, German Aristotelian scholar W. W. Jaeger argued that Aristotle started out as a Platonist and gradually moved away from Platonism, and proposed a chronological arrangement of all the works of Aristotle according to that principle. Since then some discrepancies have been found in his arrangement, and many Aristotelian scholars believe that although there are some differences, Aristotle's ethical theory is essentially similar to Plato's. I will discuss these differences when I take up Julia Annas' evaluation of Aristotelian ethics at the end of this chapter.

Nicomachean Ethics

In the beginning of this work, Aristotle examines the concept of *eudaimonia*. As explained earlier, this Greek word is usually translated as happiness but "living well" or "doing well" is a better translation. Aristotle says that though all agree that *eudaimonia* is what they aim for in life, people differ in what they think *eudaimonia* is. Thus, in Aristotelian ethics, we can equate *eudaimonia* with the highest good. Saying that, however, still does not answer what *eudaimonia* is. In 1098A15–1098A18, Aristotle gives his first preliminary definition: "activity of the soul exhibiting the highest and most complete excellence in a complete life." What is translated as excellence is ἀρετή. It is a more accurate translation than virtue. Since Aristotle thinks that reason (λόγος) is the most important function of man, the second preliminary definition of *eudaimonia* may be as follows: "activity involving the use of reason at a high level of excellence and throughout a complete life" (Urmson 1988, p. 18).

There has been a long debate among philosophers as to whether Aristotelian *eudaimonia* is inclusive or dominant. Inclusive means that *eudaimonia* must consist of all the good moral and intellectual qualities, as well as external factors such as health, good looks, and good birth. (Aristotle recognizes the possibility that external factors have an effect on *eudaimonia* but eventually minimizes their importance (see Annas, "Aristotle: An unstable view" below).) Dominant refers to the belief that a life of contemplation is exclusively the best kind of life. The dispute has arisen because in different parts of the *Nicomachean Ethics* (henceforth simply *Ethics*) Aristotle seems to subscribe to the different views. The inclusive view is presented in the first nine books and the dominant view in the last Book X.

The inclusive view is more appealing to common sense. The ideal life in this view is the life of a virtuous citizen who has all the resources, spiritual and material, to serve his *polis* well. Aristotle believed that everything has its own function and *aretē* of anything is the state in which its function is developed to the fullest. Thus, the *aretē* of the horse is running fast, the *aretē* of the eyes is seeing well, and so on. Now, according to Aristotle, man is a political (social) animal (ζῷον πολιτικόν) (*Politics*, 1253A2). Therefore, an excellent political (social) life is the best life.

However, this view seems to be too mundane. In Book X Aristotle recognizes that the true function of man, unlike the horse or eyes, is not merely to be a perfect man but to try to go beyond it. That is, to look toward God. This is the meaning of contemplation.

> But if happiness consists in activity in accordance with virtue, it is reasonable that it should be activity in accordance with the highest virtue; and this will be the virtue of the best part of us. Whether then this be the intellect, or whatever else it be that is thought to rule and lead us by nature, and to have cognizance of what is noble and divine, either as being itself also actually divine, or as being relatively the divinest part of us, it is the activity of this part of us in accordance with the virtue proper to it that will constitute perfect happiness; and it has been already stated that this activity is the activity of contemplation.
> (1177A13–18, trans. H. Rackham, Loeb Classical Library)

Such a life as this, however, will be higher than the human level: not in virtue of his humanity will a man achieve it, but in virtue of something within him that is divine.

(1177B33–35)

Compared to this life of contemplation, Aristotle regards the excellent political life as the second best: "The life of moral virtue, on the other hand, is happy only in a secondary degree" (1178A9–10).

A good account of this view is given by Nagel (1980, pp. 12–13):

> Having argued the claims of the contemplative life on a variety of grounds, he breaks in at 1177B27 with the remark that such a life would be higher than human. It is achieved not in virtue simply of being a man but in virtue of something divine of which men partake. Nevertheless this divine element, which gives us the capacity to think about things higher than ourselves, is the highest aspect of our souls, and we are not justified in forgoing its activities to concentrate on lowlier matters – namely, our own lives – unless the demands in the latter area threaten to make contemplation impossible. As he says at 1177B33, we should not listen to those who urge that a human should think human thoughts and a mortal mortal ones. Rather we should cultivate that portion of our nature which promises to transcend the rest. If anyone insists that the rest belongs to a complete account of human life, then the view might be put, somewhat paradoxically, by saying that comprehensive human good isn't everything and should not be the main human goal. We must identify with the highest part of ourselves rather than with the whole. The other functions, including the practical employment of reason itself, provide support for the highest form of activity but do not enter into our proper excellence as primary component factors. This is because men are not simply the most complex specie of animal but possess as their essential nature a capacity to transcend themselves and become like gods. It is in virtue of this capacity that they are capable of *eudaimonia*, whereas animals are incapable of it, children have not achieved it, and certain adults, such as slaves, are prevented from reaching it.

This choice between a contemplative life and a practical life is a big problem everyone faces, not just Aristotelians. It has been a critical issue in Christianity and Buddhism. In the Gospel according to Luke (10:38–42) there is a well-known story of Jesus visiting the house of sisters Martha and Mary. Martha was busy preparing dinner in the kitchen, while Mary sat at Jesus' feet and listened to him attentively. When Martha complained to Jesus that Mary was not helping her, Jesus replied that Mary had chosen the better act. Dogen (1200–1253), father of Japanese Zen Buddhism, went to China to study Zen Buddhism. When his ship arrived in a port in China, a monk came on the ship to buy Japanese mushrooms. When Dogen asked him why he was not doing Zazen (the sitting), he smiled and replied that preparing food for the monks was his Zazen.

Some people criticize the dominant view for being selfish. But I think those who have contemplated God rightly will love their fellow men and try to help them, as the philosopher-kings of Plato who have seen the sun will go back to the cave to govern the wretched people below.

Aristotle seems to have believed in altruistic love for a friend. For example, speaking of love (*philein*), he says, "we ought to wish our friend well for his own sake" (1155B31). He also says, "Let loving, then, be defined as wishing for anyone the things which we believe to be good, for his sake but not for our own, and procuring them for him as far as lies in our power" (*Rhetoric*, II. iv, trans. J. H. Freese, Loeb Classical Library).

When I discussed Plato's ethics, I said that his ethics is generally person-centered rather than act-centered. The same is true of Aristotle's ethics. Aristotle believes that excellence (ἀρετή) of character refers to the state of soul that can be achieved after long practice and training, where one behaves in a good way willingly. Just doing good things is not enough. One must do them willingly and enjoy doing them. Annas (1993, p. 130) expands this statement as follows: "virtues are concerned with choice, and with doing the right thing, from a well-informed judgment as to what is the right thing to do and a firm disposition to feel and react in the right way about it." There are three aspects to character – desire, choice, and action. The man with excellent character must be good in all three aspects. He feels good desires (desires here include not only bodily desires but also rational wishes), chooses a good act after deliberation, and is able to carry it out.

The behavior of a man of excellent character is signified by the rule of the mean (μέσον).

> Fear and confidence and appetite and anger and pity and in general likes and dislikes may be felt both too much and too little, and in both cases not well; but to feel them at the right time, with reference to the right objects, towards the right people, with the right motive, and in the right way, is what is both intermediate and best, and this is characteristic of excellence.
>
> (1106B19–23, trans. Urmson, p. 33)

Thus, Aristotle's concept of the mean is not a simple middle; it is, rather, the optimal considering all the situations. This was also the teaching of Confucius (551–479).

Ethics, Book VII

Aristotle examines Socrates' well-known doctrine "a man does not do bad things knowingly." Does a man have knowledge (ἐπιστήμη) and yet do bad things? Aristotle's answer is a conditional "yes." If a man knows something is bad and yet does it succumbing to a desire, his knowledge is temporarily abated and not working to its fullest extent. It is analogous to reciting a poem without comprehending its value. This phenomenon is called the weakness of will (ἀκρασία). A weak-willed man is at least better than a man who willingly does bad things. The latter characteristic is called self-indulgence (ἀκολασία). A man with ἀκρασία feels remorse after doing a bad thing, but a man with ἀκολασία does not. Urmson (1988, p. 32) gives the following table (I have modified the words a little) illustrating the differences of these traits in terms of desire, choices, and action:

	Desire	Choice	Action
Excellence of character	Good	Good	Good
Strong will	Bad	Good	Good
Weak will	Bad	Good	Bad
Self-indulgence	Bad	Bad	Bad

Why, then, did Socrates not recognize the possibility of ἀκρασία? It seems to be because Socrates used the word "knowledge" in a deeper sense: the knowledge that is equipped with the ability to act correctly. The Greek word φρόνιμος carries such a connotation.

Ethics, Book X

In this chapter Aristotle presents his theory of pleasure. His attitude toward pleasure is somewhat more positive than Plato's but is essentially the same in that he thinks there are both good pleasures and bad pleasures and therefore pleasure should not be the aim of action. Aristotle wrote

> Also there are many things which we should be eager to possess even if they brought us no pleasure, for instance sight, memory, knowledge, virtue. It may be the case that these things are necessarily attended by pleasure, but that makes no difference; for we should desire them even if no pleasure resulted from them. It seems therefore that pleasure is not the Good, and that not every pleasure is desirable, but also that there are certain pleasures, superior in respect of their specific quality or their source, that are desirable in themselves.
> (1174A4–A10, trans. H. Rackham, Loeb Classical Library)

An example of the superior pleasure referred to here is the pleasure of contemplating God. Like Plato, Aristotle says an excellent person does good deeds for the sake of goodness (1105A31–A32).

There is a common misconception that pleasure is a feeling produced by an activity and that it is homogeneous among activities and can therefore be added up. Bentham, father of utilitarianism, fell into this mistaken idea. Aristotle forcefully dispels this misconception. According to Aristotle, pleasure is the same thing as enjoying an activity and therefore particular to an activity. Therefore, different pleasures cannot be compared to each other. Urmson explains this by saying (p. 104), "Every activity has its own 'proper' or special pleasure; one could not chance to get the pleasure of, say, reading poetry from stamp collecting."

Urmson (1988, p. 106) points out, however, that in addition to the pleasure identified with the enjoyment of an activity, there is also pleasure as a feeling generated by an activity. For example, there is definitely the Aristotelian pleasure of enjoying the activity of eating good food, but at the same time we do feel a pleasant sensation on our palate. This does not diminish the value of Aristotle's contribution in recognizing an important aspect of pleasure that is different from a sensation.

Julia Annas, *The Morality of Happiness*

Virtue and morality

Annas' (1993) main theme in this section is that the Aristotelian concept of virtues is broader than the modern concept of morality in that it includes both moral and nonmoral desirable traits. To illustrate this point, Annas refers to 1104B30 where Aristotle mentions three desirable things – the noble (καλόν), the expedient (σύμφερον), and the pleasant (ἡδύ). Of these three characteristics, only the first is a moral term. However, Annas proceeds to minimize the difference between Aristotelian and modern moral philosophy by quoting the passages from *Ethics* where the noble dominates the other criteria: "The virtuous person does the virtuous action for its own sake (1105A31–32)"; "The *kalon* is the aim of virtue (1115B11–13)" (p. 123).

Annas writes

> It is a mistake to bend the notion of virtue to fit happiness; in the ancient way of thinking it is happiness which is the weak and flexible notion, which has to be modified when we understand the nature of the demands which virtue makes in our lives.
>
> (p. 129)

Burnyeat (1980, pp. 86–8) also quotes the same passage 1104B30 and states that *akrasia* arises only because these three kinds of good cannot be compared by a single measure. In the utility maximization model Socrates used to deride Protagoras with, the three kinds of good can be measured by a single unit. However, for a truly wise man, the three kinds of good coincide and, therefore, *akrasia* does not arise. That is the state Confucius attained at age 70, which I mentioned earlier in my discussion of Plato's ethics.

Aristotle: an unstable view

By "an unstable view" Annas means that Aristotle was oscillating between the view that virtues are sufficient for happiness and the view that external goods are also necessary. Annas refers to the same passages she refers to in the previous section and argues that Aristotle's preferred position is that virtues are sufficient for happiness.

We can support her thesis by the following quotations from *Ethics*

> Yet nevertheless even in adversity nobility shines through, when a man endures repeated and severe misfortune with patience, not owing to insensibility but from generosity and greatness of soul ... since we hold that the truly good and wise man will bear all kinds of fortune in a seemly way, and will always act in the noblest manner that the circumstances allow; even as a good general makes the most effective use of the forces at his disposal, and a good shoemaker makes the finest shoe possible out of the leather supplied him.
> (1100B30–A5)

After pointing out that a political life requires external goods such as wealth and friends, Aristotle says, "the wise man on the contrary can also contemplate by himself, and the more so the wiser he is; no doubt he will study better with the aid of fellow-workers, but still he is the most self-sufficient of men" (1177A30).

Nevertheless, it is true that there are other passages in *Ethics* which indicate that Aristotle could not completely shake off the fetters of conventional goods. The stoics, who hold that virtue is sufficient for happiness, regard the Aristotelian view that happiness requires conventional goods as well as virtue "unworthy concessions to everyday prejudices" (Annas 1999, p. 50). Annas says that Atticus called this a "low and false view" and quotes, "Aristotle's works on this, the *Nicomachean* and *Eudemian Ethics* and the *Magna Moralia*, have ideas about virtue which are petty and groveling and vulgar. They are the kind of thing that an ordinary person would come up with, an uneducated person, a child – or a woman." After this quotation, Annas makes the following comments: "In view of Aristotle's own views about women, this complaint is rather amusing" and "Personally, I find this outburst rather refreshing" (ibid., p. 51).

10 Plato's economics

Introduction

Plato did not write much about economics in the narrow sense. An exception is the explanation of division of labor in the *Republic*, Book II. In this chapter, I will first discuss this and, later, the *Laws*, in which many economic regulations for his ideal city are put forth. Both of these works abound in admonitions against greed and profit-taking.

Republic II

The first part (beginning–368C) is a continuation of the discussion about justice as it pertains to man. I have already discussed this in Chapter 8, "Plato's ethics". In 368D, Socrates says that if we consider the justice of a state, we will obtain a better understanding of the justice of a man, much as we can see a small letter better by seeing it through a magnifying glass. Then he goes on to discuss the division of labor.

It is interesting to compare Plato's theory of the division of labor with that of Adam Smith (*The Wealth of Nations*, Chapters I and II). Smith was well-read in classics and there is no doubt that he had read the *Republic*.

Socrates says

> So, then, when one man takes on another for one need and another for another need, and, since many things are needed, many men gather in one settlement as partners and helpers, to this common settlement we give the name city, don't we? Now, does one man give a share to another, if he does give a share, or take a share, in the belief that it's better for himself?
>
> (369C, trans. Alan Bloom, Basic Books, 1968)

Smith, on the other hand, says

> This division of labor, from which so many advantages are derived, is not originally the effect of any human wisdom, which foresees and intends that general opulence to which it gives occasion. It is the necessary, though very

slow and gradual, consequence of a certain propensity in human nature which has in view no such extensive utility; the propensity to truck, barter, and exchange one thing for another.

(Chapter II)

Note that Plato, who firmly believes that a human being should always act according to reason, would not want to give such an importance to "a natural propensity."

Plato believes that the division of labor originates in the natural differences of people in their abilities and preferences. Thus, Socrates speaks

> I myself also had the thought when you spoke that, in the first place, each of us is naturally not quite like someone else, but rather differs in his nature; different men are apt for the accomplishment of different jobs. Isn't that your opinion?
>
> (370A–370B)

That is how one man becomes a farmer, another a housebuilder, and another a shoemaker, and Plato does not allow for much social mobility in his city. On the contrary, Smith believes that the human difference is the result, rather than the cause, of the division of labor, as he writes

> The difference of natural talents in different men is, in reality, much less than we are aware of; and the very different genius which appears to distinguish men of different professions, when grown up to maturity, is not upon many occasions so much the cause, as the effect of the division of labour. The difference between the most dissimilar characters, between a philosopher and a common street porter, for example, seems to arise not so much from nature, as from habit, custom, and education.
>
> (Chapter II)

Plato expands the division of labor to a greater dimension and defines three classes in his city – guardians, warriors, and workers, and he does not allow much social mobility among these classes either. Remember that Plato's definition of justice in the *Republic* IV was "doing one's own thing and not meddling with other people's business." However, he does recognize the possibility that a child of a guardian may not be good enough to belong to the guardian class and that a child of a warrior may have enough talent to be educated to become a guardian (415C).

Plato and Smith generally agree about the benefits of the division of labor. Plato says that as the result of the division of labor, production will become "more plentiful, finer, and easier" (370C). Smith says that the effects of the division of labor are (1) the increase of dexterity, (2) the saving of the time which is commonly lost in passing from one species of work to another, and (3) "the invention of a great number of machines which facilitate and abridge labour, and enable one man to do the work of many" (Chapter I). This second point is also expressed by Socrates as follows:

> And, further, it's also plain, I suppose, that if a man lets the crucial moment in any work pass, it is completely ruined. I don't suppose the thing done is willing to await the leisure of the man who does it; but it's necessary for the man who does it to follow upon the thing done, and not as a spare-time occupation.
>
> (370B–370C)

Not surprisingly, the third point did not occur to Plato.

As an example of the division of labor, Smith talks about the pin factory, where "one man draws out the wire, another straights it, a third cuts it, a fourth points it, a fifth grinds it at the top for receiving the head" (Chapter I). Although Plato did not discuss this kind of division of labor, it was familiar to ancient Greeks as one can tell from the following quote from Xenophon:

> In large cities, on the other hand, inasmuch as many people have demands to make upon each branch of industry, one trade alone, and very often even less than a whole trade, is enough to support a man: one man, for instance, makes shoes for men, and another for women; and there are places even where one man earns a living by only stitching shoes, another by cutting them out, another by sewing the upper together, while there is another who performs none of these operations but only assembles the parts.
>
> (*Cyropaedia*, VIII. ii. 5, trans. Walter Miller, Loeb Classical Library)

The discussion of the division of labor naturally continues on to the discussion of the formation of a city. At minimum a city needs a farmer, a housebuilder, a weaver, and a shoemaker. In addition we need carpenters, smiths, many other craftsmen, cowherds, and shepherds. The city will grow further as some goods need to be imported from other cities, and in order to pay for the imports, the city must produce more of the things it produces. The existence of currency as a medium of exchange is presupposed. This will necessitate merchants, traders, people who work in markets, and wage earners. At this stage the city will still be fairly simple and idyllic:

> Setting out noble loaves of barley and wheat on some reeds or clean leaves, they will stretch out on rushes strewn with yew and myrtle and feast themselves and their children. Afterwards they will drink wine and, crowned with wreathes, sing of the gods.
>
> (372B)

At this moment Glaucon interrupts Socrates and says, "You seem to make these men have their feast without relishes (ὄψον)." So Socrates adds salt, olives, cheese, onions, greens, figs, pulses, beans, myrtle-berries, and acorns (372D). At this point the description of a simple city ends and that of a luxurious city starts. The luxurious city will have, in addition, couches, tables, other furniture, perfume, incense, courtesans, cakes, painting, embroidery, gold, poets, rhapsodes, actors, choral dancers, contractors, feminine adornment, teachers, wet nurses, governesses, beauticians, barbers, relish-makers, cooks, swineherds, and doctors (373A–373D). These professions exist in any country, and it is hard to imagine that Plato was against all of them. The reason Plato describes the luxurious city is to show that as the city becomes luxurious, there will be more things to satisfy human desires and more opportunities for human greed to expand and hence more injustice. He wanted to show what kind of city is more prone to injustice.

To defend this luxurious expanded city against the attack of foreign states, the class of guardians is needed, and the rest of the book is devoted to the discussion of what kind of characteristics the guardians (φύλακες) should have and how to educate them. Later (414b) we find that the guardians in this broad sense consist of the real guardians (philosopher-kings) and the warriors (ἐπίκουροι).

Laws

Overview

The *Laws* is Plato's final work. In the *Republic* (473D) Socrates said

> Unless the philosophers rule as kings or those now called kings and chiefs genuinely and adequately philosophize, and political power and philosophy coincide in the same place ... there is no rest from ills for the cities, nor I think for human kind ...

Between the time of writing the *Republic* and the *Laws*, Plato visited Sicily twice in an effort to mold Dionysius II into a philosopher-king. Both attempts ended in failures and Plato was somewhat disillusioned. This experience, coupled with the criticisms of Aristotle and other students that some proposals of the *Republic* were too unrealistic, led Plato to modify some aspects of his ideal city and write the present work called the *Laws*. As the title indicates, Plato now recognizes the importance of laws. In stark contrast to the above quotation from the *Republic*, Plato in the *Laws* recognizes that no man is good enough to govern other men (713C–714A) and makes the Athenian say

> For wherever in a state the law is subservient and impotent, over that state I see ruin impending; but wherever the law is lord over the magistrates, and the magistrates are servants to the law, there I discover salvation and all the blessings that the gods bestow on states.
> (715D, trans. R. G. Bury, Loeb Classical Library)

Plato does not envision the laws that are forced upon the citizen with threat of punishment, however. Through education Plato hopes to attain the willing cooperation of citizens in observing the laws. Thus, the ideal city of the *Laws* is far from a totalitarian state contrary to common criticism (see Cohen 1993).

In the *Republic*, Plato instituted the revolutionary rule of common ownership of properties and spouses in the class of guardians. In the *Laws* he abandons this as unrealistic (739C). To control the extent of private properties, however, Plato proposes four property classes and sets certain limits on the amounts of property each class can possess (see "739C–745B" below).

Plato views what is proposed in the *Laws* as the second best (739A, 739E, and 875A–875D), in contrast to the ideal state expounded in the *Republic*. Whereas Plato sanctioned rule by the philosopher-kings in the *Republic*, he recommended a mixture of monarchy and democracy in the *Laws*. The Athenian says

> There are two mother-forms of constitution, so to call them, from which one may truly say all the rest are derived. Of these the one is properly termed monarchy, the other democracy, the extreme case of the former being the Persian polity, and of the latter the Athenian; the rest are practically all, as I said, modifications of these two. Now it is essential for a polity to partake of both these two forms, if it is to have freedom and friendliness combined with wisdom. And it is what our argument intends to enjoin, when it declares that a State which does not partake of these can never be rightly constituted.
>
> (694B)

As an example of the ideal mixture, Plato mentions Persian King Cyrus, who gave some degree of freedom to the ruled (694A–694B). A democratic element in his ideal state appears in the following passage: "but if it should ever be thought that a necessity for change has arisen, all the people (πάντα δὲ τόν δῆμον) must be consulted, as well as all the officials, and they must seek advice from all the divine oracles" (772D).

Three old men – an anonymous Athenian, Cleinias of Crete, and Meggilos of Sparta – discuss the constitution and laws of a new state they are about to create, called Magnesia. First, the Cretan and the Spartan proudly tell the Athenian about their ways of government and their laws, characterized by such well-known institutions as communal meals and gymnastic training, but the Athenian criticizes them on the grounds that their only purpose is to win wars. The Athenian maintains that the true purpose of the laws should be to win wars at home rather than against foreign states: that is to say, to establish a harmonious, strife-free state. For that purpose the laws should aim at fostering wisdom, moderation, justice, and courage in the souls of the citizens (631C–631D, 688B, 963A). Note that this aim is the same in both the *Republic* and the *Laws* even though the means to attain it are different. As mentioned while discussing the *Republic*, for Plato the ideal state is that in which its citizens can live ideal lives. The Athenian says, "The object of all these discourses was to discover how best a State might be managed, and how best the individual citizen might pass his life" (702B).

Throughout the book Plato discusses the details of the laws concerning various aspects of the society, but he also emphasizes the importance of the preambles of the laws (718B–718C), which should elucidate the underlying spirit and principles of the laws.

The purpose of the preambles is to educate the citizens so that they will voluntarily follow the laws. One of these principles is that soul, body, and wealth are important in this order. This theme is repeated over and over again (631C, 660E, 697B, 728A, 743E, and 870B).

Related to this is Plato's familiar theme "just is happy," which has been mentioned repeatedly in Chapter 8, "Plato's ethics". The Athenian says, "Undoubtedly, then, the unjust life is not only more base and ignoble, but also in very truth more unpleasant, than the just and holy life" (663D). He goes on to say

> And even if the state of the case were different from what it has now been proved to be by our argument, could a lawgiver who was worth his salt find any more useful fiction than this (if he dared to use any fiction at all in addressing the youths for their good), or more effective in persuading all men to act justly in all things willingly and without constraint?

This famous passage, which is sometimes called "a noble lie" argument, has been often criticized as immoral. Morrow (1993, p. 559) defends Plato saying

> Furthermore, the methods he advocates for moral instruction – the training of the feelings, the discipline of the passions, the formation of habits to supplement the teaching of principles – are precisely those used in all ages by teachers who take seriously the training of character. They try to enchant the soul so that it will instinctively love what intelligent judgment pronounces best.

See also Cohen (1993, p. 306) who states

> For Plato, it is not sufficient to produce purely habitual and mindless obedience to the norms of the community. Although, as Aristotle also recognized, habit is an indispensable starting point of socialization, it must be supplemented through that understanding of right and wrong that can alone provide the basis for the capacity for judgment essential for virtue.

In Book VI, various administrative agencies and positions for establishing and enforcing the laws are discussed. Most of the positions, as well as the method of selection – a mixture of lottery and election – are similar to what existed in classical Athens.

The most important office is that of the guardians of the laws (νομοφύλακες, appearing first in 671D and 752E). Thirty-seven members are chosen from citizens aged between 50 and 70 (755A). Although they did not actually exist in Athens in Plato's day, reference to them appears in Xenophon's *Oikonomikos* (IX. 14–15) and Aristotle's *Politics* (1298B, 1322B, 1323A), so such a post must have existed somewhere in Greece, though not in Athens. Spartan overseers (ἔφοροι) had somewhat similar roles. Five of them were elected every year from candidates over the age of 30, and they supervised the two Kings and elders (γερουσία, 28 men of age over 60) and represented the principle of law. The role of Areopagus in the days of Solon was somewhat analogous (see Chapter 3, "Athenian democracy"), but the guardians of the laws did not have all the power Areopagus had; on the other hand, they performed some of the functions of the archons as well. It is suggestive that in the *Laws*, Plato appoints νομοφύλακες, whereas in the *Republic* φύλακες (guardians) rule.

The functions of the guardians of the laws are numerous and varied. Summarizing the detailed descriptions by Morrow (1993), they are listed as follows:

1 To supervise various magistrates (ἄρχοντες) such as generals (στρατηγοί), *astynomoi* in charge of the city, *agoranomoi* in charge of the market, *agronomoi* in charge of the country, and priests and priestesses. The actual enforcement of the laws is relegated to the magistrates. The role of the guardians of the laws is mainly that of a moral authority (Morrow 1993, p. 198). If a dispute arises between magistrates and citizens, however, the guardians of the laws are to work as an arbitrator. The guardians of the laws can bring charges against the magistrates in the courts.
2 To formulate the laws as well as guard them. In other words, the guardians of the laws are *nomothetai* as well as *nomophylakes* (770A).
3 To register property and take legal proceedings against those who underreport property (754).
4 To supervise the actions of private citizens and of the family law.

Another unique position is that of the minister of education (765D), to be chosen from among the guardians of the laws. Since education plays a crucial role for the success of his ideal city, Plato bestows the greatest importance to this position. The public examiners (945B), who examine the conduct of all the administrative positions, are analogous to the Athenian auditors (εὔθυνοι) but assume a far greater role in Magnesia. They are given the highest honor of the state and serve also as the state priests.

One of the unique features of Magnesia is the institution called the nocturnal council (951E–952B). Its members are selected from the public examiners, the guardians of the laws, the minister of education, as well as specially chosen citizens who have gone abroad and studied the laws and institutions of foreign states. They meet every day early in the morning and discuss the laws. They not only discuss practical matters but also engage in basic research on the laws as well as on morality and religion.

A large part of Book X is devoted to the rebuttal of materialism and atheism. It provides useful and relevant reading even at present. Plato is acutely aware of the attraction materialism and atheism pose to many people and proceeds with his rebuttal with great care.

739C–745B

In the beginning the Athenian admits that even if ideally all properties should be communally shared, private ownership would be allowed in Magnesia as the second best policy (739A). Land and houses would be distributed equally to citizens by lot. They should not be sold and should be bequeathed to descendants, either real or adopted. The number of households should always be kept at 5,040, by means of immigration and emigration if necessary. The choice of the number 5,040 shows Plato's penchant for mathematics, for the number equals $2^4 \times 3^2 \times 5 \times 7$ and can be divided by every integer between 1 and 10.

Citizens should not engage in moneymaking or unskilled labor in manufacturing (βαναυσικός). A suitable amount of gain from honest work in agriculture is permitted (743D), however. The residents of Magnesia should use only the fiat currency, good only within the state. There should not be any gold or silver in the state. People who go to foreign states for official or other necessary reasons may use the international currency but they must return the remaining amount to the state after they come back. Dowries and lending at interest are prohibited.

With regard to wealth versus happiness, the Athenian states, "it is impossible for them to be at once both good and excessively rich" (742E). Compare this statement to "It is easier for a camel to go through the eye of a needle, than for a rich man to enter the kingdom of God" (Matthew 19:24). It is another indication of what Simone Weil called an intimation of Christianity among the ancient Greeks. Also note, "I would never concede to them that the rich man is really happy if he is not also good" (743A). That wealth is neither sufficient nor necessary for happiness was earlier emphasized by the following remark of the Athenian: "The good man, since he is temperate and just, is fortunate and happy, whether he be great or small, strong or weak, rich or poor" (660E). A great harm of greed is stressed in the following passages:

> The greatest is lust, which masters a soul that is made savage by desires; and it occurs especially in connection with that object for which the most frequent and intense craving afflicts the bulk of men, – the power which wealth possesses over them, owing to the badness of their nature and lack of culture, to breed in them countless lustings after its insatiable and endless acquisition. And of this lack of culture the cause is to be found in the ill-praising of wealth in the common talk of both Greeks and barbarians; for by exalting it as the first of goods, when it should come but third, they ruin both posterity and themselves.
>
> (870A)

A similar account can be also found in 831C.

Lands and houses are initially distributed equally among the citizens by lottery, and the buying and selling of lands and houses are prohibited. Four property classes are defined (744B–745A), and the allocation of public positions, taxes, fines, and monetary distributions is done according to the property classification.

The government should see to it that the poorest man should not be poorer than the assessed value of the allotted land, the members of the third (next poorest), the second, and the first (richest) property class should not be worth more than double, triple, and quadruple of the assessed value of the allotted land. Any amount over the quadruple of the assessed value of the allotted land must be given back to the state. The reason Plato set upper and lower limits on wealth is that he was well aware of the danger of internal strife if the difference between the rich and the poor were to increase to a level where equilibrium was broken. In the section of the *Republic* where he criticizes an oligarchic government (551D), Plato says, "Such a city's not being one but of necessity two, the city of the poor and the city of the rich, dwelling together in the same place, ever plotting against each other" (trans. Allan Bloom). This was also how Plato regarded the Athens of his day.

Any citizen can attend assembly meetings; attendance is compulsory for the first and second property classes, a ten drachmas fine being imposed on the lack of attendance, whereas it is not compulsory for the third and fourth classes (764A). Although there is no class limitation regarding participation in government, there are some restrictions regarding certain public offices: for example, only the citizens of the first class can become city wardens (*astynomoi*), and the first and second class can become market wardens (*agoranomoi*).

846D–850D

Citizens should not be skilled workers (δημιουργοί). Earlier it was mentioned that citizens should not be unskilled workers (βάναυσοι), but the reason is different. Citizens should not be unskilled workers because such work is unhealthy and demeaning. Citizens should not be skilled workers because a person should have only one job and the job of a citizen is to engage in politics and civil service. Plato has great respect for any *technē*, whether it is the *technē* of civic duties or the *technē* of a skilled worker.

All import and export except that needed for wars is prohibited. The latter is conducted by the state. Earlier in Book IV the Athenian had proposed that Magnesia should be built inland in a mountainous region. Import and export are discouraged both because the state is far from the sea and because it is not abundant in resources that can provide a source for export (705A–705B). International trade is discouraged because too much wealth obtained from it will corrupt the citizens.

Agricultural output is divided into three parts: the first part is allocated to the citizens, the second part to their slaves (we learn from 806D that all the work at the farm is done by slaves), and the third part to the foreigners including the skilled workers. Only the third part will be sold in the market. The citizens and their slaves cannot buy and sell agricultural products in the market. As for other items, they may do so. Credit sales are prohibited. There will be legal limits to the quantities sold and the prices charged. The market wardens (*agoranomoi*) will supervise the activities at the market.

914E–921D

Selling and buying are permitted only in specific markets. When one sells goods at the market, one should charge one price throughout the day. Those who sell adulterated goods will be punished.

Plato recognizes that retail trade (καπηλεία) is ideally a useful profession. In reality, however, most of those engaging in retail trade succumb to the temptation of seeking gains beyond what are justly allowed:

> small is the class of men – rare by nature and trained, too, with a superlative training – who, when they fall into diverse needs and lusts, are able to stand out firmly for moderation, and who, when they have the power of taking much wealth, are sober, and choose what is of due measure rather than what is large. The disposition of the mass of mankind is exactly the opposite of this; when they desire, they desire without limit, and when they can make moderate gains, they prefer to gain insatiably.
>
> (918D)

Thus, Plato prescribes the following policies concerning retail trade: (1) Keep the number of retail traders to a minimum. (2) Those engaging in retail trade should belong to such a class of people that their corruption will not bring a great harm to the state – in other words, metics and foreigners. (3) Find ways to prevent retail traders from falling easily into corruption and degradation. Magistrates should publish guidelines regarding a suitable profit rate retail traders are allowed to charge.

Plato recognizes that both wealth and poverty are bad: "indeed our present fight in this matter is against two foes, poverty and plenty, of which the one corrupts the soul of men with luxury, while the other by means of pain plunges it into shamelessness" (919C).

As I mentioned above, Plato regards skilled workers with respect. See 920E where the Athenian says

> Sacred to Hephaistos and Athena is the class of craftsmen (δημιουργοί) who have furnished our life with the arts (τέχναι), and to Ares and Athena belong those who safeguard the products of these craftsmen by other defensive arts; rightly is this class also sacred to these.

However, responsibility comes with the esteem, as the Athenian continues

> These all continually serve both the country and the people: the one class are leaders in the contests of war, the others produce for pay instruments and works; and it would be unseemly for these men to lie concerning their crafts, because of their reverence for their divine ancestors.

They are also admonished not to give too high an estimate for their work, but to estimate it simply at "its real worth" (921B). Plato does not explain what price is equal to the real worth of a product. Craftsmen are also protected against deceitful buyers. Anyone who breaks a contract with a craftsman and does not pay within a period specified by the contract must pay a double amount and interest. This is an exception to the general rule that prohibits lending at interest.

We have seen that citizens are banned from unskilled labor, skilled labor, and retail trade. More generally, a citizen is not supposed to work for others for pay. However, serving one's parents or elders in a way suitable for a free man is an exception.

Additional matters concerning economics

949D	Liturgies are made mandatory.
955D–E	In a year of good harvest, tax rates are calculated on the basis of income; in other years, on wealth evaluation.

Treatment of slaves

776B–778A	Plato begins his discourse on slaves by saying it is a difficult problem. He regards slaves (οἰκέτης) as household property (κτῆμα).
	He recognizes that some slaves have excellent character: "in the past many slaves have proved themselves better in every form of excellence than brothers or sons, and have saved their masters and their goods and their whole houses" (776D–776E). On the other hand, he goes on to say, some have the extreme opinion that slaves do not possess souls.
	It is advisable not to hire slaves who come from the same regions so that they should not revolt.
	Slaves should not be treated with *hybris*; they should not be over-indulged, however, and should be punished if need be.
914E–915C	The master has the right to capture slaves who have fled.
	Freed men should visit their former masters three times a month and offer service. They should not keep greater wealth than their former masters.

Treatment of women

As one can see in the following passages, Plato exhibits an ambiguous attitude toward women.

742C	As mentioned in "739C–745B" above, Plato proposes that dowries should be abolished. This would weaken the status of women (see the section entitled "Status of women" in Chapter 2, "Society and culture").

781A	"the female sex, that very section of humanity which, owing to its frailty, is in other respects most secretive and intriguing."
781B	"women are by nature inferior to men in terms of virtues (ἀρετή)" (my translation).
804E	Men and women should be treated equally in regard to education and training.
937A	Free women who have reached the age of forty should be allowed to testify in court for their defense. If they do not have husbands, they can also sue in court.
944D	A man who abandons arms in a battle should be changed into a woman (if that were possible).

11 Aristotle's economics

Ethics V (up to 1134A15)

There are two senses to justice: one general and the other special. Justice in the general sense is what we have been discussing, for example, in Plato's *Republic*. Justice in the special sense has to do with fairness in the distribution of gains. Thus, a man who sleeps with another man's wife because of sexual desire commits self-indulgence and injustice in the general sense, whereas a man who does so to gain profit is not self-indulgent but commits injustice in the special sense (1130A25).

Aristotle unsuccessfully tries to make the concept of justice conform to his theory of the mean. However, it is not helpful to understand justice as the state where the optimal amount of emotion is exhibited. So it is best to ignore the part of the chapter that concerns this point.

Aristotle states that justice (in the special sense) in distribution is governed by geometrical proportion. That is to say, if $F(A)$ and $F(B)$ are the worth (honor, wealth, etc.) of two persons A and B, and $S(A)$ and $S(B)$ are their shares, we must have $S(A)/S(B) = F(A)/F(B)$ (1131B5). An example of this distribution appears in the *Politics* (1318A10–1318A40). Here, Aristotle considers determining people's votes according to wealth, that is, if A owns twice the wealth of B, A is given twice as many votes as B.

Justice in rectification, on the other hand, is governed by arithmetic proportion. That is to say, if A gains X unjustly from B, A must return X to B. Here, unlike the case of distribution, the amount A must return to B is independent of the worth of A and B (1132A1).

Next, Aristotle presents a price theory, more precisely, an exchange rate between two commodities, and proposes that an exchange rate should also follow the principle of proportions. The main point of this argument is given in the following quotation:

> There will therefore be reciprocal proportion when the products have been equated, so that as farmer is to shoemaker, so may the shoemaker's product be to the farmer's product.
> (1133A33–35, trans. H. Rackham, Loeb Classical Library)

The vagueness of this sentence caused various different interpretations by later scholars. Let us denote farmer by N and shoemaker by K, the price of the farmer's product by $P(N)$, and the price of the shoemaker's product by $P(K)$. If the above sentence is literally interpreted, it becomes $N/K = P(N)/P(K)$, which is meaningless. Therefore, we must interpret it to mean $F(N)/F(K) = P(N)/P(K)$, where function F is appropriately defined. The question is, What is F?

The most natural interpretation is to regard F as need or utility. In this case, $F(N)$ is defined as the shoemaker's need for the farmer's product. The basis for this interpretation lies in the following quotation:

> for without this reciprocal proportion, there can be no exchange and no association; and it cannot be secured unless the commodities in question be equal in a sense. It is therefore necessary that all commodities shall be measured by some one standard, as was said before. And this standard is in reality demand, which is what holds everything together ...
> (1133A26–1133A33)

The Greek word which Rackham translates as "demand" here is χρεία, which it would be better to translate as "need" or "utility." It took the genius of Aristotle to find out how different objects can be made commensurable by *chreia*. I will call this interpretation the utility theory of value. There are subtle differences among these English words. Need is most basic. In view of Aristotle's emphasis on self-sufficiency, need seems to be the best translation. However, Aristotle was fully aware of the utility of a good arising from other factors than basic need, such as scarcity (*Rhetoric*, 1364A) or conspicuousness (*Rhetoric*, 1365B). Demand implies an active desire as well as need. For example, a rich man and a poor man may have the same amount of need for a certain food, but the former has a greater demand because he can afford more. It is unlikely that Aristotle had demand in mind.

The second interpretation is the labor theory of value. This was advocated by Thomas Aquinas and Karl Marx. In this case, $F(N)$ is considered to be the labor that was used for producing goods. Aristotle did not directly refer to labor. This interpretation is based on the following quotation:

> But in the interchange of services Justice in the form of Reciprocity is the bond that maintains the association: reciprocity, that is, on the basis of proportion, not on the basis of equality. The very existence of the state depends on proportionate reciprocity ... and it is exchange that binds them together.
> (1132B32–35)

The key word here is the maintenance of association. As mentioned earlier, Plato's ideal was to build a *polis* where citizens can live an *eudaimōn* life, and this was the same for Aristotle. The maintenance of association is necessary for this. If the cost of labor were not compensated sufficiently, there would be discontent and the maintenance of association would not be possible.

Aristotle emphasizes the strengthening of the association as a result of the exchange. This is a stark contrast to the impersonal market exchange. Compare this to what Adam Smith says: "It is not from the benevolence of the butcher, the brewer, or the baker, that we expect our dinner, but from their regard to their own interest" (*The Wealth of Nations*, Book I. Chapter II, p. 15). And

> by directing that industry in such a manner as its produce may be of the greater value, he intends only his own gain, and he is in this, as in many other cases, led by an invisible hand to promote an end which was no part of his intention. Nor is it always the worse for the society that it was no part of it. By pursuing his own interest he frequently promotes that of the society more effectually than when he really intends to promote it.
>
> (Book IV. Chapter II, p. 485)

The third interpretation is that proposed by Polanyi (1968). It interprets $F(N)$ and $F(K)$ to be the social status of farmer and shoemaker, respectively. This replaces one's shares in the aforementioned Aristotle's distribution theory with prices.

It should be noted here that Aristotle's price theory is concerned with the determination of an exchange ratio when two people bring to the market goods which have been already produced and try to exchange them. The process of production is ignored except for its psychic effect on the persons about to be engaged in exchange. The existence of other producers and consumers is also ignored. Therefore, it differs from the main objective of modern economics, which is market price determination resulting from equilibrium between demand and supply.

There are situations, however, where modern economics analyzes the problem considered by Aristotle. The most well-known example of this is Edgeworth's contract curve. Edgeworth showed that two people's exchange ratios are contained in the set of points (i.e., contract curve) where each other's indifference curves have the same tangent lines and are not uniquely determined by the principle of utility maximization alone. In Figure 11.1, the indifference curves of the trader X are shown as dotted curves. His utility becomes greater as his position moves in the direction of northeast signifying the possession of more apples and oranges. The utility remains constant on a single indifference curve. The indifference curves of the trader Y are shown as solid curves. His utility becomes greater as his position moves in the direction of southwest. Suppose the initial position of the two traders is represented by the point A, meaning X had only apples and Y only oranges. As the exchange begins, the traders will never settle at a point such as B because by moving from B to C, the trader X will become better off as he moves to a position of a higher utility whereas the utility of the trader Y remains the same. Therefore, the exchange will take place only on the curve connecting the tangency points of the indifference curves.

In reality, a unique exchange ratio must be determined and will depend on the negotiating power of the two people involved in the exchange. Since the

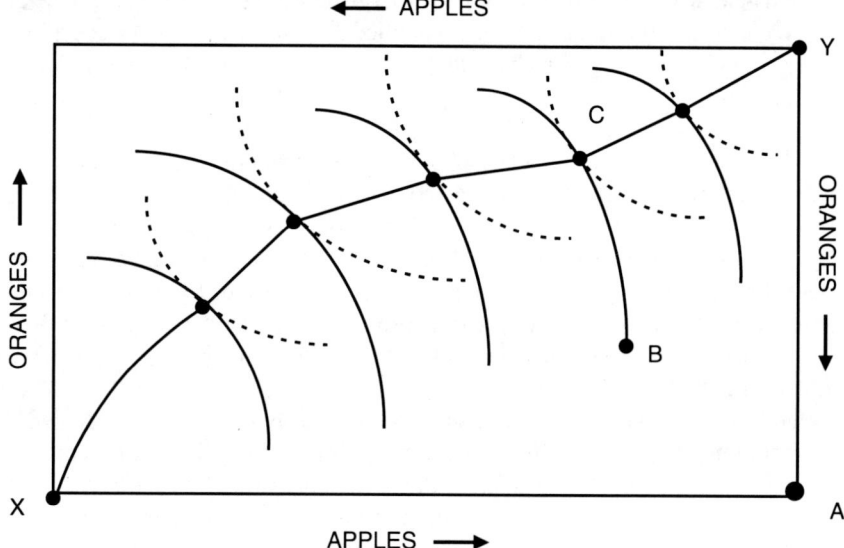

Figure 11.1 Edgeworth diagram

negotiating power is likely to be determined by things such as their status, honor, wealth, and labor used for production, all three interpretations mentioned above are somehow relevant. Aristotle, after noting that need or utility makes exchanges possible by making different things commensurable, says that what makes exchange smooth is money (1133A33) and expounds a surprisingly modern theory of money. Aristotle, like Plato, did not consider currency to have value by itself, but as legal tender or fiat money. This is not unrelated to the fact that the Greek word for currency *nomisma* has its origin in *nomos* (custom, law). Aristotle states that "money gives us a guarantee of future exchange" (1133B11) and that money changes its value like any other commodity but not as much (1133B17).

Politics, Book I

Aristotle's *Ethics* ends with the remark, "Let us then begin our discussion." Here Aristotle means the discussion of politics. In *Ethics* he considered the question of what is the best life for a man. Since for Aristotle, as it was for Plato, the best state is that in which a man can live the best life, it is natural that *Politics* follows *Ethics*. At the beginning of *Politics*, this point is clearly stated as follows:

> Every state is as we see a sort of community, and every community is formed with a view to some good (since all the actions of all mankind are done with a view to what they think to be good). It is therefore evident that, while all communities aim at some good, the community that is the most supreme of all

and includes all the others does so most of all, and aims at the most supreme of all goods; and this is the community entitled the state, the political association. (1252A1–6; I have changed "partnership" in Rackham's translation to "community" (κοινωνία))

The smallest community is a household, the next step is a village consisting of many households, and the final complete form of community is a state consisting of many villages. Aristotle believes that a household, a village, and a state all arise naturally, and the state is the final and best form of community because in a state self-sufficiency (αὐτάρκεια) is realized (1253A1). Human beings cannot exist by themselves and therefore, only when they form a state, can they satisfy all their wants and become self-sufficient. In other words, "man is by nature a political animal" (1253A2).

When Aristotle says that a state arises naturally, he does not mean it in the sense that a community of bees is formed naturally. Since reason is a part of human nature, he does expect it to play a role in the formation of a state. So we can say that Aristotle is closer to Plato than to Adam Smith, who postulated a man's propensity to truck, barter, and exchange. Unlike a community of bees, which is always of the same kind, a human community can be either good or bad. It is good only when reason and virtues pervade it (1253A35).

There is a difference between Plato and Aristotle, however, regarding the origin of the state. Plato attributes it to the division of labor between members of different professions, whereas Aristotle attributes it to the mutual needs of households and villages.

In Book I, Aristotle discusses household management (οἰκονομία). There are two parts to it: one is concerned with human relationships and the other with the procurement of necessary goods. Although Aristotle says later (1259B18–1259B19) that human relationships are more important than the procurement of necessary goods, he discusses the latter first.

Since Aristotle regards slaves as half-human and half-tool, however, slaves are discussed in both parts. He says, "a slave is a live article of property" (1253B32). Aristotle asks, Are slaves so by nature (φύσις) or by convention (νόμος)? He believes that most slaves are so by nature. But he is aware of a group of scholars who disagree with him, and later (1255B5) he rather reluctantly admits that there may be some slaves who are slaves by convention, that is, they have all the qualifications to be free men. How do slaves (those who are slaves by nature) differ from free men? "For he is by nature a slave ... who participates in reason so far as to apprehend it but not to possess it" (1254B21–22).

One of the prominent scholars of his age who disagreed with Aristotle was Antiphon (480–411), who argued that all humans belong to one specie and therefore are biologically indistinguishable (Havelock 1957, pp. 256–7). Another was Alcidamas, a pupil of Gorgias, who said, "God has left all men free; Nature has made none a slave" (a footnote to Aristotle, *Art of Rhetoric*, trans. J. H. Freese, Loeb Classical Library, 1373B2). Other men more sympathetic to slaves were Euripides (Dover 1994, pp. 114–16) and Xenophon (Pomeroy 1994, p. 66).

Before we go further with our discussion, we need to get some of the terminology straight (see the last section of this chapter). Four arts are mentioned: the art of household management (οἰκονομική), the art of acquiring property (κτητική), the art of getting wealth (χρηματιστική), and the art of retail trade (καπηλική). κτητική is a proper part of οἰκονομική, the other part being the art concerning human relationships. χρηματιστική has two meanings: proper and improper. In the proper sense it is identical with κτητική. It is the art of acquiring food and other necessary household properties including slaves, either directly or by exchanging goods with other households. In the improper sense it is identical with καπηλική. Exchange may be carried out either by barter or by use of money. Using the symbolic representations of Meikle (1979), the former transaction may be represented by C–C, meaning that a commodity is exchanged for a commodity, and the latter C–M–C, meaning that a commodity is exchanged for money and then money for another commodity. Aristotle would approve them because the purpose of both kinds of transactions is the procurement of necessary goods and, therefore, there is a natural limit to the amount acquired. Here money is used just as a mode of exchange and is not an object of acquisition.

As soon as money was invented, however, the improper sense of χρηματιστική. arose, namely, the art of retail trade (καπηλική). Unlike the proper art of getting wealth, there is no natural limit to the amount of money one seeks to acquire (1257B24). Greed compels a man to try to get more and more money. The symbolic representation of this kind of activity is M–C–M. καπηλική is fundamentally contrary to οἰκονομική. However, some people have mistakenly thought that increasing wealth was the purpose of household management (1257B39), and καπηλική has intruded into the sphere of household management, thereby giving rise to the improper sense of χρηματιστική. Aristotle does not approve of M–C–M. What he denounces even more strongly, however, is lending at interest, saying it is the most unnatural of all modes of getting wealth (1258B37). Symbolically, this activity can be represented as M–M.

As examples of shameful ways to make money, Aristotle mentions the stories of the philosopher Thales and a Sicilian man. In order to show that a philosopher can do something useful, Thales predicted a big harvest of olives with his knowledge of astronomy, bought up all the oil presses of the region beforehand, and made a great profit (1259A7–17). A Sicilian man bought up iron, charged a monopoly price, and made a great profit (1259A24–27).

The discussion of the part of household management concerned with human relations starts at Section 12 (1259A37). Aristotle discusses proper relationships between a man and a slave, a man and a wife, and a man and a child. They are to be defined on the basis of his belief that " the slave has not got the deliberative part at all, and the female has it, but without full authority, while the child has it, but in an undeveloped form" (1260A13–15). Since slaves can "participate in reason" (1259B29), however, it is a mistake to use command only, "for admonition is more properly employed with slaves than with children" (1260B6–7). Unlike Socrates, who believed that the virtues are the same for everybody, whether a person is man, woman, or child (Plato, *Meno*, 72A–73C), Aristotle believes that the virtues must be specific to each category of people (1260A22–23).

Political theory

Since Aristotle was a resident alien (metic), he was not allowed to participate in politics. In *Politics*, however, he puts forth his own political ideas making use of an extensive empirical study of the various political forms that existed in Greece at the time. Also, in *The Constitution of Athens*, he presents the political history of Athens from ancient times to the latter half of the fourth century. As Aristotle, like Plato, had an aristocratic tendency, he was sympathetic to aristocracy (i.e., government by those who excel – *aristos*); however, he recognized the advantages of democracy more readily than Plato. In *Politics* (1281B and 1286A), Aristotle recognized an advantage of democracy by stating that even if each individual comprising a majority may be inferior in wisdom, the total wisdom of the majority can surpass that of a few superior people, just as a dinner prepared by many people, each bringing a dish, is better than that prepared by one person. Aristotle seemed to regard a combination of aristocracy and democracy as ideal, like the one advocated by Plato's *Laws*. Aristotle was less democratic than Plato, however, in that he was more discriminatory toward women and slaves, as mentioned earlier. In contrast to Xenophon's Ischomachos, who recognized his wife's individuality and treated slaves as humans, *Politics*, Book I, describes an ideal interpersonal relationship within a household, in which the wife is completely subordinated to her husband and slaves are managed as property.

Aristotle strongly criticized Plato's proposal in the *Republic* that the philosopher-kings should not own private property and should share their wives and children. His reason was that people care only for the things that they own, and if one does not own private property, there would be no occasion for showing benevolence, and that the common possession of women would deprive men of the virtue of moderation.

Although Aristotle could not participate in politics himself, he commended participating in politics as an *eudaimōn* life, except in the *Nicomachean Ethics*, Book X. There he advocates a life of contemplation as *eudaimōn* and relegates participation in politics to second best, as mentioned earlier.

Polanyi, "Aristotle discovers the economy"

Polanyi is a primitivist and a substantivist. Even though he is basically a primitivist, his remarks are occasionally contradictory. On p. 105 he states, "the supply–demand–price mechanism was unknown to Aristotle." But on p. 106, he acknowledges

> The Athenian *Agora* preceded, therefore, by some two centuries the setting up of a market in the Aegean which could be said to embody a market mechanism. Aristotle, writing in the second half of this period, recognized the early

instances of gain made on price differentials for the symptomatic development in the organization of trade which they actually were.

And, even more significantly, on p. 101 Polanyi notes

> The first authentic record of the Agora is of the fifth century BC. when it was already definitely established, though still contentious. Throughout the course of its early history the use of small coin and the retailing of food went together. Its beginnings in Athens should therefore coincide with the minting of obols in the early sixth century BC.

Evidence does not seem to support his primitivist thesis as I have pointed out earlier.

On pp. 87–93 Polanyi describes the characteristics of primitive societies reported by anthropologists like Margaret Mead and Malinowski. Whether or not their reports are accurate, Polanyi's primitivist and substantivist thesis seems to apply more appropriately to these primitive societies as depicted by these anthropologists than to classical Athens. Polanyi's definition of the economy is as follows: An instituted process of interaction between man and his environment which results in a continuous supply of want-satisfying material means. Note that Polanyi carefully avoids a reference to the involvement of man's conscious, rational deliberations in economic decisions. In contrast, the modern formal definition of the economy is "the allocation of scarce means to alternative ends" (Robbins 1984). Here, whether or not the allocation is done by a state or by the market, man's rational decisions are implied.

Polanyi's interpretation of Aristotle's famous passage (1133A33–35) about the determination of the exchange rate between a farmer (or a builder) and a shoemaker is best represented by the following quotation:

> The rate of exchange must be such as to maintain the community. Again, not the interests of the individuals, but those of the community were the governing principle. The skills of persons of different status had to be exchanged at a rate proportionate to the status of each: the builder's performance exchanged against many times the cobbler's performance; unless this was so, reciprocity was infringed and the community would not hold.
>
> (p. 107)

Aristotelian terminology

Art of household management (οἰκονομική)
  Human relations
  Art of acquiring property (κτητική)   The proper sense of the art of
  (C–C, C–M–C)   getting wealth (χρηματιστική)
  Art of retail trade (καπηλική)   The improper sense of the art of
  (M–C–M, M–M)   getting wealth (χρηματιστική)

12 Utilitarianism

Bentham

Jeremy Bentham (1748–1832) is usually regarded as the father of utilitarianism. Although Francis Hutcheson (1694–1746) and David Hume (1711–1776) had ideas similar to Bentham's, Bentham used the word "utilitarian" for the first time and developed the idea systematically in *An Introduction to the Principles of Morals and Legislation* published in 1789. Bentham's major aim in this publication was a reform of the British penal code, which was still based on the medieval idea that criminals should be punished for punishment's sake. Bentham argued that the penalty should be determined so as to maximize the utility or happiness of society. He states, "all punishment in itself is evil" (Methuen 1970 edition, p. 158). In his humanist approach, Bentham was a part of the philosophy of the European Enlightenment.

Bentham's utilitarianism is crude and has many defects, some of which have been remedied by later writers. One of his elementary errors was to assume that pleasure is sensation, which had been refuted by Aristotle more than two thousand years earlier. Bentham defined utility as follows: "By utility is meant that property of any object, whereby it tends to produce benefit, advantage, pleasure, good, or happiness (all this in the present case comes to the same thing)" (p. 12). It is misleading to say that utility is a property of an object because it is not something belonging to an object independent of the person who uses it. We must always talk of the utility U of object X to person A so that we can express U as a function of X and A as in the equation $U = f(X, A)$. For Bentham, utility, benefit, advantage, pleasure, good, or happiness denote the same thing. Bentham recognizes four different sources of pleasure and pain: physical, political, moral, and religious. Thus, we can characterize Bentham's ethical theory as psychological hedonism. He thinks all pleasures, regardless of the source, are homogeneous and can be measured. Moreover, he believes pleasures (utilities) of different people can be compared and added. This gives rise to a formidable problem of interpersonal comparison of utility, which has been a hotly debated issue among moral philosophers. The sum of the utilities of all the people in society is called social welfare. Bentham calls the maximization of social welfare the "principle of utility," which is the core of his ethical theory. He epitomized this idea by the rule "the greatest happiness for the greatest number."

There are ambiguities about Bentham's principle of utility. It is not clear whether Bentham thought an individual should act in such a way as to maximize social welfare or only his own utility. In the following passage, Bentham regards the former as public ethics and the latter as private ethics (p. 293):

> Private ethics teaches how each man may dispose himself to pursue the course most conductive to his own happiness, by means of such motives as offer of themselves: the art of legislation (which may be considered as one branch of the science of jurisprudence) teaches how a multitude of men, composing a community, may be disposed to pursue that course which upon the whole is the most conductive to the happiness of the whole community.

Bentham starts his book with the remark: "Nature has placed mankind under the governance of two sovereign masters, pain and pleasure. It is for them alone to point out what we ought to do, as well as to determine what we shall do" (p. 11). The same idea had been espoused by Democritos more than two thousand years earlier (see Karayiannis 1988). If his principle of utility is the maximization of social welfare, it is not clear how a man's individual interest can be subordinated to the general welfare. One possible explanation is that Bentham hoped, somewhat vaguely, that the two interests could be reconciled through sympathy and benevolence, as the following passages indicate: "What motives can one man have to consult the happiness of another?" "In the first place, he has, on all occasions, the purely social motive of sympathy or benevolence: in the next place, he has, on most occasions, the semi-social motives of love of amity and love of reputation" (p. 284). It seems doubtful that these social motives are sufficient to make individuals forgo their search for pleasure in order to maximize general welfare. It is a valid criticism of utilitarianism to say that individuals are sacrificed too much for the sake of general welfare (see Rawls' criticism in the section entitled "Further comments on utilitarianism").

The following unkind but apt characterization of Bentham was given by Karl Marx in *Das Kapital*, Vol. 1, p. 571 (quoted by Miller 1992, p. 279):

> Bentham is a purely English phenomenon. Not even excepting our philosopher Christian Wolff, in no time and in no country has the most homespun commonplace ever strutted about in so self-satisfied a way. The principle of utility was no discovery of Bentham. He simply reproduced in his dull way what Helvetius and other Frenchmen said with *esprit* in the 18th century. To know what is useful for a dog, one must study dog-nature. This nature itself is not to be deduced from the principle of utility. Applying this to men, he that would criticize all human acts, movements, relations, etc., by the principle of utility, must first deal with human nature in general, and then with human nature as modified in each historical epoch. Bentham makes short work of it. With the driest naivete he takes the modern shopkeeper, especially the English shopkeeper, as the normal man. Whatever is useful to this queer normal man, and to his world, is absolutely useful. ... Had I the courage of my

friend, Heinrich Heine, I should call Mr. Jeremy a genius in the way of bourgeois stupidity.

John Stuart Mill

John Stuart Mill (1806–1873) was given a private education at home by his father James Mill from a very early age. It had a strong utilitarian bias because James Mill was a close friend of Bentham and was himself a staunch utilitarian. J. S. Mill (henceforth, simply Mill) was also well-educated in Greek philosophy. As he reached adulthood, he was disillusioned by Bentham and revolted against his father; it seems appropriate to say that at this stage of his career he was a lot closer to Aristotle than to Bentham. In his essay entitled "Remark on Bentham's philosophy" published in 1833, Mill "firmly dismissed Bentham's claims to contribute anything of importance to ethical theory" (Scarre 1996, p. 88). In his essay entitled "Bentham" published in 1838, Mill wrote

> Man is never recognized by him as a being capable of pursuing spiritual perfection as an end; of desiring, for its own sake, the conformity of his own character to his standard of excellence, without hope of good or fear of evil from other sources than his own inward consciousness.
>
> (Scarre 1996, p. 88)

In the 1840s and 1850s, however, Mill softened his criticism of Bentham under the influence of the feminist Harriet Taylor, whom he married in 1851 after a friendship lasting 20 years. In the autobiography published in 1873, Mill wrote

> In this third period (as it may be termed) of my mental progress, which now went hand in hand with hers, my opinions gained equally in breadth and depth, I understood more things, and those which I had understood before, I now understood more thoroughly. ... I had now completely turned back from what there had been of excess in my reaction against Benthamism.
>
> (Scarre 1996, pp. 90–91)

It was in these changed circumstances that Mill wrote *Utilitarianism*, published in 1861.

Mill's utilitarianism

I will present important passages from his work *Utilitarianism*, either in direct quotation or indirectly, followed by my commentaries. In this work we observe Mill's wavering attitudes toward utilitarianism. The page numbers in the parentheses refer to those in John Stuart Mill, *Utilitarianism*, ed. by George Sher, Hackett Publishing Company, 1979.

> Socrates listened to the old Protagoras and asserted the theory of utilitarianism against the popular morality of the so-called sophist" (p. 1).

Shows Mill's superficial understanding of Plato's *Protagoras*. (See "Protagoras" in Chapter 8, "Plato's ethics".)

> It is quite compatible with the principle of utility to recognize the fact that some kinds of pleasure are more desirable and more valuable than others. It would be absurd that, while in estimating all other things quality is considered as well as quantity, the estimation of pleasure should be supposed to depend on quantity alone.
>
> (p. 8)

Once one starts discussing about quality of pleasure, simple hedonic calculus becomes impossible. This leads inexorably to a departure from Benthamite utilitarianism.

> Mill believes that one should choose a higher quality pleasure to a lower one "even though knowing it to be attended with a greater amount of discontent" (p. 8).

Since discontent is the opposite of pleasure, this remark is tantamount to discarding pleasure altogether as a criterion of action.

> A being of higher faculties requires more to make him happy, is capable probably of more acute suffering, and certainly accessible to it at more points, than one of an inferior type; but in spite of these liabilities, he can never really wish to sink into what he feels to be a lower grade of existence.
>
> (p. 9)

An admirable anti-utilitarian manifesto.

> ... a sense of dignity, which all human beings possess in one form or other ...
> (p. 9)

Mill is a "dignitarian," not a utilitarian.

> It is better to be a human being dissatisfied than a pig satisfied; better to be Socrates dissatisfied than a fool satisfied.
>
> (p. 10)

Mill would also have to say "better to be Socrates in pain than a fool in pleasure."

> "Neither pains nor pleasures are homogeneous" (p. 11). Mill goes on to say that a comparison of pleasures of different qualities and quantities must be made by competent judges, and if they disagree, by a majority rule.

Mill is substituting majority rule for objectivism.

> [I]f it may possibly be doubted whether a noble character is always the happier for its nobleness, there can be no doubt that it makes other people happier, and that the world in general is immensely a gainer by it. Utilitarianism, therefore, could only attain its end by the general cultivation of nobleness of character.
>
> (p. 11)

If everyone is noble, we don't need any ethical theory. This is Platonic and Aristotelian person-centered ethics.

> Mill defines the ideal human being as the one who has "cultivated a fellow-feeling with the collective interests of mankind" and "finds sources of inexhaustible interest in all that surrounds it: in the objects of nature, the achievement of art, the imaginations of poetry, the incidents of history, the ways of mankind, past and present, and their prospects in the future" (pp. 13–14).

Is this what Mill meant by nobility? Marx would have called it petty bourgeois ethics. It is pitifully complacent compared to the harsh austerity of Plato's image of a just man without any praise and honor. Weil (1987, p. 143) wrote, " only the penitent thief has seen justice as Plato conceived it, naked and perfect, veiled beneath the appearance of a criminal."

> [I]t (to forgo one's happiness) often has to be done voluntarily by the hero or the martyr, for the sake of something he prizes more than his individual happiness. But this something, what is it, unless the happiness of others or some of the requisites of happiness.
>
> (p. 15)

> ... but he who does it or professes to do it for any other purpose is no more deserving of admiration than the ascetic mounted on his pillar.
>
> (p. 16)

> ... the only self-renunciation which it [utilitarianism] applauds is devotion to the happiness, or to some of the means of happiness, of others, either of mankind collectively or of individuals within the limits imposed by the collective interests of mankind.
>
> (p. 16)

These passages show that Mill's philosophy is completely secular. He does not recognize a man's actions done for the sake of God. Abraham is either crazy or stupid. Even on a secular level, he does not recognize a man's actions done according to what he believes to be his mission in this life or any commitment in general.

> In the golden rule of Jesus of Nazareth, we read the complete spirit of the ethics of utility.
>
> (p. 16)

Mill adopts for his benefit only the innocuous, most banal part of Christianity. It is highly unlikely that the man who shouted at the moment of death, "My God, my God, why hast thou forsaken me?" (Matthew 27:46) lived by the principle of utility.

> [H]e who betrays the friend that trusts him is guilty of a crime, even if his object be to serve another friend to whom he is under greater obligations.
>
> (p. 18)

This remark sounds more like that of a deontologist than a utilitarian. Deontology is the theory of ethics that is based on the belief that duty should be always done for its own sake, regardless of consequences. The German philosopher Emmanuel Kant is the most famous proponent of this theory. Two central maxims of Kant's moral theory expounded in *Foundations of the Metaphysics of Morals* are (1) "act only according to that maxim by which you can at the same time will that it should become a universal law" (categorical imperative) and (2) "treat humanity always as an end and never as a means only." Kant regarded these as the necessary consequences of rationality.

> the occasions on which any person (except one in a thousand) has it in his power to do this on an extended scale – in other words, to be a public benefactor – are but exceptional; and on these occasions alone is he called on to consider public utility; in every other case, private utility, the interest or happiness of some few persons, is all he has to attend to.
>
> (p. 19)

This is a repetition of Bentham's private ethics/public ethics distinction mentioned earlier.

> We not uncommonly hear the doctrine of utility inveighed against as a *godless* doctrine.
>
> (p. 21)

Mill's answer to this criticism, which I raised myself above, is rather shamelessly self-serving. He in effect says, if God is a utilitarian, a utilitarian will believe in God. It reminds one of Protagoras, who said that if a horse had invented God, God would have looked like a horse.

> On p. 22, Mill answers the criticism of utilitarianism as being expedient. For example, a utilitarian has been criticized for breaking the rule "do not tell a lie" expediently. Mill would not break this rule so easily. He says, "we feel that the violation, for a present advantage, of a rule of such transcendent

expediency is not expedient." "Yet that even this rule, sacred as it is, admits of possible exceptions is acknowledged by all moralists."

Kant would disagree. According to his famous example recounted in his *Critique of Practical Reason*, if an evil man pursuing an innocent victim asked Kant where the victim was hiding, Kant would tell the evil man the truth.

> Mill notes that one of the criticisms against utilitarianism is "that there is not time, previous to action, for calculating and weighing the effects of any line of conduct on the general happiness" (p. 23). Mill answers that we can use age-old general rules of conduct, such as "murder and theft are injurious to human happiness" (p. 23). Mill calls utility maximization the first principle and these general rules the secondary principle. He likens the first principle to telling a traveler his destination and the secondary principle to "landmarks and direction-posts" (p. 24).

This is a variation of so-called "rule utilitarianism." Act utilitarianism determines each act so as to maximize general welfare. There are several variants of rule utilitarianism, depending on the relative importance of rules and maximization.

> In Chapter III, "Of the ultimate sanction of the principle of utility," Mill asks the important question of whether there is a moral force that compels a man to follow the principle of utility. To put it simply, Mill believes that a man's natural feeling of sympathy provides much of this moral force. He hopes that education and a better environment brought about by the progress of society will perfect the foundation of utilitarian morality. The belief in the progress of society is a reflection of the optimism prevalent in the enlightenment movement of his days.

I think that a feeling of sympathy is a feeble basis for moral force. As Mill himself admits, without a firm moral force, education would be reduced to mere brainwashing.

> It maintains not only that virtue is to be desired, but that it is to be desired disinterestedly, for itself.

> They are desired and desirable in and for themselves; besides being means, they are a part of the end.
>
> (p. 35)

These remarks are completely Platonic and Aristotelian, but after a few paragraphs Mill degenerates into Benthamism at its worst.

> Those who desire virtue for its own sake desire it either because the consciousness of it is a pleasure, or because the consciousness of being without is a pain, or both reasons united.
>
> (p. 36)

This is extremely objectionable because a man does a good thing because of his conviction and not because of whatever good feeling he might get by doing so.

> If "the mind can recognize justice by simple introspection of itself, ... it is hard to understand why that internal oracle is so ambiguous" (p. 53).

Here Mill admits that the internal foundation of any moral theory, including utilitarianism, is weak; therefore, he must brainwash people into utilitarianism. However, the fact that many people have different ideas of justice does not imply that there is no correct one.

> [T]he truths of arithmetic are applicable to the valuation of happiness, as of all other measurable quantities.
>
> (p. 61)

This is another lapse into Benthamism and contradicts his earlier remark that pleasures differ in quality.

Further comments on utilitarianism

Scarre (1996, p. 1) aptly summarizes the opposing attitudes toward utilitarianism as follows.

> Seen by its enthusiasts as a down-to-earth and liberating theory which enjoins an empirical attitude to practical decision making and refuses to accept the tyranny of questionable moral conventions, utilitarianism has been condemned by the more severe of its critics as a pernicious doctrine which treats our most precious values with scorn and prescribes the universal sacrifice of principle to expediency.

For example, Dickens (*Hard Times*, 1854) wrote that utilitarian theory was dour, dry, and informed by the lowest estimate of human possibilities (Scarre 1996, p. 4). Scarre says he somewhat sides more with utilitarians, but presents a very fair picture of both sides of the argument. He succinctly describes his own attitude as follows: "it [utilitarianism] is a very bad form of moral philosophy, but that all the others are so much worse" (p. 2).

Scarre reports that John Plamenatz announced the death of utilitarianism in 1949, but it was still alive in 1973 when Bernard Williams hoped, "The day cannot be too far off in which we hear no more of it." "Twenty years further on we hear so much about utilitarianism as we ever did, and the flow of new writings on the subject is unceasing" (p. 2). Scarre concludes his introductory remark by saying, "Utilitarianism is to the present day the moral philosophy *par excellence* which people love to hate."

My own feeling about utilitarianism is as follows. In certain situations, such as when deciding whether to go to McDonald's or a French restaurant for dinner, it may be useful to assume that the action which yields higher utility (pleasure, happiness, satisfaction, or value) is chosen. It is not valid, however, in situations which involve morality. In deciding whether to steal a book or not, we should not compare utilities. We do not steal because it is wrong to steal. When we follow our sense of right and wrong, we are not maximizing utility. If one equates "Choose A over B" with "$U(A) > U(B)$," however, everyone is a utilitarian by definition. Such a theory does not have any meaningful content and is utterly uninteresting. If one asked Antigone, Simone Weil, and Mother Teresa if they were glad, happy, and satisfied that they did what they did, they would probably say yes, but that does not mean they did what they did to become happy. They did so because they believed it was the right thing to do.

Another forceful argument against utilitarianism has been presented by philosophers who emphasize the importance of basic individual rights, such as John Rawls (1971). These philosophers complain that "utilitarianism not only condones but positively encourages the infringement of individuals' rights in the name of the general good" (Scarre 1996, p. 21).

An important issue in utilitarianism is the question of whether utility is subjective or objective. If we adopt the subjectivist stance, we must forgo an objective standard and treat a fool's utility equally with a sage's utility. Also, interpersonal comparison of utilities becomes impossible. If we adopt the objectivist stance, however, there is a danger of arbitrarily imposing a standard on everybody. Brink (1989) suggested that the objective standard should be set by a rational, well-informed person, but even rational, well-informed people can make mistakes. Harsanyi (1976), on the other hand, takes the subjectivist stance, saying, "I want to be treated in accordance with my own wants." But he hopes that subjective differences among people will not be large if wants are determined "on due reflection and in possession of all relevant information" (Scarre 1996, p. 7). In spite of his subjectivism, Harsanyi believes that interpersonal comparison of utilities is possible by means of "imaginative empathy" (Scarre 1996, p. 16).

Economic theory of utility maximization

I have mentioned Adam Smith's doctrine of an invisible hand; when consumers and producers seek their selfish interests, society will benefit as a result (see Chapter XI). This doctrine has been later made precise by economic theorists as follows. If producers maximize profits and consumers maximize utilities under the assumption of perfect competition and perfect information, and also assuming that a person's utility does not depend on another person's utility, resources will be efficiently utilized and the so-called Pareto optimum will be reached at equilibrium. The Pareto optimum is the point at which any movement away from that point will make at least one person worse off. It depends on the initial endowment of wealth and therefore can be unfair if the initial endowment is unfair. Also, the whole process that leads to the Pareto optimum may be contrary to some ethical standards. Marx offered a cogent criticism of the famous remark of Smith earlier quoted in Chapter XI: "It is not from the benevolence of the butcher, the brewer, or the baker, that we expect our dinner, but from their regard to their own interest" (*The Wealth of Nations*, Book I, Chapter II, p. 15). Kain (1992, p. 227) summarizes Marx's argument as follows:

> To act morally, one must know rationally what the good is, and the act must be motivated by this rational knowledge. To act selfishly and allow a good to come about behind your back – no matter how effective it might be – is not moral.

In *The Theory of Moral Sentiments*, however, Smith somewhat qualifies the doctrine of an invisible hand:

> How selfish soever man may be supposed, there are evidently some principles in his nature, which interest him in the fortune of others, and render their happiness necessary to him, though he derives nothing from it except the pleasure of seeing it.
> (Part I, Section I, Chapter i. 1)

I have mentioned that economists have a tendency to believe that anything resulting from a market equilibrium is good. Hausman and McPherson, *Economic Analysis and Moral Philosophy* (Chapter 2), give the following most radical example of this tendency. In December of 1991, Lawrence Summers, who was then the chief economist at the World Bank, sent a memorandum to some colleagues (apparently in all seriousness), in which he proposed that developed countries should export pollution to less developed countries and pay a certain amount of money in compensation. Summers obviously thought that as long as both parties were made happier by the transaction and were willing to engage in it, it was good.

The theory of utility maximization is less objectionable and may be actually useful in the small private economic decision of a consumer. For example, in deciding whether I should have dinner tonight at a high-class French restaurant or at McDonald's, it may be useful to compare the utilities derived from both choices. Even in such a simple case, however, it may be difficult to quantify exactly the utility of eating at a French restaurant and that of eating at McDonald's, although we can say the former is greater than the latter. Now it is true that if we gradually increase the price of dinner at the French restaurant, at a certain point McDonald's becomes more attractive. To explain this phenomenon, economists try to abstain from specifying cardinal functions $U(F, P_F)$ and $U(M, P_M)$. Instead, they assume a preference ordering between the choice of (F, P_F) and (M, P_M). A preference ordering is necessary for decision making, but it does not imply the existence of a cardinal utility function.

Sen, "Rational fools"

Amartya Sen, a well-known critic of utilitarian economics, begins this article by quoting Edgeworth's assertion that "the first principle of Economics is that every agent is actuated only by self interest" (Sen 1977). Sen goes on to say, "the nature of economic theory seems to have been much influenced by this basic premise."

In the rest of Section I, Sen states that the Pareto optimum (see my discussion above) may not be good from the point of view of social welfare if the initial endowment of wealth is unjust.

In Section II, Sen explains the economist's theory of "revealed preference" in a situation analogous to my restaurant choice.

> If you are observed to choose x rejecting y, you are declared to have "revealed" a preference for x over y. Your personal utility is then defined as simply a numerical representation of this "preference", assigning a higher utility to a "preferred" alternative. With this set of definitions you can hardly escape maximizing your own utility, except through inconsistency. ... But if you are consistent, then no matter whether you are a single-minded egoist or a raving altruist or a class conscious militant, you will appear to be maximizing your own utility in this enchanted world of definitions.

Sen notes, "This approach of definitional egoism sometimes goes under the name of rational choice, and it involves nothing other than internal consistency." In other words, the revealed preference theory of utility has too little structure. It seems too broad and innocuous. However, Sen thinks that even though it is so broad (or, might I say, because it is so broad), it cannot explain the concept of commitment. Utility theory can incorporate sympathy by making the utility of a person depend on the utility of another person. Of course in that case the theory of the Pareto optimum must be modified, but Sen thinks it can be done. But commitment cannot be incorporated into the theory of utility because it may make a person choose the action that will bring a smaller amount of utility. Sen suggests the model of meta-ranking (ranking of rankings) as a way to incorporate commitment.

Glossary of Greek names and terms

References

Cartledge, Millet, and Todd, eds, *Nomos: Essays in Athenian Law, Politics and Society*, Cambridge 1990.
Joint Association of Classical Teachers, *The World of Athens*, Cambridge 1984.
Liddell and Scott, *An Intermediate Greek–English Lexicon*, Oxford.
The Oxford Classical Dictionary.

Aeschines Αἰσχίνης (*c.*397–*c.*322): Athenian orator famous for his two exchanges with Demosthenes in 343 and 330. In the earlier year Demosthenes accused Aeschines of his misconduct in his role as ambassador to Macedonia in 346, in his speech titled "On the Embassy," to which Aeschines replied in the speech with the same title. In the latter year, Aeschines in his speech titled "Against Ctesiphon" challenged Ctesiphon's motion to give a gold crown to Demosthenes in recognition of his services to the state. Demosthenes defended Ctesiphon in the speech titled "On the Crown."

Alcibiades Ἀλκιβιάδης: Athenian general. See "Sicilian expedition" in "Classical age".

alphita ἄλφιτα: barley meal.

Anthestēria Ἀνθεστήρια: festival in honor of Dionysos.

antidosis ἀντίδοσις: a man who was nominated to perform a liturgy could avoid this duty if he could name another citizen who was richer and better qualified to perform the task. If the man challenged agreed that he was richer, he had to take over the liturgy; if he claimed to be poorer, then the challenger could insist on the exchange of all their property to test the claim – in which case the challenger would himself perform the liturgy as the new owner of the greater estate.

apoikia ἀποικία: a colony.

archōn ἄρχων: the leading officers of the state under Solon's constitution. See "Solon's constitution" in Chapter 3.

atimia ἀτιμία: loss of honor. Loss of some or all of a man's active rights as a citizen.

autarkeia αὐτάρκεια: self-sufficiency.

banausikos βαναυσικός: a derogatory adjective characterizing a simple mechanical work which does not require a skill.

chorēgia χορηγία: a liturgy of defraying the cost of staging a chorus.
chrēmatistikē χρηματιστική: art of getting wealth.
Cimon Κίμων: wealthy and noble Athenian, son of Miltiades. Was often *strategos* since 479. Together with Aristides, he was instrumental in the formation of the Delian League and commanded most of its operations in 476–463. Defeated Persians at the battle of Eurymedon. After the earthquake in Sparta in 464, Cimon led the Athenian army that tried to help the Spartans to suppress the uprising of the helots, but this offer of help was rejected by the Spartans. This humiliation led to Cimon's ostracism in 461. After returning from the ostracism, he arranged the Peace Treaty with Sparta in 449.
Cleon Κλέων: Athenian politician, the son of a rich tanner. Became influential after the death of Pericles. In 427 he unsuccessfully argued for executing all the men of Mytilene. He, together with *strategos* Demosthenes (not the orator of the fourth century), succeeded in defeating the Spartans in Pylos in 425. Was killed in a battle outside Amphipolis in 422. A constant object of ridicule by Aristophanes.
dēmiurgos δημιουργός (one who works for the people): a skilled workman.
diaitētēs διαιτητής: arbitrator, served by a 60-year-old citizen, to arrange arbitration (δίαιτα).
Dionysia Διονύσια: festival held every year in honor of Dionysos, at which the major tragic and comic competitions were staged.
dokimasia δοκιμασία: an examination which state officials and the members of the Council underwent before taking up office.
eisangelia εἰσαγγελία: impeachment.
eisphora εἰσφορά: a special tax on capital, often levied at the time of war.
Eleusis Ἐλευσίς: a *dēmos* of Attica where there was a sanctuary of Demeter and Persephone, goddesses of fertility. Famous for a mystery cult which attracted initiates from all over Greece.
emporikē dikē ἐμπορική δίκη: a lawsuit involving traders.
emporion ἐμπόριον: a trading place.
emporos ἔμπορος: a merchant.
enktēsis ἔγκτησις: tenure of land or house by a noncitizen. It was one of various privileges (see also *isoteleia*) which could be granted at Athens to individual metics.
ephēbos ἔφηβος: a young man becoming a citizen at the age of eighteen.
Ephialtes Ἐφιάλτης: Athenian politician, about whom little is known. Was the leading opponent of Cimon and resisted the sending of the troops to Sparta. With the help of Pericles, he passed measures to take from Areopagus its judicial powers of political importance in 462. He was murdered soon afterward.
ephoros ἔφορος: an overseer. One of the five Spartan magistrates.
epidosis ἐπίδοσις: voluntary contribution to the state following a decree passed by the Assembly.
epiklēros ἐπίκληρος: heiress.
epōbelia ἐπωβελία: one-sixth of damages assessed to the plaintiff if he does not get one fifth of the votes cast by the juries.

eranos ἔρανος: means both a private club and what its members pay for a common activity such as a common meal. It also has a specific meaning of an interest-free loan.

Eubulos Εὔβουλος (*c*.405–*c*.335): probably the most important Athenian statesman of the period 355–342. After the conclusion of the Social War (355), by means of his position as a commissioner of the theoric fund gradually assumed control of the whole of Athens' finances, and raised public and private prosperity to a level probably not attained since the fifth century. He passed a law which made it difficult for the Assembly to draw on the routine revenues of the state for inessential military operations. The distribution of money to the people engaged only a small part of the moneys controlled by the theoric commission. Initially he made an effort to contain the power of Philip, but later argued for peace, and by 342 was eclipsed by Demosthenes who was eager to fight against Philip.

euthuna εὔθυνα: an examination of accounting for outgoing state officials.

graphē paranomōn γραφὴ παρανόμων: a lawsuit brought by an individual against another for proposing a law or decree which is contrary to an existing law in form or content.

hetaira ἑταίρα: professional female entertainer, mistress, call girl. Cf. *pornē* πόρνη (prostitute).

Hippias Ἱππίας: tyrant of Athens in 527–510, son and successor of Peisistratos, in association with his brother Hipparchus. His rule was at first mild. The Attic owl coinage began in his reign, as did the building of the temple of Olympian Zeus. His rule became harsher after Hipparchus' assassination (514) by Harmodius and Aristogeiton.

horos ὅρος (boundary): an inscribed stone marking the boundary of a piece of property.

isēgoria ἰσηγορία: freedom of speech in the Assembly.

Isocrates Ἰσοκράτης (436–338): Athenian orator of central importance. He taught rhetoric to many famous writers. He is known for his pan-Hellenism and is said to have inspired Philip to try to conquer Persia. In contrast to Plato, his philosophy was very practical.

isonomia ἰσονομία: equality under the laws.

isoteleia ἰσοτέλεια (equality of taxation): the privilege of exemption from the *metoikion* granted by individual decree to particularly favored metics.

kalos kagathos καλός κἀγαθός (fine and good): a self-approbatory term used by Athenian aristocrats to describe themselves.

kapēlikē καπηλική: retail trade.

klēros κλῆρος: that which is allotted. Inherited estate.

krithē κριθή: barley.

leitourgia λειτουργία: voluntary contributions for various public enterprises and services such as payment for participation in political and judicial processes, festivals, welfare, and military expenditures, the most important of which was the construction and manning of warships.

Lycurgos Λυκοῦργος (*c*.390–*c*.325): Athenian statesman of great importance after the battle of Chaironea (338). He played the major part in the control of the city's finances for a period of 12 years, raising the revenue to perhaps 1,200 talents a year, and financing military and building projects. The powers by which he did it all are obscure. In politics he was bitterly suspicious of Macedonia.

Lysias Λυσίας (*c*.459–*c*.380): Athenian orator. His father Cephalos, a Syracusan, was invited by Pericles to take up residency in Athens. He and his brother Polemarchos left Athens after Cephalos' death to live in Thurii in southern Italy. They were expelled after the Sicilian expedition and returned to Athens in 412. In 403 the Thirty Tyrants arrested both brothers and confiscated their substantial property. Polemarchos was executed but Lysias escaped. This incident is described in Lysias' most famous speech titled "Against Eratosthenes."

metoikion μετοικίον: tax paid by metics – 12 drachmas for men and 6 drachmas for women per year.

misthos μισθός: wage. Public pay.

Mitiades Μιλτιάδης: Athenian aristocrat and general from a wealthy and powerful family. He played a major role in defeating Persians in the battle of Marathon (490). Later he was condemned to pay a fine of 50 talents on account of a military failure at Paros but died before he paid the fine. His son Cimon paid the fine after his death in 489.

Nicias Νικίας: Athenian statesman who reluctantly led the Sicilian expedition and was killed. Was wealthy and said to have owned 1,000 slaves in the silver mines.

nomos νόμος: law, custom, convention. Often contrasted with *physis* (nature).

ostracism ὀστρακισμός: a method of banishing a citizen for ten years. It was held once a year in a special session of the Assembly. Each citizen who wished to vote wrote on a fragment of pottery (ὄστρακον) the name of the citizen whom he wished to be banished. If more than 6,000 votes were cast, the one who collected the largest number of votes was ostracized. The practice started in the early fifth century and lasted until 417, after which it was replaced by *graphē paranomōn*. An ostracized citizen had to leave the country within ten days and remain in exile for ten years, but he did not forfeit his citizenship or property, and at the end of the ten years he could return to live in Athens without any disgrace or disability.

Panathenaia Παναθήναια: a festival in honor of Athene celebrated every year, with the Great Panathenaia being held every fourth year.

Pasion Πασίων (died in 370): the wealthiest banker and manufacturer of his time in Athens. He began his career as a slave with a banking firm in Peiraieus, was made a freed man and subsequently acquired ownership of the bank. He later became an Athenian citizen, having spent lavishly on donations to the city. He bequeathed an estate worth about 80 talents. His banking business was given to his slave Phormion, who also later became an Athenian citizen.

peltast πελταστής: soldiers carrying small round shield called πέλτη.

Philocrates Φιλοκράτης: Athenian politician principally connected with the Athens–Macedonia Peace Treaty of 346. Athenian dissatisfaction with the outcome exposed him to prosecution and he fled into exile in 343.

physis φύσις: nature. Often contrasted with *nomos* (custom).

polētai πωληταί: sellers. Officers who sold the state right to collect taxes, etc.
politeia πολιτεία: the conditions and rights of a citizen, a form of government (often translated as a constitution).
proxenos πρόξενος: a foreign citizen bringing benefits to the state. A public guest.
puros πυρός: wheat.
Pythia Πυθία: the priestess who pronounced the oracle in Delphi.
sitos σῖτος: grain.
stasis στάσις: internal strife.
sycophant συκοφάντης: a false accuser. An exceedingly litigious person (different from the English meaning).
technē τέχνη: skill, art. Plato's examples of the objects of *technē* are mathematics, medicine, music, and ethics (politics). His nonexamples are rhetoric, cosmetics, and gourmet cooking.
theōrika θεωρικά: the money given to the poor citizens to pay for seats in the theater (at two obols the seat), but also for other purposes.
Theramenes Θηραμένης: Athenian politician. He played an active part in establishing the Oligarchy of Four Hundred in 411, but four months later he was active in overthrowing them and establishing the Five Thousand, a more moderate but still not fully democratic regime which succeeded Four Hundred briefly. At Arginusai (406) he commanded a ship but came out free unlike the six generals who were held responsible for not rescuing survivors and were executed. In 404 he was involved in setting up the Oligarchy of Thirty, and was himself one of the Thirty, but he soon quarreled with the extremists, especially Critias, who had him executed. A critical view of him is as an adroit politician, but others view him as a moderate seeking a genuine political mean.
Thesmophoria Θεσμοφόρια: women's festival in honor of Demeter.
Thrasybulos Θρασύβουλος: Athenian general and statesman. In 411 he was a leader of the democratic state formed by the navy at Samos in opposition to the Four Hundred. In 404 he was banished by the Thirty and fled to Thebes, where he organized a band of exiles and occupied Phyle and later seized Peiraieus and defeated the troops of the Thirty. During the Corinthian War (395–387) he played a prominent part in reviving Athenian imperialism. Killed in 388.
timē τιμή: honor, status.
Timotheus Τιμόθεος: Athenian general. Played a major role in establishing the Second Athenian League (377).
triērarchy τριηραρχία: an important type of liturgy responsible for the construction, upkeep, and manning of triremes.
trirēmē τριήρης: a three-decked warship.
xenia ξενία: a friendly relation between two foreigners, or between an individual and a foreign state.

References

Adams, John (1994) "The institutional theory of trade and the organization of intersocial commerce in ancient Athens", in A. M. Duncan and D. W. Tandy, eds, *From Political Economy to Anthropology*, Black Rose Books, pp. 80–104.
Amyx, D. A. (1958) "The Attic Stelai: Part III. Vases and other containers", *Hesperia*, Vol. 27, Issue 3 (July–Sep), pp. 163–254.
Andreades, A. M. (1933) *History of Greek Public Finance*, Vol. I, Harvard University Press.
Annas, Julia (1981) *An Introduction to Plato's Republic*, Oxford University Press.
—— (1993) *The Morality of Happiness*, Oxford University Press.
—— (1999) *Platonic Ethics, Old and New*, Cornell University Press.
Austin, M. M. and P. Vidal-Naquet (1980) *Economic and Social History of Ancient Greece, An Introduction*, 2nd edn, University of California Press.
Beazley, J. D. (1963) *Attic Red-Figure Vase-Painters*, 2nd edn, Oxford University Press.
Benedict, Ruth (1948) *The Chrysanthemum and the Sword: Patterns of Japanese Culture*, Houghton Mifflin.
Blaug, M. (1992) *The Methodology of Economics*, 2nd edn, Cambridge University Press.
Blue Guide, 4th edn, London 1981, p. 402.
Blundell, Sue (1995) *Women in Ancient Greece*, Harvard University Press.
Boeckh, Augustus (1842) *The Public Economy of Athens*, John W. Parker.
Brink, David O. (1989) *Moral Realism and the Foundations of Ethics*, Cambridge University Press.
Brown, A. and A. Deaton (1972) "Models of consumer behavior: A survey", *Economic Journal*, Vol. 82, Issue 328, 1145–1236.
Buchanan, James J. (1962) *Theorika*, J. J. Augustine Publisher.
Burke, Edmund M. (1992) "The economy of Athens in the classical era: Some adjustments to the primitivist model", *Transactions of the American Philological Association*, Vol. 122, pp. 199–226.
Burkert, Walter (1992) *The Orientalizing Revolution*, Harvard University Press.
Burnyeat, M. F. (1980) "Aristotle learning to be good", in A. M. Rorty, ed., *Essays on Aristotle's Ethics*, University of California Press, pp. 69–92.
Camp, John M. (1992) *The Athenian Agora*, Thames and Hudson.
Cartledge, Paul (1985) "Rebels & sambos in classical Greece: A comparative view", in P.A. Cartledge and F. D. Harvey, eds, *CRUX: History of Political Thought*, Imprint Academic, Vol. VI, Issue 1/2, pp. 16–46.
Cartledge, Paul, Edward E. Cohen, and Lin Foxhall (2002) *Money, Labour and Land*, Routledge.

Casson, Lionel (1976) "The Athenian upper class and new comedy", *Transactions of the American Philological Association*, Vol. 106, pp. 29–59.
Chadwick, John (1976) *The Mycenaean World*, Cambridge University Press.
Christ, Matthew R. (2001) *Classical Quarterly*, Vol. 51, Issue 2, 398–422.
Cipolla, Carlo M. (1993) *Before the Industrial Revolution*, W. W. Norton & Company.
Clark, Colin (1957) *The Conditions of Economic Progress*, 3rd edn, Macmillan.
Cohen, David (1993) "Law, autonomy, and political community in Plato's laws", *Classical Philology*, Vol. 88, Issue 4, pp. 301–17.
Cohen, Edward E. (1992) *Athenian Economy and Society: A Banking Perspective*, Princeton University Press.
Crosby, M. (1950) "The leases of the Laureion mines", *Hesperia*, Vol. 19, Issue 3 (July–Sep), pp. 189–297.
Davidson, James (1998) *Courtesans and Fishcakes*, St. Martin's Press.
Davies, J. K. (1981) *Wealth and the Power of Wealth in Classical Athens*, Arno Press.
—— (2001) "Temple, credit, and the circulation of money", in A. Meadows and K. Shipton, eds, *Money and Its Uses in the Ancient Greek World*, Oxford University Press, pp. 117–28.
Dickinson, Oliver (1994) *The Aegean Bronze Age*, Cambridge University Press.
Dodds, E. R. (1951) *The Greeks and the Irrational*, University of California Press.
Dover, K. J. (1994) *Greek Popular Morality in the Time of Plato and Aristotle*, Hackett Publishing Company.
Drews, Robert (1988) *The Coming of the Greeks*, Princeton University Press.
—— (1993) *The End of the Bronze Age*, Princeton University Press.
Easterling, P. E. and J. V. Muir, eds (1985) *Greek Religion and Society*, Cambridge University Press.
Fine, V. A. John (1983) *The Ancient Greeks*, Harvard University Press.
Finley, M. I. (1981) *Economy and Society in Ancient Greece*, B. D. Shaw and R. P. Saller, eds, Chatto and Windus.
—— (1999) *The Ancient Economy*, Updated Edition, University of California Press.
Fischer-Hansen, T. (2000) "Ergasteria in the western Greek world", in P. Flensted-Jensen, T. H. Nielsen, and L. Rubinstein, eds, *Polis and Politics: Studies in Ancient Greek History*, Museum Tusculanum, pp. 91–120.
Foxhall, L. and H. A. Forbes (1982) "The role of grain as a staple food in classical antiquity", *Chiron*, Vol. 12, pp. 41–90.
Frede, Dorothea (1992) "Disintegration and restoration: Pleasure and pain in Plato's *Philebus*", in Richard Kraut, ed., *The Cambridge Companion to Plato*, Cambridge University Press.
Fujisawa, Norio (1980) *Girisya Tetsugaku to Gendai* (Greek Philosophy and the Present Age) (Japanese), Iwanami Publishing Company.
Gabrielsen, Vincent (1994) *Financing the Athenian Fleet*, Johns Hopkins University Press.
Gadamer, Hans-Georg (1986) *The Idea of the Good in Platonic–Aristotelian Philosophy*, Yale University Press.
Gallant, Thomas W. (1991) *Risk and Survival in Ancient Greece*, Stanford University Press.
Garlan, Yvon (1988) *Slavery in Ancient Greece*, Revised and Expanded Edition, Cornell University Press.
Garnsey, Peter (1988) *Famine and Food Supply in the Fourth Century B.C.*, Cambridge University Press.

Garnsey, Peter (1998) "11. Grain for Athens", in Walter Scheidel, ed., *Cities, Peasants and Food in Classical Antiquity: Essays in Social and Economic History*, Cambridge University Press, pp. 183–95.
Goldsmith, Raymond W. (1987) *Premodern Financial Systems*, Cambridge University Press.
Green, Peter (1973) *Ancient Greece*, Thames and Hudson.
Guthrie, W. K. C. (1975) *The Greek Philosophers From Thales to Aristotle*, Harper Torch Books.
Hansen, M. H. (1986) *Demography and Democracy: The Number of Athenian Citizens in the Fourth Century, B.C.*, Systime.
—— (1991) *The Athenian Democracy in the Age of Demosthenes*, Blackwell.
Hanson, V. D. (1992) "Thucydides and the desertion of Attic slaves during the Decelean War", *Classical Antiquity*, Vol. 11, Issue 2, pp. 210–28.
Harris, Edward M. (2002) "Workshop, marketplace and household", in Paul Cartledge, Edward E. Cohen, and Lin Foxhall, eds, *Money, Labour and Land*, Routledge, pp. 67–99.
Harsanyi, John C. (1976) *Essays on Ethics, Social Behavior, and Scientific Explanations*, Reidel.
Hausman, D. M. and M. S. McPherson (1996) *Economic Analysis and Moral Philosophy*, Cambridge University Press.
Havelock, Eric A. (1957) *The Liberal Temper in Greek Politics*, Yale University Press.
Heidegger, Martin (1984) *Early Greek Thinking*, Harper & Row.
Hodkinson, Stephen (1988) "Animal husbandry in the Greek polis", in C. R. Whittaker, ed., *Pastoral Economies in Classical Antiquity*, The Cambridge Philological Society, pp. 35–86.
Hoepfner, W. and E. L. Schwandner (1994) *Haus und Stadt im klassischen Griechenland*, Deutscher Kunstverlag.
Hopper, R. J. (1953) "The Attic silver mines in the fourth century B.C.", *Annual of the British School at Athens,* Vol. 48, pp. 200–54.
—— (1979) *Trade and Industry in Classical Greece*, Thames and Hudson.
Irwin, T. H. (1996) "Kant's criticism of eudaemonism", in S. Engstrom and J. Whiting, eds, *Aristotle, Kant, and the Stoics*, Cambridge University Press.
Isager, Signe and M. H. Hansen (1975) *Aspects of Athenian Society in the Fourth Century B.C.*, Odense University Press.
Ito, Sadao (1981) *Kotenki no Polis Shakai* (The Polis Society of the Classical Period) (Japanese), Iwanami Shoten.
J.A.C.T. (Joint Association of Classical Teachers) (1984) *The World of Athens*, Cambridge University Press.
Jameson, Michael H. (1977–78) "Agriculture and slavery in classical Athens", *The Classical Journal*, Vol. 73, Issue 2 (Dec–Jan), pp. 122–45.
—— (1988) "Sacrifice and animal husbandry in classical Greece", in C. R. Whittaker, ed., *Pastoral Economies in Classical Antiquity*, The Cambridge Philological Society, pp. 87–119.
Johnson, A. C. (1915) "Studies in the financial administration of Athens", *American Journal of Philology*, pp. 424–52.
Jones, A. H. M. (1986) *Athenian Democracy*, Johns Hopkins University Press.
Kain, Philip J. (1992) "Aristotle, Kant, and the ethics of the young Marx", in George E. McCarthy, ed., *Marx and Aristotle*, Rowman & Littlefield, pp. 213–42.
Karayiannis, A. D. (1988) "Democritus on ethics and economics", *Rivista Internazionale di Scienze Economiche e Commerciali*, Vol. XXXV, Issue 4–5, pp. 369–92.

Kim, Henry S. (2001) "Archaic coinage as evidence for the use of money", in Andrew Meadows and Kirsty Shipton, eds, *Money and Its Uses in the Ancient Greek World*, Oxford University Press.
Kraut, Richard (1992) "Introduction to the study of Plato", in Kraut, ed., *The Cambridge Companion to Plato*, Cambridge University Press, pp. 1–50.
Lewis, David M. (1959) "Attic manumissions", *Hesperia*, Vol. 28, Issue 3 (Jul–Sep), pp. 208–38.
Loomis, W. T. (1998) *Wages, Welfare Costs and Inflation in Classical Athens*, Michigan University Press.
MacDowell, Douglas M. (1978) *The Law in Classical Athens*, Cornell University Press.
Markle, M. M. (1985) "Jury pay and assembly pay at Athens", in P. A. Cartledge and F. D. Harvey, eds, *CRUX: History of Political Thought*, Vol. VI, Issue ½, Imprint Academic, pp. 265–97.
Mattingly, H. B. (1968) "Athenian finance in the Peloponnesian War", *Bulletin de Correspondance Hellénique*, Vol. 92, Issue 2, pp. 450–85.
Meikle, Scott (1979) "Aristotle and the political economy of the polis", *Journal of Hellenic Studies*, Vol. 99, pp. 57–73.
Michell, H. (1957) *The Economics of Ancient Greece*, Barnes and Noble.
Miller, Richard W. (1992) "Marx and Aristotle: A kind of consequentialism", in George E. McCarthy, ed., *Marx and Aristotle*, Rowman & Littlefield, pp. 275–302.
Millett, Paul (1990) "Sale, credit and exchange in Athenian law and society", in Paul Cartledge, Paul Millett, and Stephen Todd, eds, *Nomos: Essays in Athenian Law, Politics and Society*, Cambridge University Press, pp. 167–94.
Moravcsik, Julius (2000) *Plato and Platonism*, Blackwell.
Morris, Ian (2004) "Economic growth in ancient Greece", *Journal of Institutional and Theoretical Economics*, Vol. 160, Issue 4 (Dec), pp. 709–42.
Morrow, Glenn R. (1993) *Plato's Cretan City*, Princeton University Press.
Nagel, Thomas (1980) "Aristotle on eudaimonia", in A. O. Rorty, ed., *Essays on Aristotle's Ethics*, University of California Press, pp. 7–14.
Ober, J. (1989) *Mass and Elite in Democratic Athens*, Princeton University Press.
Oliver, G. J. (1995) *The Athenian State under Threat; Politics and Food Supply, 307 to 229 BC*, Ph.D. thesis, Oxford University.
Osborne, Robin (1985) *Demos: The Discovery of Classical Athens*, Cambridge University Press.
—— (1991) "Pride and prejudice, sense and subsistence: Exchange and society in the Greek city", in John Rich and Andrew Wallace-Hadrill, eds, *City and Country in the Ancient World*, Routledge, pp. 119–45.
Polanyi, Karl (1968) "Aristotle discovers the economy", in George Dalton, ed., *Primitive, Archaic and Modern Economies. Essays of Karl Polanyi*, Doubleday & Co., Inc., pp. 78–115.
Pomeroy, Sarah B. (1975) *Goddesses, Whores, Wives, and Slaves*, Schocken Books.
—— (1994) *Xenophon Oeconomicus*, Oxford University Press.
—— (1997) *Families in Classical and Hellenistic Greece*, Oxford University Press.
Pomeroy, S. B., S. M. Burstein, W. Donlan, and J. T. Roberts (2004) *A Brief History of Ancient Greece*, Oxford University Press.
Popper, Karl R. (1963) *The Open Society and Its Enemies*, Vol. 1, Harper Torchbooks.
Pritchett, W. Kendrick, and Anne Pippin (1956) "The Attic Stelai: Part II", *Hesperia*, Vol. 25, Issue 3 (July–Sep), pp. 178–328.

Raaflaub, Kurt A. (1994) "Democracy, power, and imperialism in fifth-century Athens", in J. P. Euben, J. R. Wallace, and J. Ober, eds, *Athenian Political Thought and the Reconstruction of Athenian Democracy*, Cornell University Press, pp. 103–46.

Raepsaet, George (1973) "A Propos de l'utilisation de statistique en démographie grecque. Le nombre d'enfants par famille", *L'Antiquite Classique* Vol. 42, pp. 536–43.

Rawls, John (1971) *Theory of Justice*, Harvard University Press.

Rhodes, P. J. (1982) "Problems in Athenian *Eisphora* and Liturgies", *American Journal of Ancient History*, Vol. 7, Issue 1, pp. 1–19.

Robbins, Lionel (1984) *An Essay on the Nature and Significance of Economic Science*, Macmillan.

Sakurai, Mariko (1992) *Kodai Girisha no Onna Tachi* (Women of Ancient Greece) (in Japanese), Chuko Shinsho.

Scarre, G. (1996) *Utilitarianism*, Routledge.

Scheidel, Walter, ed. (1998) "Addendum to 11. Grain for Athens", in Peter Garnsey, *Cities, Peasants and Food in Classical Antiquity*: *Essays in Social and Economic History*, Cambridge University Press, pp. 195–200.

Sealey, Raphael (1993) *Demosthenes and His Time*, Oxford University Press.

Sen, A. K. (1977) "Rational fools: A critique of the behavioural foundations of economic theory", *Philosophy and Public Affairs*, Vol. 6, Issue 4, pp. 317–44.

Starr, Chester G. (1991) *A History of the Ancient World*, Oxford University Press.

Ste Croix, G. E. M. de (1966) "The estate of Phainippus", in E. Badian, ed., *Ancient Society and Institutions*: *Studies Presented to Victor Ehrenberg*, Oxford University Press, pp. 109–14.

Stockton, David (1990) *The Classical Athenian Democracy*, Oxford University Press.

Stone, I. F. (1988) *The Trial of Socrates*, Little, Brown and Company.

Strauss, Barry S. (1991) "On Aristotle's critique of Athenian democracy", in Carnes Lord and David K. O'Connor, eds, *Essays on the Foundations of Aristotelian Political Science*, University of California Press, pp. 212–33.

Urmson, J. O. (1988) *Aristotle's Ethics*, Blackwell.

van Wees, Hans (2000) "The city at war", in Robin Osborne, ed., *Classical Greece*, Oxford University Press, pp. 81–110.

Vlastos, Gregory (1991) "Socrates *contra* Socrates in Plato", in *Socrates*: *Ironist and Moral Philosopher*, Cornell University Press, pp. 45–80.

Weil, Simone (1987) *Intimations of Christianity among the Ancient Greeks*, Ark Paperbacks.

Whitby, Michael (1998) "The grain trade of Athens in the fourth century BC", in Helen Parkins and Christopher Smith, eds, *Trade, Traders and the Ancient City*, Routledge, pp. 102–28.

Wolin, Sheldon S. (1994) "Norm and form: The constitutionalizing of democracy", in J. Peter Euben, John R. Wallach, and Josiah Ober, eds, *Athenian Political Thought and the Reconstruction of American Democracy*, Cornell University Press.

Wood, Michael (1985) *In Search of the Trojan War*, New American Library.

Index

accounting identities xii, 62–3
adultery 23–4; *see also* marriage
Aeschines 43, 169; *Against Timarchos* 43, 44
Aeschylus 19; *The Persians* 19
Agora: *see* Athenian Agora
agriculture 74–80; improvements in 63–4; Plato on 146; slaves in 29–30, 33; Xenophon on 119
Alcibiades 8, 9, 169; as landowner 75; and rhetoric 53; and Socrates 35; warlike 49, 50
Alcidamas 154
Alcmaionidai (aristocratic family) 51
Anaxagoras 23
Anaximander 22
Anaximenes 22
Andreades, A. M. 91, 96, 97, 111n
animal husbandry 78–80, 83
Annas, Julia 125, 126, 129–30, 134, 136–7
antidosis (liturgy-substitute) 64, 78, 169
Antipater 11, 45
Antiphon 154
archons (officers of state) 37, 43, 44, 51, 169
Areopagus (retired archons) 37, 44, 144
Aristarchos 59; and female workers 19, 66
aristocracy: in Aristotle 156; *see also Alcmaionidai*, elite
Aristophanes 20, 50; *Acharnians* 20, 40, 47, 50, 67; *Babylonians* 46–7; *Clouds* 79; on coins 84; *Ecclesiazusae* 26, 39, 68, 84, 105; *Frogs* 20, 84; on liturgies 94; *Lysistrata* 24–5, 25, 26, 50; *Peace* 50; on prices 62; *Thesmophoriazusae* 25; *Wasps* 80; on wealth 53
Aristophon 43
Aristotle, 131; *arête* (function) xiii, 132; on community 153–4; *The Constitution of Athens* 37, 42, 44, 68, 78, 100, 156; contemplation 132–3, 137, 156; on democracy 156; Democritus and 23; economics xiii, 151–8; ethics xiii, 123, 132, 154; on household management 154, 155; on justice 150; on love 35, 134; Lyceum of 131; *Nichomachean Ethics* xiii, 35, 124, 131–6, 156; on money 153; on need 151–3; on philosopher kings 156; on Plato 154, 156; on pleasure 135–6; *Politics* 153–6; on price theory 150–1, 152; on property 155; on retail trade 155; *Rhetoric* 151; on rule of the mean 134, 150; on slaves 118, 154, 155; on tragedy 19–20; utility theory of value 151–3; on virtue 132–3, 134, 136, 156; on wealth 155; on women 25–6, 118, 156
armed forces, cost of 101–2
Asia Minor 5
Assembly (*Ekklesia*) 14, 35, 45; in Aristophanes 40; of Cleisthenes 38–44; as court 39; election of *stratēgoi* 39; influence in 52; and lawgivers 48; paid attendance 31, 39; in Plato 146; and public finance 91; role 43; of Solon 37, 38
Athenian Agora 38, 42, 66, 67, 112n, 156–7
Athenian economy xi–xii. 62–114; agriculture 74–80; definition 117; did it exist? 105; growth in 63; market 64–8; model of 106–11; money 102–6; prices 68–72; primitivist view 156–7; public finance 91–102; strengthening (Xenophon) 119; wages in 72–4
Athenian League 8, 43, 44
Athens 5, 7, 43
atomic theory 21, 23
Attica 5

banking 104–6; Demosthenes on 105, 106
barbarians 28, 145
battles: Aigos potamoi (405) 8–9; Arginusai (408) 8, 42, 46, 173; Chaironea (338) 11, 171; Eurymedon (467) 170; Issus (333) 11; Marathon (490) 7, 41, 172; Pylos (425) 170; Salamis (480) 7, 19, 41
Benedict, Ruth 16
Bentham, Jeremy xiv, 128, 135, 158–60; ethical theory 158–9, 163, 164, 165; Marx on 159
Berkeley, Bishop 121

Index

Blaug, M. 63
Blue Guide 15
Boeckh, Augustus 71, 76–8, 97–8
Boetia 67
Bosporus; grain imports 80–1; trade to 87
bottomry loans (against ship losses) 86–7, 105
boulē (council) 37
Bouleutērion 42
Brink, D. O. 166
Buddhism 14

capital liquidity 103
Cartledge, P. 31
catharsis 20
cavalry, cost of 101
charis (reciprocal favours) 52–3
Chinese philosophy 22
Cimon 7, 10, 41, 170
citizens 27; and banking 107; in Cleisthenes' constitution 38; duties 17, 52; numbers in classical Athens 28, 65; in Plato 146
city-states 5, 6, 10
Clark, Colin 77–8, 112–13
classical Greek economy: choice of term 58; and modern American 58; substantivism in 59; *see also* Athenian economy
Cleisthenes 51; constitution of 38–44; and democracy 6, 7, 45
Cleon 45, 46, 50, 170; criticized by Aristophanes 47, 50; hawkish 49; and rhetoric 53
Cohen, E. E. 64, 104–6
coinage 30, 64, 157; absence of paper money 106; circulation 80; copper 84; silver 64, 65, 84
comedies 20, 26
Confucius 123
Corinth 20
corruption, 40, 44
cost of living: clothes 72; rent 77, shoes 77; total 77–8; *see also* food, grain
Council (*boulē*) 44; budget of 91; and Cleisthenes 38–9, 40, 41–2; paid attendance 31, 42; and Plato 144; role 43; and Solon 41
courts (*dikastēria*) 42–3; Assembly as 39; Demosthenes and 32; paid jury 41; role 43
Critias 9
Ctesiphon 43, 169
cultural relativism 58–9

Davies, J. K. xiv, 28–30, 64, 71, 93–8, 100, 102–4, 108
Decelea 30, 84
decrees (*psēphisma*) 39, 48
Delian League 7, 170
Delphi 15; Amphictiony 10; oracle 15; Temple of Apollo 18
dēmagōgos (people-leader) 49, 80
demand: *see* utility
Demetrius of Phaleron 11

Demetrius Poliorectes 12
democracy: and modern American 48–9; Athenian 45–54; failure of 45–6; freedom of speech 46–7; and income redistribution 50; in Plato 142; radical or moderate? 47–9; success of 46; in war and peace 49–50
Democritos 21, 23, 121, 159
dēmos 38, 42, 44
Demosthenes: *Against Aphobos I* 31–2, 33–4, 105; *Against Ctesiphon* 169; *Against Dionysodoros* 59, 82; *Against Eubiledes* 25, 54; *Against Leptines* 62; *Against Meidias* 52; *Against Phainippos* 64; and the Assembly 53; on banking 104, 105; on cost of living 78; on dowry 26; on moneylending 103; and Navy Board 95, 96; *On the Cheronese* 52; *On the Crown* 43, 54, 169; *On the Embassy* 47; on the poor 18; on prices 107; on shame 16; and slavery 31–4; speeches 10, 11; on war expenditure 46, 49; and workshops 65
deontology 125, 163
de Tocqueville, Alexis 48
Dickens, Charles 165
diōbelia (payments to citizens) 50, 99
Diodotos 46, 49
Diogenes Laertios 27
Dionysia 14, 15, 19, 20, 170; City Dionysia 19; Great Dionysia 51
"disembedded economy" (Finley) 58
Dodds, E. R. 16
Dorians 5
Dover, K. J. 17, 18, 29
Dracon 6

economic indicators 34
economics: defined 17, 167
economy, Athenian: *see* Athenian economy
Edgeworth's contract curve 152, 167
education 21; in Plato 121, 122, 123–4, 125, 128, 143, 144; and women 21, 26
eisphora (tax on capital) 64, 96–7, 170
elections: in Plato 143; of *stratēgoi* 39, 44; *see also* lottery
Eleusinian Mysteries 8, 14, 15, 170; slaves in 77; social structure of sanctuaries 65, 111n
elites 51–2
"embeddedness" (Finley) x, 57, 60
Ephialtes 44, 47, 170
ephēboi (adolescent group) 38
epidosis (emergency tax) 98, 170
epōbelia (damages awards) 17, 42, 170
Eubolos 91, 119, 171
eudaimonia (good living): Aristotle and 131, 156; defined xiii, 123, 125, 129, 131–2; dominant 131; inclusive 131; in Plato 151
Euripedes 19
Evans, Sir Arthur 3
exchange ratios: in Aristotle 151–2, 155, 157; in Edgeworth 152; in Smith 152; in Xenophon 118; *see also* liturgy

Index 181

export-import tax 97
exports xii, 110; manufactured goods 86; marble 85–6; olive oil 85; silver 845; vases 85; wine 86

factory, types of: bed (Demosthenes' father) 30, 31–3, 34, 66, 86; flute (Isocrates' father) 86; leather (Timarchus) 33; lyre (Cleophon) 86; shield (Lysias) 30, 86; shield (Pasion) 30; sword (Demosthenes' father) 30, 31–3, 66, 86; value of 66
festivals 14, 19, 20, 42
financial institutions 48, 50
Finley, M. I. x, xiii, 57, 58, 59, 60–1, 65, 112n, 118
food: cost of 76, 77, 78; dairy products 80; meat 77; *opson* (relish) 76–7, 78; Socrates on 140–1
formalist x, 57, 58, 59, 60

Gabrielsen, Vincent xiv, 94–6, 100–1
generals: *see stratēgoi*
Glaukos 16
Gorgias 21
government: defined 107; in model 107; revenue and expenditure 110, 112n; transfer payments 114
grain: biological need for 75–6, 107, 113; comparative country cost 77, 113; consumption 114; cost 76, 113; imports xii, 80–3, 112n; market 68; output 74–5; prices 68–9, 107–11
graphē paranomōn (lawsuit) 11, 38, 43, 171; replaces ostracism 48
greed: in Aristotle xiii; in Plato xiii
Guide to Greece (Pausanias) 20

Hansen, M. H. xiv, 30, 39, 43, 66, 80–1, 83–8, 90–1, 96–7, 100, 106, 111n1, 111n10, 112n21, 112n23
Harris, E. M. 65, 66, 68
Harsanyi, J. C. 166
Heraclitus 22
Herodotos 7, 25, 78
Hippias, 6, 7, 171
history, periods of Greek: Archaic Age (800–510) 5–7, Classical Age (510–322) 7–11, Dark Age (1200–800) 5; Hellenistic Age (322–30) 11–12; Mycenaean Age (1600–1200) 3–5
Hodkinson, S. 79–80
Homer 6, 15, 16; *Iliad* 6, 16; *Odyssey* 6
homosexuality 35–6; Plato on 35
honor 16, 17; loss of (*atimia*) 169; love of (*philotimia*) 17; and shame 16
hoplites (large-shielded soldiers) 3, 7, 44, 45; estimated number 111n
household management: in Aristophanes 26; in Aristotle xiii, 154, 155; in Lysias 26; in Xenophon xii, 24, 26, 117–19

hybris (ill-treatment of citizens) 17, 18, 51; in Plato 148

imports: grain xii, 80–3, 112n; in Hermippos 83; in model 108, 109, 110; other types of 83–4; in Plato 146
income redistribution 50
Indo-Europeans 3–4
institutions, Athenian 43
interest 31–2; in Aristotle xiii, 155; on bottomry loans 87; rates 102–3
invisible hand (Smith) 152, 166–7
Ionia 5, 6, 21
isēgoria (freedom of speech in Assembly) 47, 171
Isager, Signe xiv, 30, 39, 43, 66, 80–1, 83–8, 90–1, 96–7, 100, 106, 111n1, 111n10, 112n21, 112n23
Isocrates 21, 171; *Against Lochites* 51; *Areopagaticos* 103; *On the Peace* 52
Ito, Sakurai xv, 34, 85–6

Jameson, Michael H. xv, 29–30, 70–1, 75, 77, 80, 83, 99
jurors 42–3, 48, 52, 54
justice: in Plato 125–6, 127

Kant, Emmanuel 122; on ethics 163, 164; on eudaimonism 129
Karayiannis, A. D. xv, 23, 159
Knossos, palace 3, 4

labor, attitude to 18; division of, in Aristotle 137, 154; in Democritos 23; in Plato xiii, 125, 138–41, 145, 154; in Smith 138–40; in Xenophon 140
labor theory of value 151
Laureion: *see* silver
laws (*nomos*) 39, 48; in Plato 141–9
lawgivers (*nomothetai*) 39, 48; in Plato 143
lawsuit: confiscation 98; court fees 98; Demosthenes 51; *dikē* (injured party) 42, 43; fines 98; *graphē* (public concern) 42, 43; of Isocrates 51
leitourgia (wealth tax) 19, 50
Lesbos 45, 49
litigiousness 17, 42
liturgy (voluntary gifts) 52, 53, 59, 171; examples 93–4; festivals 94; in Plato 148; trierarchy 94–5, 96, 173; *see also antidosis*
loans 34, 103, 105–6; example of Dionysodoros 82; *see also* bottomry
lottery 17, 39, 43; and Council 41, 42; and jurors 42, 48; in Plato 143
Luke, gospel according to 133
Lycurgos 46, 48, 91, 92, 119, 171–2
Lysias, 172; *Against the Corn Dealers* 59, 81–2; *Against Diogeiton* 26; *Defense Against a Charge of Subverting the Democracy* 52; on cost of living 79; on liturgies 93–4; *On the*

Murder of Eratosthenes 13, 23, 25, 26, 172; on *opson* 77; *On the Refusal of a Pension to the Invalid* 51, 100; slaves of 30; on traders 66; on women 23

MacDowell, D. M. 44
manufacturing: defined 107, 112n; estimates of revenue and expenditure 109, 110–11; in model of Athenian economy 104, 107–11; slaves in 30; *see also* factory, workshop
marble, trade in 85–6
market: Athenian 64, 65, 66, 156; defined 58; embeddedness of 60, equilibrium 167
marriage: arranged 27; divorce 26; dowry 26, 31, 148; mistresses 27, 35–6; and property 26, 27
Marx, Karl: on Bentham 159–60; on Mill 162; on Smith 166
Matthew, gospel according to 145
Megacles 51
Meikle, S. 155
Melos 8
Menander 20
metics (foreign residents) 6, 18, 44, 119; Aristotle as 156; and banking 1-6; in court cases 43; numbers 28, 65; property-owning 75; tax paid 97, 172; trading in Agora 66; in workshops 65; Xenophon on 119
metoikion (tax paid by metics) 97, 172
military service 38, 44; conscription 44
Mill, John Stuart 160–5; and education 164; and utilitarianism 160–5
Minoan civilization 3, 4; and Mycenaean 4
Mitiades 172
modernist x, 57, 58, 60
monarchy: in Plato 142
money: in Aristotle 153; in Plato 153
moneylending: defended by Demosthenes 103; and by Isocrates 103
Moravcsik, Julius xv, 123, 127
Morris, I. 61
Mycenae: civilization 4–5, 6; and Minoan 5; palace 4; script 4

Nagel, T. 133
naval warfare 8, 41; Demosthenes on 95; money voted for 46; power in Aegean 80
net income (Demosthenes' father) 33–4
Nicias 6, 172
nomophylakes (guardians of the laws) 11
nomos (custom, law) 153, 172

Ober, J. 47, 51–4
occupations (Harris list) 65
oikos (home) 16–17
Old Comedy 65
Old Oligarch 45
oligarchy 45, 53
Oligarchy of Four Hundred 8, 173; in Aristophanes' *Frogs* 20

Oligarchy of Thirty 9, 46, 173
oracles 15, 47
Orphic cult 14
Osborne, R. 39, 64, 85, 86
ostracism (banishing a citizen for ten years): Cimon and 170; origin 38; as strategy 17, 48, 172; *see also graphē paranomōn*

paidagōgos (slave-tutor) 21
palace-kingdoms 4–5
Pareto optimum 58, 166, 167–8
Parmenides 22
parrhēsia (general freedom of speech) 47
Parthenon 7, 22; and Pericles 41
Pasion 29, 30, 172; as banker 105, 106
pawnbrokers 105, 106
Peiraieus, port, xii, 7, 80, 97, 119
Peisistratos 6, 19, 51
Peloponnesian Alliance 8
pensions (to invalids) 51, 100
Pericles: and Aspasia (mistress) 26, 27; and Athenian imperialism 41; citizenship decree (451) 24, 27, 35; elected general 39; funeral speech 41, 45, 83; political skills 40; and Thucydides 16, 18, 41; as trader 64; on women 25
Persia 95
Pheidias 20
Philip, king of Macedonia 10, 11
Philocrates 172
philosophy 21–3
phratia (clans) 27, 40
phylai (kinship groups) 40, 42; in Cleisthenes 38; in Solon 37, 38
Plato xxi, 120–30; Academy 21; and beauty 121; the cave (*Republic*) 122, 123; and the city 140–2, 144; and democracy 156; Democritus and 23; and division of labor 138–41; and economics xiii, 138; and education 121, 122, 123–4, 125, 128, 143, 144; and ethics xii, 123; and the good 121, 125; *Gorgias* 21, 127, 128; guardians of the laws 125–6, 141, 142, 143–4; and justice 126, 129, 138, 139, 143, 150, 162; and love 122; *Laws* 26, 141–9; *Phaedo* 10, 128; *Philebus* 130; and philosopher kings 125–6, 127, 128, 134, 142, 156; and pleasure 124, 125, 127, 129–30; *Protagoras* 127–8, 130, 161; *Republic* 122–3, 124–6, 150, and retail trade 147; and slaves 148; and Socrates 10, 120; and the sophists 121, 127–8; *Symposium* 35; and the state 126, 142–3, 151; and tax rates 148; theory of forms 120–4; and unity of virtues 121, 128, 129; on wealth 145–6; on women 26, 118, 148–9
pleasure: in Aristotle 124; in Bentham 158–9; in Democritos 23; in Mill 161–2; in Plato 124, 125, 127, 129–30
Plutarch 119

Pnyx 40
Polani, K. 152, 156–7
polis (the state) 16–17; in Plato 126, 142–3, 151; wealth good for 18
political skills 49; Assembly 40; and influence 41
Pomeroy, S. B. 21, 63–4
population: estimates 36, 75, 107; in model 106–11
pottery 5, 7, 20, 85
poverty 18, 106–7; estimates of revenue and expenditure 108; number of "poor" 107–8; in Plato 145–6, 147
price theory: in Aristotle 152; in model 107; in Plato 147–8; in Xenophon xii
prices: barley 68–9; bread 69; clothes 70–1; figs 70; fish 70; furniture 72; funeral 72; *hetairai* 72; honey 69; land 71–2; livestock 70; ointment 71; olives 69; shoes 71; vases 72; voyage 72; wheat 68; wine 67
primitivist x, 57, 58, 156, 157
private ownership: in Aristotle 156; in Plato 145
productive capital: Demosthenes' father 34
profit x, 18, 57, 60; of Demosthenes' father's sofa factory 111n; as goal 59; maximization difficult 59; as threat to norms 59
profit-output ratio: for Demosthenes' father's bed factory 103–4
property 25, 26, 27; in Aristotle 155; bequeathed in male line 25; mines as 85; in Plato 142, 145–6, 148; prices 71–2; slaves as 154; slaves leaving 29; visible and invisible 53, 105; in Xenophon 118
Protagoras 21
proxenos (foreign citizen benefiting state) 80, 173
prytaneis (presidents) 40, 42
Pseudo-Aristotle: *Oikonomikos* 26, 68
Pseudo-Demosthenes 86–7
Pseudo-Xenophon 29, 53
public finance: Andreades on 91, 96, 97, 111n; bottomry 86–7, 105; confiscations 98; court fees 98; *diōbelia* 50, 99; *epidosis* 98; *eisphora* 64, 96–7; expenditure 99–102; export-import tax 97; fines 98; leases on mines 97; liturgies 52, 53, 59, 93–6, 171; *metoikion* 97, 172; military expenses 100–2; pensions 51, 105; revenue 92–9; spoils 99; state pay 99; theoric fund 50, 99–100, 173; tributes 10, 92; trierarchies 94–5, 96, 173
public officers: election 44; lottery 44
public service 52–3; Aristotle on 68; in market 67–8
public works 41
Pythagoras 22; and Plato 121

Raaflaub, K. A. 49–50
rate of return: on bed factory (Demosthenes' father) 33–4, 103; on land 103; on leather workshop (Timarchos) 33; on money (Demosthenes' father) 33; on silver mines 33, 103; on slaves (Demosthenes' father) 33
Rawls, John xiv, 166
reality: in Aristotle 121; in Plato 120–2
rebellions, against Athens: Lesbos 45, 49; Melos 45–6
reciprocal proportion (Aristotle) 150–1
religion 13–15, 21
rents 64
retail trade (*kapēlikē*): in Aristotle xiii, 155; in Plato 147
rhetoric 53–4; in *Gorgias* 21, 127
Rome: conquers Athens 11, 12

Sakurai, Mariko xv, 23
Scarre, G. 165, 166
Scheidel, W. 76, 107
Schliemann, Heinrich 4, 6
Schumpeter, J. 61
science/natural science 21–3
scripts: Linear A 3; Linear B 4, 5; Phoenician alphabet 6
sculpture 20
Scythian archers 30, 40
Second Athenian League 10
Sen, Amartya xiv, 167–8
shame 16; and honor 16, 126; Plato on 126; Socrates on 65
Shinto 13–16
shipowners 86–7
Sicilian Expedition 8, 46, 49, 50, 172
silver: in Aristophanes 84; leases on mines 97, 111n; mining in Laureion xii, 7, 30, 31, 84–5; and money 64, 65; and naval warfare 46; output 97, 111n; slaves and 30–1, 33, 84, 111n; and Spartan occupation 84; state and 59, 84; in Xenophon 119
slaves/slavery 6, 18, 28–34; abundance weakens technology? 31, 63; Alcidamas on 154; Antiphon on 154; Aristotle on 154; and banking 106; Demosthenes on 31–4; domestic 29–30, 33; enable democracy? 30–1; Euripedes on 154; imports of 87–91; manumission 28, 28–30, 90, 106; model 88–91; numbers of 28, 31, 90–1; occupations of 29–30; ownership of 30–2; Plato on 148; price of 33; productivity of 33–4; in silver mines 30–1, 33, 84, 111n; source of 28; trade in 28; Xenophon on 118, 154
Smith, Adam xiii, 59–60, 138–40, 152, 154, 166, 167
Socrates 8; and Alcibiades 35; on animals 79; and citizen 17; cross-examination method 120, 124–5; and democracy 45; and education 120, 127; and the good 125; and Ischomachos 59; and justice 124–5, 127; Mill and 161; and Plato 10, 120; and rhetoric 53; on shame 65; trial and execution 9–10, 46; on

virtues 128, 155; and women 19, 25; and Xenophon 117–18
Solon 6, 37; constitution 37; laws 6
sophists 21, 121, 127–8
Sophocles 19; *Antigone* 15, 17
sōphrosynē (soundness of mind) 17–18
Sparta 5; and Athens 8, 9, 10, 45, 46, 49, 170; and Delian League 7; occupation of Decelea 30, 84; slaves in 30; soldiers 78
state, the: in Aristotle 154; in Plato 154
status x, 51, 57, 59
Stone, I. F. 9
Strabo 80–1
stratēgoi (generals) 39, 42, 43, 44, 46, 173
Strauss, B.S. 48
substantivist x, 57, 58, 59, 156
sycophants 17, 173
Syracuse 46

technē (skill, art) 173
temple 13, 18, 104
Thales 22, 155
Themistocles 7, 46
Theophrastus 67, 76, 77, 79, 104; *Characters* 67, 98
theoric fund (*theōrika*) 50, 91, 99–100, 173; Demosthenes and 46, 50; Eubolos and 171
Theramenes 173
Thesmophoria (festival for women) 14, 25
thētes (serfs) 6, 37; numbers 111n
Thrasybulus 173
Thucydides: *Pelopennesian War* 16, 46, 50; on Sparta 80; on war 49, 79; on wealth 18; on women 25
Timotheus 173
trade 21, 80–91, 119; Plato on 146–7; Xenophon on 85, 119
tragedies 19–20
treasury 48
tributes 10, 92
trierarchy (liturgy for triremes) 94–5, 96, 173
triremes 30, 41, 46, 94, 100–1, 173
Troy 6

Urmson, J. O. 135, 136
utilitarianism xiv, 158; act 164; Aristotle and 124, 135; Bentham and 158; critics of 165–6; Mill and 160–5; Plato and xii, 123; Socrates and 128; rule 164
utility x, 57, 60; in Aristotle 151–3, 158; in Bentham 158–9; critics of 165–8; in Edgeworth 152–3; in Kant 163; maximization xiv, 58, 128, 166–7; in Mill 160–5; in Sen 168
utility theory of value 151–3

Ventris, Michael 4

wages: Assembly attendance 72; Council 72, courts 73; military 73–4; public offices 73; theater 73; welfare 73
wall paintings 4
wars: Corinthian (395–387) 10, 173; Lamian (323–322) 11; Macedonian 49–50; Peloponnesian (431–404) 7–8, 19, 20, 27, 28, 49, 97; Second Punic (201) 12; Social (357–355) 10; Trojan 6
wealth 18, 106–7; in Aristotle 155; boasting of 52; concealment of 53; duties of 52, 54; distribution of 93; estimates of 108; numbers of wealthy 108; Phainippos and 64; in Xenophon 118
Wealth of Nations (Smith) 60, 138–40
Weil, Simone 122–3, 125, 145, 162, 166
wine 66, 86
Wolin, S. S. 48, 49
women: in Aristophanes 24–5, 26; in Aristotle 25–6, 137; Demosthenes and 25, 26; dowry 26, 31, 148; education of 21, 26; Herodotos and 25; Lysias and 23–4, 26; as oracles 15; in Minoan society 4; and Pericles' decree 24, 25; in Plato 24–5, 148–9; in Pseudo-Aristotle 26; status 23–6; Thucydides and 25; and work 19, 25; in Xenophon 24, 25, 26, 118, 156
workshops 35, 65; artisans 60; size of 34; slaves owning 29; *see also* factories

Xenophon: and economics xii; on love 36; *Memorabilia* 9–10, 59, 65, 79; *Oikonomikos* 24, 25, 26, 28, 59, 117–19, 143; on Socrates 9–10, 19; *Ways and Means* xii, 50, 59, 85, 119

Zen Buddhism 122, 133